THE BLESSING
OF A SKINNED KNEE

USING JEWISH TEACHINGS
TO RAISE SELF-RELIANT CHILDREN

Wendy Mogel, Ph.D.

PENGUIN COMPASS

PENGUIN BOOKS

Published by the Penguin Group

Penguin Group (USA) Inc., 375 Hudson Street, New York, New York 10014, U.S.A.

Penguin Group (Canada), 90 Eglinton Avenue East, Suite 700, Toronto, Ontario,
Canada M4P 2Y3 (a division of Pearson Penguin Canada Inc.)

Penguin Books Ltd, 80 Strand, London WC2R 0RL, England

Penguin Ireland, 25 St Stephen's Green, Dublin 2, Ireland (a division of Penguin Books Ltd)

Penguin Group (Australia), 250 Camberwell Road, Camberwell, Victoria 3124,
Australia (a division of Pearson Australia Group Pty Ltd)

Penguin Books India Pvt Ltd, 11 Community Centre, Panchsheel Park, New Delhi – 110 017, India

Penguin Group (NZ), 67 Apollo Drive, Rosedale, North Shore 0745,
Auckland, New Zealand (a division of Pearson New Zealand Ltd)

Penguin Books (South Africa) (Pty) Ltd, 24 Sturdee Avenue, Rosebank, Johannesburg 2196, South Africa

Penguin Books Ltd, Registered Offices: 80 Strand, London WC2R 0RL, England

First published in the United States of America by Simon & Schuster 2001
Published in Penguin Books 2001

27 29 31 33 35 34 32 30 28

Copyright © Wendy Mogel, Ph.D., 2001
All rights reserved

"This Be the Verse" from *Collected Poems* by Philip Larkin.
Copyright © 1988, 1989 by the estate of Philip Larkin. Reprinted with
permission of Farrar, Strauss and Giroux, LLC, and Faber & Faber.

THE LIBRARY OF CONGRESS HAS CATALOGED
THE HARDCOVER EDITION AS FOLLOWS:
Mogel, Wendy (date).
The blessing of a skinned knee : using Jewish teachings
to raise self-reliant children/ Wendy Mogel.
p. cm.
Includes bibliographical references and index.
1. Child-rearing—Religious aspects—Judaism.   2. Parenting—
Religious aspects—Judaism.   3. Parenting—Psychological aspects.
4. Self-reliance in children.   I. Title.
HQ769.3.M64 2001
296.7'4—dc21   00-061243
ISBN 0-684-86297-2 (hc.)
ISBN 978-0-14-219600-7 (pbk.)

Printed in the United States of America
Set in Dante / Designed by Erich Hobbing

PENGUIN
COMPASS

THE BLESSING OF A SKINNED KNEE

Wendy Mogel, Ph.D., a clinical psychologist, lectures widely to parents, teachers, clergy, and school administrators on meeting the challenges of modern family life. She is a member of the board of directors of the Council for Spiritual and Ethical Education, a century-old interfaith organization serving independent schools. Dr. Mogel lives in Los Angeles with her husband and their two daughters. You can visit her on the Web at www.wendymogel.com.

To Michael

Ben Bag Bag says: Delve in the Torah and continue to delve in it, for everything is in it; look deeply into it; grow old and gray over it, for you can have no better portion than it. Ben Hie Hei says: The reward is in proprtion to the exertion.
—The Ethics of the Fathers 5:26

Better a broken bone than a broken spirit.
—Lady Allen Hurtwood

Acknowledgments

"Just transcribe tapes of your lectures," colleagues and friends advised me. "You'll have a book!" Were it only so. Even the most scintillating set of lectures yield tapes that are buzzy, repetitive, full of gaps. No, I countered, I'll just sit down and write a book from scratch. But even my best intentions yielded text that was buzzy, repetitive, full of gaps.

Then one day Betsy Amster, literary agent sent from above, called and asked simply, "Would you like to write a book?" Yes, I told her. I certainly would. So Betsy guided me. Her hand is everywhere in this book—she is a strong coach and an enthusiastic cheerleader. It is an honor to know her.

The Blessing of a Skinned Knee would not exist without the expert editorial help of Lynette Padwa. Lynette is a meticulous surgeon ("Even though you love these five long quotes from first-century philosopher Philo, they have to go!") and landscape architect ("Too many flowers here; we need more trees"). Her humor and patience have been a blessing.

Jane Rosenman, my editor at Scribner, understood right from the start just what this book was meant to be. She was adamant about finding the right voice and tone for its message. Because of her clarity and dedication to the cause, we got there.

Thank you to Miriam Parrish, my hardworking, good-spirited assistant, and to Ethan Friedman, editorial assistant at Scribner.

There is much talk of tensions and divisions among Jewish denominations. As a student of Judaism, teacher, and writer, I approached rabbis representing a broad spectrum of theological positions. They gave me generous help without judgment every time. I am grateful to the following rabbis (in alphabetical order!): Rabbi Yitzchok Adlerstein of Yeshiva of Los Angeles for sharing the depth of his knowledge of texts and law; Rabbi Mark Borovitz of Beit Tshuvah for being on call for rabbinic texts; Rabbi Mordecai Finley of Ohr HaTorah for his thoughts on theology; Rabbi Karen Fox of Wilshire Boulevard Temple for friendship, sources, and support; Rabbi Yosef Kanefsky of Bnai David Judea for his help with sources for Chapter 6 ("The Blessing of Work"); Rabbi Danny Landes of the Pardes Institute in Jerusalem for providing a model of warm and authoritative teaching; and Rabbi Daniel Swartz of the Religious Action Center in Washington, D.C., for starting the ball rolling.

I give special thanks to Rabbi Laura Geller of Temple Emanuel, who read the entire manuscript and offered her guidance, insight, and knowledge, and to Rabbi Jonathan Omer-Man of the adult Jewish education academy, Metivta, and his ever-enthusiastic program administrator, Rema Nadel, for giving me the opportunity to teach and therefore to learn what I needed to know to write this book.

Thank you to colleagues: Jewish educators Judy Aronson of Leo Baeck Temple and Linda Thal of the Union of American Hebrew Congregations for believing that what I have to say matters in a bigger forum than our little slice of the planet.

And thank you to friends: Claudia Weill for putting together the first Jewish parenting class and for knowing how to criticize and elevate; Laurie Levit for her droll observations of our local subculture; Priscilla Wolff, academic dean at Curtis School, for her articulate formulations of the problems families face and for supplying articles I would have otherwise missed; Laura Bellotti and Debbie Attanasio for help in the early stages; Robin

Swicord and Nick Kazan, who invited me to get a start on Chapter 1 in their breezy writer's aerie and who kept me motivated by capping each day with homemade blueberry pie; and to my running partner of ten years, Dr. Jill Ruesch-Lane, for many fine tales from the trenches.

Thanks to my parents, Ann Mogel, for her experienced reading of the manuscript, and Leonard Mogel, for his publishing wisdom.

When the stretches of writing were long and bleak, my husband, Michael Tolkin, said, "You have to put this book before everything. Before your children. Before your marriage. You have to finish it." I thank you, Michael, for your prescience.

Finally, thank you to my daughters, Susanna and Emma, who teach me all about life and who accepted the long gestation of our third child, "The Book," with their usual grace.

Contents

Contents

Author Notes

ON THE USE OF THE WORD *GOD*

When writing about children in general, I randomly alternated the use of female and male pronouns for the sake of equality. While I believe that God transcends gender, it was impossible for me to completely eliminate pronouns ("God, in God's wisdom") or to alternate them ("God, in Her wisdom") without sounding awkward. Instead, I've resorted to the grammatical convention of using the pronoun *He* when referring to God, for the sake of the graceful flow of ideas and language, not because I think of God as either anthropomorphic or male.

ON THE USE OF THE WORD *TRADITIONAL*

Determining what is holy in God's eyes is under constant examination by serious, involved Jews. In the past two decades there have been many invigorating shifts and readjustments in the practices of each denomination. Orthodox Jews are experimenting with new roles for women and engaging in active interdenominational dialogue. Reform Jews are reclaiming traditional practices and celebrations and taking on rituals rejected by the founders of their movement.

When I refer in the text to "traditional" Jews and "traditional"

Jewish practices, I am pointing to the set of teachings, rules, and traditions that are most commonly followed by Orthodox Jews. I'm using these practices to illustrate the principle of religious teachings in action, not as an exclusive model or blueprint for holy living.

CHAPTER 1

How I Lost One Faith
and Found Another

For fifteen years I practiced child psychology, and for fifteen years I loved doing it. From my seventh-story office window, I had a beautiful panoramic view of the Hollywood Hills to the north and Beverly Hills to the west. From inside my consulting room, I had a view of the families who lived in these privileged neighborhoods. Most of my time was spent conducting psychological tests and doing psychotherapy with children. Like anyone who enters a healing profession, I gained great satisfaction from discovering the roots of a problem and then showing both parents and children what could be done to help remedy it. I was successful. I made a good living.

From the outside, the families who came to see me looked as if they had ideal lives. The parents were committed to raising successful, happy, well-adjusted children. They attended every soccer game. They knew to shout, "Way to go, Green Hornets!" to cheer the whole team, not just their Nicole. Father and mother went to school conferences and listened hard and well. They were involved. They could recite without hesitation the names and most telling personality traits of their child's three closest friends. If a child scored low in school, the parents hired a tutor or educational therapist right away.

Ten years ago I started to feel that something fundamental

was amiss. My discontent began when I first noticed an odd pattern in my testing practice. I had grown accustomed to dealing with all levels of psychological distress, from severely disturbed children to those who were mildly unhappy. Often I had to deliver news that was painful and disappointing for parents to hear. I might have to say, "Even though Jeremy knows lots of TV jingles by heart and seems bright and alert to you, his IQ falls well below normal and he needs to be in a special school program." Or, "The reason Max washes his hands so much isn't because he is fastidious. This behavior is a symptom of an obsessive-compulsive disorder that showed up on every psychological test I gave him."

I thought of these as the "hard news" days, and I never looked forward to them. Parents nearly always reacted to my report with great resistance. It's understandable—parental denial is born of fierce love and fear, and it's a hard defense to break through. But most of the mothers and fathers rose to the challenge, tackling their child's problems with compassion and commitment.

Fortunately, there were also plenty of "good news" days, when I could report to parents that their child's problems were within normal limits, meaning they fell within the broad range of expectable attitudes, moods, and behaviors for that particular age. It was a relief to deliver the reassuring message that a child was simply going through a difficult phase, and that his or her overall psychological profile was healthy.

Then I began to see a curious new pattern: some of the "good news" parents were not welcoming my good news. Instead of feeling relief, they were disappointed. If nothing was wrong, if there was no diagnosis, no disorder, then there was nothing that could be fixed. "My child is suffering!" complained the worried parents. And I had to agree. The children of these fine parents were not thriving.

Some children had difficulties throughout the day. In the

morning there were complaints: "My tummy hurts. . . . I'm not going to school because Sophie used to be my best friend and now she's always mean to me. . . . Coach Stanley is unfair. He wants us to run too many laps in P.E." After school there were battles over when and by whom homework would be completed, or unceasing demands for goods and services: "Everyone has platform shoes. . . . All the other kids in my class get to watch PG-13 movies. . . . All the other parents let their kids get their ears pierced. . . . All my friends get more allowance than I do."

At the dinner table there was conflict about the desirability of the food that had been prepared and whether or not the child was in the mood to eat it. At bedtime there were more complaints: "I just need to watch one more TV show. . . . My ear hurts . . . I have bad pains in my legs and my arms. . . . I'm afraid to sleep without the light on." When the parents tried to explain themselves to the children ("You need to go to school because . . . You need to eat dinner because . . . You need to go to sleep because..."), the children turned into little attorneys, responding to each explanation with a counterargument.

It may sound as if these problems are mild, typical of normal friction in the relationship between young children and their parents. But the scenarios these parents described to me were not mild. The daily problems were unremitting and the only let-up came in very specific circumstances. The perfect alignment of the planets looked like this: if the children felt protected from any sort of danger, relieved of pressure to perform or take responsibility, and sufficiently stimulated by having lots of fun things to do, they were able to relax and be cooperative, pleasant, and respectful. But these moments were rare. Much of the time both the parents and the children were miserable and frustrated.

Some of these children were on the outer edge of "normal limits." I was often asked to treat cases of bed-wetting, constipation, poor grades in children with high IQs, or children with serious difficulty making and keeping friends. But none of these children fit the category of the hard news cases. None seemed to be suffering from any kind of real psychopathology. Instead, everyone—parents and children—seemed off course, unmoored, and chronically unhappy.

LOSING MY FAITH

I was trained to believe in psychology, the talking cure. I had been taught to provide psychological support without being judgmental, but I began to have more and more judgments. Something was wrong, but I couldn't locate the problem in my diagnostic manual. Working with children, I started to feel like the highly-paid baby-sitter. Working with parents, I felt as if I were prescribing Tylenol for acute appendicitis. In need of supervision and guidance, I consulted two senior clinicians whose opinions I deeply respected. I went back into therapy myself to see if I had some unconscious resistance to perceiving my clients and their children clearly. Nothing worked. The words that came to my mind to describe these troubled youngsters were old-fashioned: petulant, obstinate, rigid, greedy, cowardly, lethargic, imperious. I started wondering whether their problems fell into a different category than I was considering, whether they might be problems that psychotherapy alone could never repair—problems of character. My training was failing me.

THE LAMENT OF THE MODERN MOTHER

I was thirty-seven years old when I began to search for a different approach to counseling. During most of the ten years it took me to find a new philosophy of parenting and put it to good use, my life, both externally and internally, was very much like the lives of the families I counseled. Like them, I felt burdened. My husband, Michael, and I had two young daughters, and although we hired a housekeeper, we did most of the daily child tending ourselves. As the girls grew older, I vowed to stay involved in all the small details of their lives: to make fresh sandwiches and tear off a ragged piece of lettuce if it looked unappetizing, to run the baths, supervise the homework, plan the play dates, and wave good-bye each morning like Harriet Nelson. Like so many of the mothers I counseled, I wanted to be a hands-on parent, and like them, I had plenty of other ambitions as well. I wanted to continue to do fulfilling professional work, to stay fit and healthy, go to the movies, keep up with my gardening, read at least one professional journal and a book a week plus the newspaper every day, head committees at the girls' schools, bake . . . and take saxophone lessons.

Of course, I wanted my children to have every opportunity for success and fulfillment as well. So, in addition to schoolwork, homework, and play dates, they each had a private music lesson once a week and occasionally a tutor for the academic weak spots. The younger one played soccer. Every appointment went on two calendars, a big one in the kitchen and my own appointment book. There was no time for anyone to waste.

I got up at 6:15 each weekday to make the lunches and launch the carpools. Most mornings I went to the gym or on a power walk with a friend, then to work. By four, when the children were back home, I was worn down, and by ten I was nearly catatonic. That wasn't part of the plan—I had meant to spend the evening hours with my husband, to watch a movie, make love, or simply talk about things beyond our little domestic sphere. Each evening I would make a pledge that the next night I would stay up late with him, but when the next night came I would again be an adulterer—my lover was sleep.

Despite my exhaustion, I didn't sleep soundly. I'd wake up, look over at the clock, and see unfriendly numbers like 1:25 or

3:30 A.M. There hadn't been enough time in the day for all my concerns, so they had overflowed into dreamtime. Occasionally I welcomed these opportunities for quiet reflection. More often, though, I spent the time choreographing the hundreds of moving parts that would make up the day to come: *Susanna's teacher sent home a note saying "bring a paper towel roll" tomorrow. I think this is different from a roll of paper towels. I think it means just the empty roll. Should I neatly unroll the one in the kitchen and make a pile out of the towels, or send her to school without a paper towel roll and risk having her left out of the art project?*

I worried most at night about my age. I had had Susanna when I was thirty-five and Emma when I was thirty-nine, and I couldn't help calculating the future. . . . *When Emma is twenty-one I'll be sixty. If I were younger, would I have more energy for them? How old will I be when my daughters marry? Will I be seventy? Will I be breathing? None of my friends is likely to see her grandchildren married. What have we done?*

AN INVITATION

I would never have imagined it at the time, but the teachings of Judaism would eventually relieve much of my doubt and anxiety. It didn't happen overnight, but over months and years I discovered a new set of priorities and values that began to ease my apprehensions and give me a sense of optimism about the future.

It all began shortly after the fruitless consultation I'd had with the two senior clinicians. I had decided that more therapy wasn't going to help me and temporarily abandoned my search for a new direction. I cut down my practice to spend more time with Susanna, who, at two, was eager to explore the world. On a lark, I accepted an invitation from my friend Melanie to join her at a Rosh Hashanah service at a Reform temple near Bel Air. Could be nice, I thought. Susanna and I like cultural anthropology. We had had a good time at an international mask and dance festival in the park the previous week. Now we could see how these people, the Jews of West Los Angeles, celebrated their ancient holy day. In no way did I expect this outing to change my life.

I'd been raised (by two Jewish parents) knowing so little of Jewish tradition that I sometimes think of myself as a convert. By the time I was eight I knew the difference between cherrystone and littleneck clams and Manhattan and New England clam chowder. My knowledge of nonkosher fish far exceeded my knowledge of Torah. In a typical year of childhood, my family's Jewish rituals lasted under five hours total: the blessing over the Hanukkah candles (five minutes to light the candles, times eight nights), plus a four-hour seder at Aunt Florrie's house. Every year my father went to High Holy Day services by himself at a neighborhood synagogue to which our family did not belong.

Although I knew almost nothing about Judaism, I knew that I didn't like rabbis. The few I had heard spoke in a pompous, deliberate way. I wondered if they thought that all congregants were slow learners. They defined us as victims and warned us to watch out for the inevitable moment when "the lion of anti-Semitism rears its ugly head." There was never talk of God or where you went when you died or why bad people got away with it or the other things I wondered about when I was eleven years old.

But that afternoon at Leo Baeck Temple in Los Angeles didn't fit my childhood prejudices. The rabbi, Sue Elwell, was a friendly-looking woman with short hair, no makeup, and such a normal way of speaking that I was startled. She didn't stand on a podium but down near the congregants. She was accompanied by a young man playing the guitar. The scene was pleasant, but I found myself in tears. I'm not an easy cry, so I was puzzled. Something had been stirred in me, but I didn't know what it could be.

On Yom Kippur, Melanie and I and our little daughters returned to this temple for a children's service. This time Susanna, just out of diapers, peed on my lap and I sat there with a wet lap and a wet face from more tears. By now, I sensed that I might be on to something meaningful. I came up with a hard test of my synagogue-evoked emotions: I would go by myself to a Friday night adult service at Temple Israel of Hollywood, a synagogue near my home.

I didn't know any of the melodies or prayers. The rabbi was Daniel Swartz, a twenty-nine-year-old who had been ordained after leaving a career as a geologist. Everyone called him Rabbi Daniel. He wore a bow tie, was very ardent, and had the same happy-relaxed demeanor as Sue Elwell. What my concept of Judaism was losing in majesty, it was gaining in accessibility.

I liked this friendly scene so much that the next morning I went to Rabbi Daniel's learner's service. He read the section of the Bible, Exodus 28, that describes the vestments of Aaron, the high priest:

> The robe was made of a weaver's craft, entirely of turquoise wool. On the hem of the robe they made pomegranates of blue, purple and scarlet yarns, twisted and finely woven linen. They made bells of pure gold, and they placed the bells amid the pomegranates on the hem of the robe, all around. . . . They made the frontlet for the holy diadem of pure gold, and incised upon it the seal inscription: "Holy to the Lord." They attached to it a cord of blue to fix upon the headdress above— as the Lord had commanded Moses.

Unfamiliar with biblical texts beyond children's stories, I was moved by the power and poetic beauty of this image. But there was more—a sermon. Rabbi Daniel explained that the *bigdei kodesh*, the holy clothing of the high priests, was meant to elevate them, to give them special status and honor and to distinguish them from the rest of the people. He then spoke about the costs and benefits of our casual southern California culture. "Adults and children dress alike here and wear the same informal styles on most occasions," he pointed out. "While it's good that we no longer feel an obligation to dress up to display our status and can instead be comfortable, too much informality has its disadvantages. A house of God is different from the carpool line or supermarket. Wearing jeans and running shoes to temple can be an obstacle to feeling awe and transcendence." And he made a specific request: he asked the congregants to dress up a bit more to come to services.

I immediately thought of Becky and Jeff, a couple I had counseled that week. They were typical of the distressed but not disturbed families who made up such a large percentage of my clientele. Both parents were successful and happy at work (she was a partner in a law firm, he was a fund-raiser) but increasingly miserable at home. They believed in helping their young son and daughter learn to express themselves, and worked hard to make sure their children understood the rationale for family rules. But their daughter, Jenna, was critical and angry with them and was doing poorly in school. Their son, Nate, had twice bitten other children at preschool. He screamed when it was time to leave the park or a friend's house. Nate's standard bedtime routine was to tear all the sheets off the bed and throw everything out of his drawers.

At work Becky and Jeff were both effective leaders, but at home they had little authority over time, space, or actions. The house was filled with toys, not just in the children's bedrooms but in the family room, the bathroom, the kitchen, even between the sheets in Jeff and Becky's bed. In this home the children's interests ruled. No place was sacred.

Although I did not expect to get insight into a therapeutic problem from a sermon, this idea of *bigdei kodesh*—the need to reinforce valid authority with signs or symbols—fit the situation

Becky and Jeff were struggling with. When I told them that they needed to become the "high priests in the Holy Temple of their home," they laughed, but later it began to make sense to them. They realized that they had been so kind and democratic with their children that there was no order in the universe of their home. The children were tuned in to their own desires but not to their obligations. Becky and Jeff began to make changes. They declared their bedroom off-limits except with explicit permission. They told their children that they needed to say "Yes, please" or "No, thank you" when they were offered something. Most important, they stopped giving the children so much attention for every emotional and physical ache and pain. Their home life improved immeasurably. I was surprised and pleased.

ONE TOE AT A TIME

At my suggestion, our family began going to temple once a month. Later I discovered that many nonpracticing Jewish husbands have a lot of resistance to attending services; it's a common issue in the parenting groups I teach. In many households, the woman is more attracted to spirituality while the husband holds back, usually citing childhood experiences that prove the hypocrisy of religion (I've heard this is true for Catholic and Protestant husbands as well as Jewish ones). Like most couples, my husband, Michael, and I have a "mixed marriage"—we don't always agree when it comes to matters of religious practice. But in our case, it's Michael who would prefer our family to be more strictly observant than I'm comfortable with. Ten years ago, however, we were pretty much at the same place: he had had a bar mitzvah and been confirmed but neither of us had been involved with Judaism as adults, and we were both curious.

At synagogue I felt like an utter novice. I didn't know the name or shape of *aleph*, the first letter of the Hebrew alphabet.

I didn't know any of the liturgy beyond what I thought was pronounced "burruch ha taw" and later learned was *baruch atah*, "blessed are you." I was embarrassed about my lack of synagogue skill and my general ignorance of Judaism. But we persisted. During the spring of our first year going to services, we went to a weekend retreat where we had our first real experience with Shabbat, the day set aside for rest and reflection. After that we began to go to temple every week.

I bought a blessing tape and stayed up late memorizing prayers. I took a Torah study class and made small changes at home. At first, we simply lit some candles on Friday nights at dinnertime, stumbled through the blessings in transliteration, said "Good Shabbos," and went to a Thai restaurant for shrimp dinner. Later we added *kiddush* (the blessing over wine) and had dinner at home. After about a year, we graduated to staying home every Friday night for a full Shabbat dinner with all the traditional blessings. We stopped eating shellfish and pork or mixing meat and dairy products at meals.

At the start of the dinner we mixed the prescribed blessings with our family rituals. We lit the candles in honor of specific family members who were ill that week or needed a blessing for some other kind of suffering. For example, Susanna might say, "I'm lighting this candle tonight to bring a blessing to my friend Jessica, who has the flu." We then whispered a traditional blessing to each child, "May the divine face shine upon you in the coming week." We went around the table and took turns describing the best things that happened during the week and catching up on one another's good news. We discussed ethical dilemmas from the news or from our daily lives using principles from Jewish law. We ended the meal with song. Occasionally the formal meal and rituals seemed trite and self-serving, but mostly these were the least hurried, most tender moments of the week, and they brought us closer together.

Another year passed and I considered taking a year's leave of absence from my practice. I was longing to study Judaism full-time and see if there might be some way to integrate what I learned into my practice. My longtime officemate, a child psychiatrist who loves his work, was skeptical. "This is not a job," he said, "it's a calling. Think about what it means to leave your patients."

Rabbi Daniel was just as adamant in his advice: "Read the prophet Isaiah, Chapter 6, where he gets the prophetic call," he urged me in a long letter. "Ultimately the decision you're making is a personal one, if not an intensely private one. I'm never certain of anything as a matter of principle, but I'm pretty sure of two things: if you do make the leap into Judaism, you will have the chance to do a great service to the Jewish community and to serve God." That letter had a huge effect on me. While I was dubious about Rabbi Daniel's prediction that I would do a great service for the Jewish community, his words gave me the courage to close my practice.

Although Rabbi Daniel is a Reform rabbi, he advised me to do some of my studies with the Orthodox. They have a lifelong familiarity with biblical texts and teachings that enables them to introduce others to Jewish thought in an utterly familiar yet nonacademic way. I dressed in *frum* (pious) garb, with sleeves covering my elbows, a long skirt, and a hat, and I studied difficult texts and the laws of making a Jewish home with Orthodox teachers. In the beginning I spent most of my time with the Hassids, who had a combination of traits that impressed me: joy in their faith and blazing intellect. But when I went to their homes for Shabbat dinner, I saw another side. The lively debate at the table featured the men and boys—the wives and daughters stayed in the background. I could not make this sort of home, and I wasn't going to subordinate my daughters this way. But I continued to study with these pious men and women and with other inspiring teachers from each branch of Judaism.

During the course of the year I absorbed every bit of Jewish knowledge I could find, especially if it pertained to child-rearing. I discovered the many fine Jewish parenting books written by liberal rabbis and teachers. The books raised issues that were new and interesting to me: how to solve the "December dilemma" (resisting the allure of Christmas for Jewish children without building Hanukkah up into a high-stature holiday it was never meant to be), how to decorate and enjoy a sukkah, how to approach children's questions about God. Designed to help parents guide children in building a positive Jewish identity within our contemporary culture, these books existed comfortably shoulder to shoulder with secular society.

In my neighborhood, there were three or four Orthodox Jewish bookstores. I wandered in and discovered tables covered with stacks of parenting books I'd never seen before. When I started reading them I was thrilled. They painted a vivid picture of the dangers and seductiveness of the materialistic, anxious, oversexed, highly competitive world around me. They elevated practical, everyday parenting concerns—how much television children were allowed to watch, their attitude toward helping out at home, what kinds of clothes they were permitted to wear—to questions of holiness. These books knew their enemy and offered ways to protect children from it. They were well written, psychologically sound, and filled with traditional Jewish wisdom in the form of parables and lessons in Jewish law and theology. But these Orthodox parenting guides all prescribed strict observance as the *only* possible path for raising wholesome, moral children. So, along with the teachings and rich insights into living came the *mehitzah* (the divider that separates women from men in the sanctuary), plus many other strictures and an insistence on separation from the wider community that neither I nor my clients were willing to embrace. I welcomed the diagnosis but not the cure.

I began to wonder if I could be a bridge. Psychology provides powerful theories for understanding children's emotional problems, but the theories shift too frequently to be an anchor and give short shrift to problems of character. In the time-tested lessons of Judaism, I discovered insights and practical tools that spoke directly to both psychological and spiritual problems. Maybe I could find a way to bring those insights to the very modern families I counseled; maybe I could integrate psychology and Jewish teachings.

A WORD OF TORAH

Not long after I started my year of study, John Rosove, the senior rabbi at Temple Israel asked me to give a talk on parenting on Yom Kippur afternoon at the synagogue. The little that I knew unfolded in me, and I spoke for an hour without notes. After the lecture, a group of women who had been studying Judaism informally together asked if I would be their teacher. I was taken aback, but I gladly agreed and ended up teaching their group for two years. Often I felt that I was only a day ahead of them, but I sustained myself against my fear of being discovered as a fraud with a saying Rabbi Daniel told me: "Whoever knows a word of Torah is obliged to teach it." The classes became the model for all my Jewish parenting classes.

Each week in my parents' group I would take an upcoming holiday, a Bible story, or a teaching from the Talmud, and tie it to a modern parenting problem. From the teaching I would extract an intervention or approach to the dilemma. The participants in the classes would go home and apply the principle and report in the next week about what worked and what didn't. The classes led to lectures, and I found that I was indeed bridging two worlds. I had two sets of lectures: one on Jewish spirituality and parenting, which I gave at religious schools and synagogues, and an identical one with just a sprinkling of Jewish references that I gave at secular schools and churches.

The lectures and parenting groups exposed me to many more types of parents than I had seen in private practice. Instead of focusing on the specific problems of individual children, I was now hearing about more general issues. Many parents told me they felt adrift after Mommy and Me. They found themselves raising young children in a world that was changing at a dazzling pace, one that was very different from the one they had grown up in. They didn't have a tradition to follow or a community to join. The community of their child's school, even if it was close-knit and supportive, was not adequate as a moral and spiritual centerpiece of the family. The parents told me that my classes filled their need for parent guidance during the elementary school years and provided a way for them to learn basic Judaism without having to commit themselves to "studying religion." Many of the participants joined synagogues and continued their study and home observance.

I never returned to practicing psychology the way I had before my crisis of faith. Instead, I have shifted my focus from diagnosis and treatment to prevention; from private therapy sessions to lecturing, teaching parenting classes, and consulting with parents and schools. For many years now, I have taught a course called "Homework, Food, Bedtime, Sex, Death, and the Holy: Jewish Wisdom for Parents." My purpose in that course—as in this book—is to help mothers and fathers develop a spiritually based parenting philosophy that will enable them to handle the rough spots in their children's development themselves rather than feel they must turn to an expert every time a child veers off track.

ANGUISHED PARENTS, ANXIOUS CHILDREN

What have I learned from my years of leading parenting groups? The hidden secret in the community of abundance in which I live is its anguish. Unsure how to find grace and security in the complex world we've inherited, we try to fill up the spaces in our children's lives with stuff: birthday entertainments, lessons, rooms full of toys and equipment, tutors and therapists. But material pleasures can't buy peace of mind, and all the excess leads to more anxiety—parents fear that their children will not be able to sustain this rarefied lifestyle and will fall off the mountain the parents have built for them.

In their eagerness to do right by their children, parents not only overindulge them materially, they also spoil them emotionally. Many parents have unhappy memories of their own childhoods, memories of not being allowed to express their feelings or participate in decisions. In trying to undo these past violations, they move too far in the other direction—they overvalue their children's need for self-expression and turn their households into little democracies. But the equality they maintain at home does not give their children a sense of self-esteem. Instead, it frightens them by sending the message that their parents are not firmly in charge. By refusing to be authority figures, these parents don't empower their children, they make them insecure.

An especially troubling aspect of modern child-rearing is the way parents fetishize their children's achievements and feelings and neglect to help them develop a sense of duty to others. I saw an example of this when a child died at a secular high school where I lecture. The day after the tragedy, adults were stationed around the campus so the children would have someone to talk to if they felt bad. There were no *mitzvot* (sacred good deeds) to be done on behalf of the dead child, no organized lessons in social obligation. In the religious community the students might help to prepare and deliver dinners to the family or escort the younger brother home from school. The emphasis in this purely secular community was to keep the children's self-regard intact and their mood elevated.

The current trend in parenting is to shield children from emotional or physical discomfort. I can't blame parents for reacting with horror to nightly news reports about our violent, dangerous society, but many of them overprotect their sons and daughters. They don't give them a chance to learn how to maneuver on their own outside of home or school. It's not only violence these parents fear; they are also alarmed by what they perceive to be a wildly uncertain future. Wishing to prepare their children for this unknown territory, they try to armor them with a thick layer of skills by giving them lots of lessons and pressuring them to compete and excel.

In this hothouse environment, children receive plenty of attention and worldly goods, but they pay a price for it. They learn very quickly that they are not to show too much unhappiness, frustration, or disappointment. They must be good at everything and cheerful all the time because they are emblems of their parents' success.

I've come to believe that many of the problems in the children I counseled arose from two sources: the heavy pressure in a competitive world and their unconscious recognition of how preternaturally important they were to their parents. I recalled the children's chronic complaints, their social woes, their learning disabilities and problems paying attention in school. What better way for children to rebel against their parents' unrealistic expectations, take back some control, and resist being worshiped like an idol than to get sick or fail to excel?

THE JEWISH WAY:
MODERATION, CELEBRATION, SANCTIFICATION

Through the study and practice of Judaism, I learned that the parents I counseled had fallen into a trap created out of their own good intentions. Determined to give their children everything they needed to become "winners" in this highly competitive culture, they missed out on God's most sacred gift to us: the power and holiness of the present moment and of each child's individuality.

Judaism provides a very different kind of perspective on parenting. By sanctifying the most mundane aspects of the here and now, it teaches us that there is greatness not just in grand and glorious achievements but in our small, everyday efforts and deeds. Judaism shows us that we don't have to be swallowed up by our frenzied, materialistic world—we can take what is valuable from it without being wholly consumed.

Three cornerstone principles of Jewish living are moderation, celebration, and sanctification. Through these principles we can achieve a balanced life, no matter what culture we happen to inhabit. The Jewish way is to continually study, learn, question, and teach these principles. By applying them to our family life, my husband, my children, and I have found some mooring and meaning in an unsteady world. In my professional life, I've seen families transformed by this new perspective on their problems in living.

The principle of moderation teaches us to do two seemingly incompatible things at once: to passionately embrace the material world that God has created—"And God saw that it was good"—while exercising self-discipline. Judaism clarifies our proper perspective on engagement with the world. We are not to emulate animals, who act on instinct; the pagans, who worship nature and the senses for their own sake; the angels, who don't struggle with longing; or the ascetics, who shun earthly pleasures. God created us with intense desire and free will on purpose, and it is up to us to use this endowment for good or ill.

Moderation leads to the second principle, celebration. We are obliged to embrace God's gifts moderately but enthusiastically; in other words, we are obliged to give thanks and to party. Celebration takes hundreds of forms: the Jewish liturgy contains blessings over food, rainbows, new clothes, a narrow escape from danger, a day of rest, doing something for the first time, and even earthquakes (this last prayer can be loosely translated as "Wow, God, you are one powerful being!"). The requirement to party is easily fulfilled by a nonstop, year-round cycle of major and minor holidays.

The Jewish concept of celebration is beautifully illustrated in a story related by the leading rabbi of nineteenth-century Germany, Sampson Raphael Hirsch: "A rabbi told his congregation that he was planning a trip to Switzerland. 'Why Switzerland?' they asked him. 'There is hardly any Jewish community there. What reason could you have for traveling so far?' The rabbi replied, 'I don't want to meet my maker and have Him say to me, "What? You never saw My Alps?"'"

Celebration and gratitude are key concepts in Judaism and Jewish child-rearing. We are commanded to be constantly on guard for opportunities to be grateful for the richness of the world and for our good fortune, whatever form it takes. Through its spiritual calendar, rituals, and blessings, Judaism offers families many ways to practice and teach gratitude and joy.

Sanctification, the third principle, is the process of acknowledging the holiness in everyday actions and events. Since the Second Temple in Jerusalem was destroyed in 70 C.E., the place of greatest holiness has become not the synagogue but our own homes. One traditional Jewish expression for *home* is the same as the word for a house of worship: *mikdash me'at,* or "little holy place." Our dining table with our children is an altar. It has the potential to be the holiest spot on the planet.

In Jewish tradition, there are rules designed to help us sanctify all our daily enterprises, from the way we treat our spouses to the way we treat our children, our household help, even our pets. There are rules for reproof, for praise, for greeting in the morning and going to sleep at night, because in Jewish tradition each of these activities is holy.

THE PRACTICE OF RAISING CHILDREN

The purpose of having children, according to the teachings of the Torah, is not to create opportunities for our glory or for theirs. The purpose of having children and raising them to be self-reliant, compassionate, ethical adults is to ensure that there will be people here to honor God after we are gone. So the rules regarding child-rearing are not primarily about making children feel good, but about making children into good people.

The Torah, the Talmud, and the writings of learned Jewish thinkers over the centuries provide invaluable wisdom to help parents with the great task of raising their children. I've tried to distill this wisdom into a form that contemporary mothers and fathers will find not just inspiring in theory but also effective during the day-to-day scramble. Each of the chapters that follow is devoted to an aspect of parenting that Jewish thinkers have deemed crucial to raising children:

- Accept that your children are both unique and ordinary.
- Teach them to honor their parents and to respect others—family, friends, and community.
- Teach them to be resilient, self-reliant, and courageous.
- Teach them to be grateful for their blessings.
- Teach them the value of work.
- Teach them to make their table an altar—to approach food with an attitude of moderation, celebration, and sanctification.
- Teach them to accept rules and to exercise self-control.
- Teach them the preciousness of the present moment.
- Teach them about God.

This is the blueprint Jewish parents have followed for three thousand years, and I believe it will work in any era, any city, any home.

FINDING YOUR OWN WAY
IN YOUR OWN TIME

A beautiful element in Judaism is its tradition of tolerance, revealed by the ancient saying, "The holy one does not come to His creatures with excessive demands." God does not demand of people more than they can give, but we are required to try to give something. In The Ethics of the Fathers (a collection of ethical maxims dating back to before the first century), Rabbi Tarfon teaches, "It is not your responsibility to complete the work [of perfecting the world] but you are not free to desist from it either."

The Torah understands that we all come into the world, and to God, differently. In the Book of Exodus, reference is made to the "mixed multitude"—a phrase used to describe all the people whom Moses led across the Red Sea and into the Promised Land. The group was composed of people at different levels of Egyptian society, from widely divergent backgrounds. Then and now, we all need different things from God, and God expects different things from each of us.

I continue to struggle with every aspect of Judaism—with theology, ritual, and community. Anything close to perfect faith escapes me, although I never doubt that there is a distilled truth in religion, a truth that can be defined as the recognition that a created universe gives us both meaning and obligation. But struggling with God does not diminish my commitment, because in Judaism struggle is built into the theology. Look at Moses, who spent his entire career in a lively debate with God! Just as we are never supposed to stop studying Torah, we are never supposed to stop questioning it, either. In that spirit, I offer this book as either a philosophy for child-rearing or an introduction to Judaism. Any parent—unaffiliated, Reform or Orthodox, Jewish or not—can benefit from the wisdom of the rabbis and scholars whose ideas I've mined for these pages.

Even after learning Jewish principles of living that stunned me with their psychological insight and common sense, I have not entirely escaped the perils of parenting today. I have not liberated myself from having grand aspirations for my children or from overindulging and overscheduling them, but I have moved a few degrees out of the zone of competition, pressure, and anxiety that led me to ruminate so often in the night. I don't worry about my age as much as I used to, because my children are part of a solid and portable community. I hope they will develop a robust relationship with God that will supplement their relationship with their mortal parents. When confronted with ethical dilemmas, they will have a framework for evaluating right and wrong, and a sense of a higher power to whom they are accountable. On a lonely Friday night away at college, they will be able to find something they grew up with at home—warmth in the candles at a Shabbat dinner on campus, familiar songs and prayers. We are giving them a tradition they can pass on to their children.

This book is not a formula for foolproof parenting. It is a lens, a way to look at the world, your life, and your family. Judaism has given my family unexpected moments of closeness and harmony, clarity about daily ethical dilemmas, and a sense of the holy potential of everyday life. It has guided me as a parent more profoundly than any other way of thinking I've yet found, and I hope it will do the same for you.

There is one question that sums up everything I have learned about the power of Jewish teachings to guide us in every generation. It's a question that rabbis like to ask schoolchildren:

What's the most important moment in Jewish history?

The giving of the Torah on Sinai?

No.

The parting of the Red Sea?

No. Right now. This is the most important moment in Jewish history.

CHAPTER 2

The Blessing of Acceptance:

Discovering Your Unique and Ordinary Child

I recently read a third-grade school newsletter that used the word *special* five times on two pages. The Thanksgiving Sing was special. So was the Spellathon. The Emerging Artists exhibition was special. Even the unassuming Pie Drive was, for reasons not clearly revealed by the newsletter coverage, special indeed. And, finally, this year's third-grade class was in itself a very, very special group.

I wondered, Is it possible? So much specialness concentrated in one place? A cosmic coincidence? Or was this really an extraordinary school with unusually dazzling children, committed teachers, generous and energetic families? In fact, this school is a fine and good one. The children are intelligent and well behaved, the teachers care, the parents give of their time and money. But it is not a terribly unusual school, and I questioned the benefit of believing otherwise.

The third-grade newsletter was not unique. At nearly every campus I visit, the staff, the posters on the walls, and the overall atmosphere emphasize that this is not merely a place of learning, it's a breeding ground for enlightened, compassionate champions. The schools are not to blame for their hubris. Parents, with their grand expectations for their children, have sparked the outbreak of specialness.

My friend Paula, who runs a terrific elementary school, told of taking a mother on a prospective parents' tour of the campus. The mom said that her daughter Sloane had a strong interest in science. "At another school I visited, the kindergarten teachers put streamers in the trees to demonstrate the properties of wind to the students," she reported. "I'm hoping you would do that here too. I wouldn't want Sloaner to miss out."

"We have leaves on our trees," Paula responded. "They do the same thing. Can't guarantee we'll be using streamers." Sloane's mother sent her daughter to the school with the streamers.

The principal of another school complained to me about his frustration with parents' expectations:

Too many parents want everything fixed by the time their child is eight. They want academic perfection, a child as capable as any other child in the Western hemisphere. Children develop in fits and starts, but nobody has time for that anymore. No late bloomers, no slow starters, nothing unusual accepted! If a child doesn't get straight A's, his parents start fretting that he's got a learning disability or a motivation problem. The normal curve has disappeared. Parents seem to think that children only come in two flavors: learning disabled and gifted. Not every child has unlimited potential in all areas. This doesn't mean most kids won't be able to go to college and to compete successfully in the adult world. Almost all of them will. Parents just need to relax a little and be patient.

What's going on here? Why does the newsletter shout hosannas? Why is Sloane's mother so anxious for her daughter to experience a miniature physics lab in kindergarten? Why can't parents let their eight-year-olds develop at a natural, raggedy pace?

When I began studying Judaism, one of the first things that struck me was how directly it spoke to the issue of parental pressure. According to Jewish thought, parents should not expect their children to be anyone other than who they are. A Hasidic teaching says, "If your child has a talent to be a baker, don't ask him to be a doctor." Judaism holds that every child is made in the divine image. When we ignore a child's intrinsic strengths in an effort to push him toward our notion of extraordinary achievement, we are undermining God's plan.

If the pressure to be special gets too intense, children end up in the therapist's office suffering from sleep and eating disorders, chronic stomachaches, hair-pulling, depression, and other ailments. They are casualties of their parents' drive for perfection. It was children such as these who spurred me to look outside standard therapeutic practices for ways to help. In Judaism I found an approach that respects children's uniqueness while accepting them in all their ordinary glory.

MISSION: PERFECTION

In Chapter 1 I described my surprise and confusion when, after conducting tests and telling parents that their child was "within normal limits," the parents were frequently disappointed. In their view, a diagnosable problem was better than a normal, natural limitation. A problem can be fixed, but a true limitation requires adjustment of expectations and acceptance of an imperfect son or daughter. Parents feel hope if their restless child is actually hyperactive, their dreamy child has ADD, their poor math student has a learning disorder, their shy child has a social phobia, their wrongdoing son has "intermittent explosive disorder." If there is a diagnosis, specialists and tutors can be hired, drugs given, treatment plans made, and parents can maintain an illusion that the imperfection can be overcome. Their faith in their child's unlimited potential is restored.

Why are parents so anxious to be raising perfect children? The answer is twofold: pride and fear of the future.

My Child, My Masterpiece

Janet asked for advice from me and the other members of our parenting class about how to "talk sense" to her older son.

> Do you know about the Johns Hopkins Talent Search? They offer sixth graders the chance to take the SAT. If a student scores in the same range as the average twelfth grader on either verbal or math he qualifies for a special summer academic program on a college campus. I know that Dylan would qualify in math but he says he doesn't want to sit for the test. This is crazy because the school wouldn't even know his score and if he makes it and enters the talent search program it would look great on his transcript.

Laypeople call it bragging; psychologists describe it as "achievement by proxy syndrome." Some parents use their children's achievements for their own sense of security, personal glory, or the fulfillment of unfulfilled dreams. Even parents who don't use their children as a hedge against existential fears or a badge of their own worth can find it hard not to succumb to the fever of competition.

It wasn't always this way. In the past, parents produced children for their work value (hands to labor on the farm). Today many parents see their children's achievement as an important family "product." This attitude leads to an upside-down, child-centered perspective where we cater to children's whims yet pressure them to achieve at all costs—academically, socially, and athletically. But this pressure can backfire.

Children who feel that they are expected to surpass their parents' already high level of achievement or to demonstrate skills that are beyond their capabilities will suffer. Some children are one-trick ponies, and trying to get them to master a broad variety of skills is futile and destructive. Keep at it, and they'll even forget their one trick. Other children begin to feel as if they are working only for their parents' satisfaction, and they openly rebel. Some respond to the pressure by losing their intrinsic enjoyment of mastering skills, and still others use psychosomatic symptoms to get out of the running. By exaggerating their defects, these children hope to avoid failure and to have their progress measured by more individual, realistic standards.

Your child is not your masterpiece. According to Jewish thought, your child is not even truly "yours." In Hebrew there is no verb for possession; the expression we translate as "to have," *yesh li*, actually means "it is there for me" or "there is for me." Although nothing belongs to us, God has made everything available on loan and has invited us to borrow it to further the purpose of holiness. This includes our children. They are a precious loan, and each one has a unique path toward serving God. Our job is to help them find out what it is.

Conquering the Future with Brave Little Generalists

If children were required to excel only in certain areas, they might be better able to cope with their parents' expectations. Psychologist Michael Thompson says that we make unfairly "generic" demands on our adolescents: "It is the only period in your life when you're expected to do all things well. Adults don't hold themselves to those standards. We don't interview the pediatrician about whether he can throw a basketball, or quiz our accountant on biology before we let her do our taxes. In elementary and high school we celebrate the generalist, but in the real world there is no room for the generalist except on *Jeopardy!*"

The age at which we expect children to become very good at everything is getting lower. Part of the reason for this is parents' fears of an uncertain future, one that is hurtling at us more quickly than ever before. The computer bought today can be replaced by a cheaper, lighter, snappier-looking one with a faster modem by the time we get it out of the box. Parents worry that in this hyperpaced world, only the child who excels at everything will survive. If young Maya can't design her own Web site, stay at the very top of her class, run a marathon, and speak confidently before large groups, she'll be left in the dust.

Our attempts to prepare our children for the future are limited by our own imaginations of what the future will be like. We're apprehensive, but our children are not. The high-tech, rapidly changing world that seems so mind-bending to us is normal to them. "Preparing" our children for this new world by turning them into supercompetitive generalists is useless because we can't second-guess the skills they will need twenty years from now. The only things that are certain to be valuable are character traits such as honesty, tenacity, flexibility, optimism, and compassion— the same traits that have served people well for centuries.

Fear of the Ordinary: Lake Wobegon Parenting

Remember Lake Wobegon, the fictional town created by Garrison Keillor, where "all the women are strong, all the men are good-looking, and all the children are above average"? That sunny, statistics-defying state of mind is familiar turf for elementary school teachers. They describe hearing the same song every year when it's time for parent conferences. One weary middle school director told me,

Parents are so nervous. If their child is doing well in everything it's like a badge for them that everything is OK. If their child is, God forbid, average, they panic. That's why so many teachers have started giving "Lake Wobegon" report cards. Teachers are afraid that if they give anything less than an A, parents will blame their child's poor achievement on the teacher's lack of skill rather than on the child's limitations. This is a shame, because real problems get glossed over or missed until fourth grade, when there's no more hiding it and the child's weaker areas show up on standardized tests.

Some parents can maintain the specialness myth with their children long past fourth grade. Is this good for the child's self-esteem? Listen to Isabel, a student I interviewed at an elite private school. Isabel will be entering the eleventh grade next year. She told me that she was having a hard time socially. The last two boys she wanted to have as boyfriends hadn't been interested in her. Her teachers seemed to favor other students. She felt confused and hurt:

> I know why this is so hard for me. My mom and dad always, always made me feel like I was the best: the most beautiful, the smartest, the most charming. And mostly I've done well in everything. But, now I'm finding out that I'm not that unusual. Maybe I'm good enough, but I don't know anymore.

Like so many parents, Isabel's mother and father were afraid their daughter would think she was ordinary. Whether they were also reluctant to admit to themselves that their child was "merely" average, I don't know. But their Lake Wobegon attitude has not benefited Isabel. They've put her on a pedestal and now she's stuck up there, unable to find out what level she would reach if she had a chance to bob around with everybody else.

BOYS AND GIRLS: EQUAL BUT DIFFERENT

There is another aspect of contemporary child-rearing that places still more pressure on our children. Over the past twenty years, teachers and social scientists have downplayed the differences between boys and girls. It's been done as a corrective to a history of inequality, but the result is that we've come to expect boys to behave like girls and girls like boys in circumstances where this is difficult for them. There's no question that all children should be encouraged to pursue whatever field interests them, but a gender-blind approach can sometimes increase the stress on our overstressed kids. Gone are the gender-based safe havens of the past; now both sexes have the opportunity—the obligation—to excel in every arena, from academics to sports, from being a good listener to being a leader.

God is the original maker of distinctions: light from darkness, the seventh day of rest from the six days of labor, sacred from profane. While remaining aware of the potential for discrimination, we can also remain respectful of innate distinctions between boys and girls. For example, their interests and developmental stages are often different. Instead of trying to ignore or flatten these differences, we can pay attention to the ways they are revealed in our children's behavior. If you fear that acknowledging any gender differences will lead to unfair treatment, your children may miss out on getting what they need. In order to treat our daughters and sons fairly it is sometimes necessary to treat them differently. Honoring distinctions can lead to equal opportunity.

Inappropriate Expectations of Boys

Laurie's son, Noah, was born when her daughter, Rachel, was four. "I was amazed at the differences from the start," she said. "When Noah was a baby he shouted 'Ball!' whenever he saw the letter O. He insisted that I walk on the trafficky side of the street instead of the lovely tree-lined residential side so he could see the trucks up close. He called out to every one, 'Rrruuum! Rrruuum!'"

Noah concentrated so hard that he could do only one thing

at a time. If Laurie wanted him to listen to her, she had to hold his three-year-old face in her hands. She couldn't take him with her on errands because he'd run away. Laurie and her husband, Mark, decided that they would never allow Noah to have toy guns or to watch TV, only educational videos. That didn't stop Noah from shooting at everything—he'd just cock his finger or make a gun out of his toast or a graham cracker.

What will happen when this truck-loving, hyperfocused, shoot-'em-up guy gets to kindergarten? When he has to sit still at a table for a chunk of the day and practice printing upper- and lowercase letters? When he has to cooperate nicely *all day long*? When no fart noises or finger guns are permitted? ("Noah, I know you remember how to use your words, right, Noah?")

Here's what his teacher might tell Laurie: "Noah has such a hard time sitting still and following instructions. We're wondering if this might be ADD. Of course, Noah is too young for us to know for sure yet. But you might consider having him tested next year."

Kindergarten used to be a place for making clay handprints, singing songs, and listening to stories, nothing more. The teacher's goal was to help the children learn how to be part of a group and to swim around in a pond bigger than their own home and family. But in many schools today the early elementary grades have become a time for mastering high-level academic tasks, and this takes a level of concentration, discipline, and fine motor skill that lots of boys haven't yet developed. Debbie Davis, a school-based learning specialist in Los Angeles, described a group of second-grade boys and girls she had recently evaluated. "The differences were apparent on the first day I worked with them. The girls could concentrate twice as long as the boys and wanted to do whatever they could to please me. They told me they loved my bracelets. The boys didn't last too long on the phonics assessment before they started a lively and graphic discussion of what happens when you throw up on a ship."

Most boys get by just fine in school, but many do suffer from our inappropriate expectations for their performance and comportment. As classrooms get more crowded, the problems get worse. I suspect that if Tom Sawyer were around today he might be put on Ritalin. For some boys, our inappropriate expectations are a recipe for resentment of adults, demoralization, bitterness about schoolwork, and shame about normal "boyishness."

Oppressive Standards for Girls

What of our expectations for girls? Fifteen-year-old Allegra is beautiful, capable, and articulate. She attends an all-girls' high school, where she earns straight A's. Allegra also plays the bassoon, not because she loves the sound but because she believes that this unusually difficult double-reed instrument will give her an edge on an Ivy League college admission.

Allegra doesn't have time to go to parties anymore. Most of the time she is working. Allegra is often up at midnight or 5 A.M., pounding out twice as many pages as were assigned on her English essays. Only last year she was a happy-go-lucky middle schooler; now she's ten pounds underweight, almost always has a stomachache, and by constantly winding her hair around her finger while she studies, has pulled out many tiny patches at her hairline.

If boys risk getting their spirits crushed in early elementary school, girls face a different challenge—fulfilling impossible expectations in adolescence. Allegra is under siege from the pressure to excel in everything. She believes what girls have always believed: it's important to be a sympathetic listener, good in English and the arts, as slender as a model. And she feels that in order to be genuinely worthy she has to excel in all the traditionally male domains as well: winning prizes at the science fair, making the varsity volleyball team, getting elected head of the student council. Allegra has this to say about her future: "I know I have high expectations but I sometimes feel that if I don't attend at least one summit conference in my life and personally solve the problem of hunger in Rwanda I will be a failure. Not to my parents, just to myself."

While we've made strides in actively promoting equal rights for women and recognizing emotional vulnerability in men, we've ignored some of the other protections boys and girls need—protection of young boys' natural rough-and-readiness and protection of girls from feeling they must excel in everything all the time. If we want to give our children what they need to thrive, we must honor their basic nature—boyish or girlish, introverted or extroverted, wild or mellow.

AN ANTIDOTE TO SPECIALITIS:
ORDINARY HOLINESS

A key concept in Hasidic thought expresses the idea of balance: "Keep two pieces of paper in your pockets at all times. On one write, 'I am a speck of dust.' On the other, 'The world was created for me.'" The divine and the ordinary merge in Judaism, where the holiest day of the year is not Yom Kippur, the majestic and awesome Day of Atonement, but every Saturday. This potentially average day of the week is such a distinctive time that, according to tradition, a band of ministering angels follows each person home from synagogue to help usher in the special spirit of the day.

In Judaism, a holy place is not a magnificent cathedral but the sukkah, a rickety hut erected in the backyard or on the balcony to celebrate the harvest in early autumn. Holy objects? The Torah, a length of parchment wound around two undistinguished wooden rollers. Holy food? Challah, a plain egg bread.

And on what does the future of the world rest? Not on great acts of heroism but on the breath of schoolchildren who are studying their tradition. This very democratic system gives a special grace to every child and stunning glory to none.

Within Judaism you can find an antidote to the "specialitis" our culture fosters. Judaism asks that we raise our children not in hope that they are the Messiah but to be themselves. Consider the wisdom of Rabbi Zusya, an early Hasidic leader and folk hero. Zusya was known as a modest and benevolent man who, despite his meager knowledge of Torah, attained merit because of his innocence and personal righteousness. Before he died he said, "When I reach the world to come, God will not ask me why I wasn't more like Moses. He will ask me why I wasn't more like Zusya."

In Judaism we are continually reminded to take into account our children's differences and allow natural endowment to reveal itself. Throughout the Torah, the sages make reference to the need to preach and guide in a way that will reach each person. At the Passover seder, tradition instructs us to tell the story of our escape to freedom so that it will be understood not only by the wise child, but also by the wicked, the simple, and the clueless one; each at his own level, each with the right tone and language. The Jewish message is consistent: Every child is unique. Don't treat all children the same way or you will not reach them.

How can you see your child's gifts and limits clearly? How much can and should be left in God's hands? Here are some guidelines that have been a great help to the parents with whom I work.

EXPECT DIFFERENCES

I once read a beautiful teaching attributed simply to "a modern educator." It read: "Try to see your child as a seed that came in a packet without a label. Your job is to provide the right environment and nutrients and to pull the weeds. You can't decide what kind of flower you'll get or in which season it will bloom." When we are open to the differences in our children, we'll give them the soil they need to flourish.

Learn and Accept Your Child's Temperament

Simon's parents came to see me because he was falling behind in school. The middle child of three, Simon's pace and talents were different from those of other family members: he ate more slowly, he wasn't interested in reading the comic page in the newspaper, he was a better athlete, a better artist, and more outgoing than either his parents or his siblings. If the family was on an outing and they walked past someone eating an ice cream cone, genial Simon might say, "That looks good. What flavor is it?" instantly and effortlessly acquiring a new friend.

Simon attended a high-pressure school and had a hard time keeping up academically. When I met the family, he was pale and had become withdrawn. He was being tutored in four out of five subjects and took medication for Attention Deficit Disorder. He had a poor appetite and a facial tic. After switching to a school with a slower pace and less social and academic pressure and replacing tutoring with visits to a skateboard park after school twice a week, Simon blossomed. He no longer needed medication to concentrate on schoolwork and homework. His spirits were high.

Many families have a Simon, a child whose talents and tempo and needs differ from what is assumed to be normal by the rest of the group. Your "different" child may be fast-paced, impatient, and quick to act, while your family tends to be slower and more reflective. Your child's temperament is a God-given blueprint for his personality; he couldn't change it even if he wanted to. Rather than fret because he doesn't approach the world in a way you can easily understand, try raising your tolerance for differences.

It helps to know that the psychiatric definition of "normal" is quite broad. In a landmark study of temperament, researchers Stella Chess and Alexander Thomas found a wide range of normal variations in children's natures that were obvious even in infancy. Some of the attributes they studied included:

- Emotional intensity: some babies rarely whimper and are easily pacified, while others are often frustrated or upset and will howl for hours.
- Persistence: some are easily redirected to a new activity and will take no for an answer, while others refuse to cooperate and will fight to continue in their chosen activity.
- Flexibility: some children adapt easily to change, surprise, or a break from routine, while others will resolutely reject anything new, such as toast cut in triangles instead of rectangles.
- Sensitivity: some children are easily disturbed by loud noises, smells, rough or slimy textures, or tags on clothing. These children are often also highly perceptive and aware of emotional nuances or visual details. They are the ones who notice your shifting moods, a rainbow in the gutter, Mom's new earrings, or the letter X formed by spaghetti strands.
- Energy: some children thrash around when sleeping, can't pass a door frame without jumping up to touch the header, spill their milk at every meal, and can't tolerate long car rides. Others will sit and play quietly for hours and move slowly when it is time to switch to a new activity.
- In first reactions to new situations, such as new food, a new car seat, or a new playmate, some children are always wary, while others plunge right in.
- Mood: some are happy and optimistic, others serious or bristly.

- Sociability: some children are more solitary and private and refuel by solitary activities such as playing Nintendo. Others refuel by being with people; they share thoughts and feelings easily, make others feel comfortable, and love to talk. These are the children who will follow you to the bathroom and stand right outside the door keeping up a nonstop monologue.

Too often parents interpret a child's behavior as rebelliousness when in fact she is just being true to her nature. In some ways, this goes back to wanting our children to be our opus. We expect them to be like us (only better, smarter, and more ambitious), and if they veer too far in a different direction, we assume they must be doing it to get attention or to rebel. Parents who adopt children recognize that there will be inherent differences between their children and themselves, but biological parents are sometimes slower to catch on. One of the most generous gifts you can give your child is to study her temperament, and once you've learned it, work to accept it.

Stay Tuned In to Gender Differences

Choose your targets for criticism with care. Lisa told me that once she started thinking about loosening up her standards of proper comportment for her son, Oliver, she realized that "I was always on him. I was like a diagnostician. Show me Ollie in any situation and I could tell you what he was doing wrong."

Instead of criticizing her son at every turn she chose one behavior to try to alter at a time. Her first target was jumping on the furniture. She approached the problem from a few different angles. Wanting to respect Ollie's high energy level, she provided an alternative jumping opportunity: a mini-trampoline in the family room. She also put a sign on the couch that said "No Jumping" and immediately intervened by banning Ollie from the room if he started to jump. "Sorry, Ollie, You have lost your family room privileges for today. I'm sure you won't forget the rule tomorrow." Once "no jumping" became a habit, Lisa set to work on helping Ollie to remember to use his "inside voice" instead of shouting when he was in the house. She approached other problem behaviors by protecting Ollie from temptation. Since he couldn't seem to resist racing the shopping cart down the aisle in the supermarket, she decided to avoid taking him there unless she had no alternative. Her overall goal? To avoid giving Ollie the impression that his rambunctiousness was something to feel ashamed of.

To help your daughter maintain balance in a world that fills her with mixed-up expectations—be a flawless beauty, be the next surgeon general—talk openly to her about these issues and about the pressure to be the best in everything. Encourage her to pursue hobbies and pleasurable activities instead of focusing all her energy on the big-ticket items that look good on college transcripts. Resist mocking or demeaning her early adolescent vanity or boy craziness. And watch the example you set. One mother told our class that she always took off her glasses when she looked in the mirror so she wouldn't see her beauty flaws up too close. Another confessed that she weighed herself twice a day. It's no use hiding tricks like this from your daughter. She is psychic. You can't expect her to accept herself when you are zealously self-critical. To truly set an example for her, you have to be willing to look in the mirror, get off the scale, and accept yourself as God made you.

ACCEPT "GOOD ENOUGH" FOR YOUR CHILD

Donald Winnicott, the British pediatrician and psychoanalyst, often wrote about "good enough mothering" and the "ordinary devoted mother." He says that "inherited potential will be realized" when "the environmental provision is adequate." *Adequate,* not exceptional. You can only do your part. You can't control the outcome. In our competitive world, it's often easy to forget this and to blame ourselves, our child's teacher, or other outside influences if our child is not achieving at an extraordinary level or doesn't seem terrifically happy.

Dr. Winnicott is reminding us that in order to flourish, children don't need the best of everything. Instead they simply need what is good enough. This may include good enough (but dull) homework assignments, good enough (but a little crabby or uninspired) teachers, good enough (although insect-infested and humid) summer camps, and good enough (although bossy and shallow) friends. Consider that "good enough" can often be best for your child, because when life is mostly ordinary and just occasionally extraordinary, your child won't end up with expectations of herself and those around her that can't be met on this worldly plane.

Recently an acquaintance of mine took the "good enough" plunge with her sixth-grade daughter, Gaby. Gaby was not unhappy in her private school, just unenthusiastic. Her mother had to prod her to do her homework each night. After testing showed that Gaby was qualified for a magnet program for the highly gifted, she transferred from the private school to a public middle school of two thousand students. The bathrooms at the new school were so dirty that Gaby never used them after midday. Twice during her first year students were arrested for having weapons on campus. At her previous school there were twenty-two students in each class. At the new school there were thirty-four. Here's what Gaby said about the experience:

> I never realized it before, but in my old school I thought there was something wrong with me. I love to read and no one else in my class had books all over their room. My new school is so fun. All the kids in my program have my sense of humor!

They read the same books I do and we trade them all the time. I'm working ten times harder than I did last year but it's worth it. I'm really happy here.

Gaby's mom and dad saw what their daughter needed and took a chance at providing it for her. The campus, class size, and bathrooms were far below the standards her parents would have preferred, but for Gaby the school was more than good enough.

DON'T PRESSURE YOURSELF TO BE AN EXTRAORDINARY PARENT

I meet many parents who are trying so hard to be perfect parents, to make everything just right for their children, that they're draining away their pleasure in parenting. They're too exhausted and too unconsciously resentful to enjoy the amazing show of childhood. For these parents, every minute needs to count. If Lana is playing in a puddle, Mom needs to turn the experience into a science lesson about microorganisms. If pre-teen Brandon is restless or in a bad mood, his parents strive to get to the bottom of it instead of letting him be.

There are a few varieties in the garden of perfect parents. Some stay-at-home-and-raise-the-kids moms figure that they had better do a superb job of it to prove to themselves and others that they're succeeding at the art, craft, and science of child-rearing. Some full-time working moms want things to be very special for their children because they feel guilty for not being around as much as their own mothers were. The moms who work part-time do a bit of both! And then there are all of us "geriatric" parents. Provided with these precious little vessels for our hopes and dreams, we turn them into our latest project. With midlife recognition of mortality at hand, we're set up to have unrealistic expectations of ourselves and our children.

My advice to all of these parents is to tolerate some low-quality time. Have a little less ambition for yourself and your children. Plan nothing—disappoint your kids with your essential mediocrity and the dullness of your home. Just hang around your children and wait to see what develops. Strive to be a "good enough" parent, not a great one. It can make everyone in the family relax and paradoxically make life richer.

SEE YOUR CHILD'S TEACHER AS AN ALLY

Every child cannot be good in everything, and no amount of encouragement or teacher talent can make it so. It usually falls to a teacher to deliver the news that our child is not the next Einstein or Marie Curie. Many parents are not prepared to hear this, not even in the early grades. Last year I had a call from a father who was angry and insulted about the treatment his son was getting at the hands of his second-grade teacher:

> Reed's teacher doesn't appreciate how special he is. He started talking when he was ten months old, played complicated games on the computer before he entered kindergarten, and impresses everyone he meets with his intelligence and creativity. Except for this teacher. All she seems to care about are a few missing homework assignments and the fact that he talks a little too much in class. My wife and I want to interview the other second-grade teacher and possibly have Reed transferred to her class, but the school doesn't think we have an adequate reason for doing so.

This father was not pleased to learn that in my opinion, removing Reed from his class would send at least three damaging messages: that whenever he isn't delighted with a situation he can escape it rather than see it through; that the usual rules don't apply to him; and that he needn't respect the authority of his teachers. I told Reed's dad that when a parent complains about a child's awful teacher I usually say, "Great! He'll learn a whole new set of coping skills dealing with her, skills he'll need on the job and in marriage." If you feel that every teacher in the school is underwhelming, you've got a problem. Either the school is inappropriate or your criteria are unrealistic.

The ultimate test of parents' relationship with their child's teacher comes at report card time. Today's teachers are experts in the art of constructive criticism, of affirming children and building up their strengths. At many schools, boys and girls are coddled and protected. Their report cards are lyrical essays full of detailed observations about what makes each child extraordinary. One principal observed that the report cards have become a cross between "a work of romantic fiction and a legal document."

In contrast, the Jewish day school to which I sent my two daughters was wonderfully matter-of-fact. I recall a parent-teacher conference lasting under seven minutes, including the small talk, but we learned what we needed to know about our daughter: she was doing well. If we needed flattery, we could talk to her grandparents about her. The school was not a cruise ship. When the girls graduated they would not be shocked to discover that life isn't a process of continuous encouragement. Unfortunately, this straightforward approach is the exception, not the rule.

The trend toward Lake Wobegon report cards is a recent one. For most of this century children's feelings were not spared when it came time for grades. When the writer Roald Dahl was a boarding school student in the 1920s, his English composition master had this to say about him:

I have never met a boy who so persistently says the opposite of what he means. He seems incapable of marshalling his thoughts on paper. . . . Consistently idle. Ideas limited . . . A

persistent muddler. Vocabulary negligible, sentences malcon-
structed. He reminds me of a camel. See his report on boxing.
Precisely the same remarks apply. Too slow and ponderous.
His punches are not well timed and easily seen coming.

This teacher's biting review reminded me that frank talk has
evaporated from most report cards—and that it takes time for
children's talents to develop. If you can look at your children's
early efforts and uneven report cards calmly, you'll see how they
are progressing through the hard business of thinking and
growing.

Your child's teacher spends nearly as many hours during the
week with your child as you do. While you are the expert on
your own Nora or Eli, she is the expert on seven-year-olds and
knows more about them than you ever will. By giving her the
benefit of the doubt and resisting playing either offense or
defense, you have a better chance of making her both your and
your child's ally.

Wondering whether to label your child's misbehavior as prob-
lematic or normal? Check in with the nonclinical experts all
around you. If the math and science teacher says that your
daughter is doing poorly and you're feeling demoralized about
her abilities, schedule a visit with the art and music teachers.
Learn about how she functions and what motivates her in her
areas of strength. Bring this knowledge to your conference with
the math teacher. If the problems are social, do some sleuthing
and talk to the social experts—the parents of your child's
friends—to hear about what happens on both the successful
and unsuccessful play dates and sleepovers. Find out if other parents have the same expectations and the same problems. Jewish
wisdom teaches us not to hold ourselves apart from the community but to use it for support and learning.

LOVING OUR CHILDREN FOR THEIR OWN SAKE

The sages advise us to study Torah *lishma*—"for its own sake"—rather than to impress others with our scholarship. A paradox of parenting is that if we love our children for their own sake rather than for their achievements, it's more likely that they will reach their true potential. If you place too high a value on straight-A report cards and a slateful of extracurricular activities, your child may feel that she needs to excel in all areas in order to retain your respect. But if she senses that you respect her for the qualities with which she's been naturally endowed, she'll gain the confidence she needs to truly shine, even without streamers in the trees.

CHAPTER 3

The Blessing of Having
Someone to Look Up To:

Honoring Mother and Father

One afternoon recently a woman called to ask me to speak at her son's school. Here is what her end of our conversation sounded like:

> I think you should speak on Thursday the tenth of April, did you look in the bottom drawer? Because on the third the parents of the fourth graders, try on Daddy's desk, will be picking their kids up from the retreat, not before dinner, and they'll probably want to be at home with them that evening. I said you can have it for dessert, not now. Are you available on the tenth?

I had to decode which part of the message was for me and which part was directed to Barbara's son, Sam, who, at the time of the phone call, was both searching for Scotch tape and importuning his mother for a Popsicle. Fighting irritation, I wondered if the problem was Barbara's or mine. Was she just a nice, casual person and was I persnickety and old-fashioned? Was she multitasking? Or was she harming her son by letting him interrupt and walk all over her this way?

Parents' complaints about lack of respect range from the serious—"She actually said, 'Mom, I hope you die. Soon.'"—to the seemingly trivial—children leaving Oreo crumbs on their parents' bed. In general, they complain that their children talk back, don't accept no for an answer, don't help around the house without heavy-duty prodding, and use the parents' belongings without asking. This worries me, as I envision a future populated by self-absorbed, rude, thoughtless people—our children, grown up.

There are passages in the Torah requiring us to love God, to love ourselves, and to love our neighbors. Yet nowhere does God decree that children must love their parents! The Fifth Commandment—"Honor your father and your mother"—is about behavior, not feelings. Just as God understood that it is difficult for people to feel gratitude instead of envy, he also recognized that children are not naturally inclined to treat their parents with respect, so he commanded it.

The inclusion of the Fifth Commandment in the Big Ten is proof that rude children are nothing new. But today, more than ever, we sympathetic, fair-minded parents need to make a conscious effort to establish ourselves as the honored rulers in our homes. Yet many of the parents I talk to actually feel guilty about demanding respect from their children. They tell me they have an aversion to being authority figures, that it feels presumptuous, rigid, and undemocratic. Many prefer to think of themselves as their children's friends. I've heard mothers boast that they like the same styles, the same movies, and the same music their kids do.

But your children don't need two more tall friends. They have their own friends, all of whom are cooler than you. What they need are parents. You alone can guide them so they grow up strong and secure; you alone can teach them the rules of our culture so that when they're adults, they'll know how to fit in. The catch is, your children will only accept your guidance and heed your advice if they respect you. In fact, it's fair to say that if you don't teach your children to honor you, you'll have a very hard time teaching them anything else.

Judaism, with its two-thousand-year-old perspective on family dynamics, can help you take your rightful place at the head of the family table. Torah teaches that there are three partners in the creation of a person—God, the father, and the mother: "When a person honors the parents, God says, 'I consider it as though I lived with them and they honored me.'" On this earthly plane, parents are the holy stand-ins. By revering them, children have an opportunity to show their reverence for God. Honoring parents at home also helps children make the leap from family to community; it is a way to grow a civilized society.

HONORING THE OLDER GENERATION

Children learn by our example. If your children are to develop genuine respect for you, they need to know what respect looks like in action. More than listening to your words, they observe how you and your spouse treat your own parents. In Jewish theology, deed carries more weight than creed. This means that God is more interested in our actions than in pledges of faith, in how we treat others than in the quality of our prayer. The sages of the Talmud taught that God said, "Better that my people should forsake me but observe my laws, than believe in me but not observe my laws."

This truth is elegantly expressed in the story of the burgher Schmuel, whose elderly father kept spilling soup on the tablecloth because of his trembling fingers. One evening the old man dropped a fine teacup and it fell to the floor and broke.

"From now on you will eat in your room, Father," declared Schmuel. "Here is a wooden bowl for you to use. This, you cannot break!"

The next day Schmuel came home and saw his very young

son sitting on the floor trying to carve out a chunk of wood. "Dearest Yitzik, what are you doing?" Schmuel asked the boy.

"It's for you, Father," the son explained, "so you can use it to eat in your room when you are old and your hands start to shake."

For any of us with aging parents, this parable can be chilling. Do we give our parents the respect they deserve, or are we so busy accomplishing things and improving ourselves that it's more convenient to toss them a wooden bowl?

To be fair, it's not always easy to demonstrate respect for our parents even if we want to. We aren't the blacksmith, son of a blacksmith, so they can't teach us their trade. Nor do we necessarily see them very often. Many older people are independent and live far away; they have pension plans, condos in retirement communities, and enough money for their medical care. They don't need us for financial support, and they don't live near enough to help us care for our young children. The less we need one another, the less we see of one another. Often, families come together only on the High Holy Days of Thanksgiving, Passover, and Mother's Day.

The pace of our lives and the appliances and services available to us also erode our connection with the older generation. Observe the scene at the next birthday party your child attends: even relatively young and healthy grandparents can seem like tokens at these events, creatures from an ancient civilization unable to ascertain which of the varied, tiny buttons to press to make the video camera function. Willing but superfluous, they're not needed to cook the meal or supervise musical chairs because the food is provided by Domino's, the cake by the bakery, and the entertainment by the Lizard Lady.

Instead of having a practical need for one another, love alone becomes the hook that the whole relationship hangs on. This connection with our parents mostly takes place in an abstract realm of greeting cards, gifts, and checks. Even gift giving has become a problem in affluent families. One grandmother lamented, "I don't know what to buy for my granddaughter. She already has three hundred dresses." To remedy the situation, you need to maximize those times when you all come together, and consciously create opportunities to honor your parents. In our deed-centered religion, honor and love are best demonstrated by doing. So consider giving your parents a chance to "do."

This doesn't mean simply asking them to baby-sit or pick something up for you at the market. The purpose of this enterprise is not to help you out or save you time. The purpose is to demonstrate to your children that you cherish the unique contribution your parents make to the family. My husband's grandfather could bray, honk, and bleat a medley of startlingly accurate animal noises to amuse the children; my father-in-law accompanies our children's dancing and singing at the piano. My own father is a wonderful storyteller. We ask him to tell us about how he and the other young ice cream vendors would run into the ocean at Brighton Beach holding the heavy boxes of their wares over their heads until the police, aching to fine them for not having licenses but wanting to keep their feet dry, gave up in frustration. He delights me and my daughters with tales about entering (and losing) dance contests at the Savoy Ballroom in Harlem and about selling men's suits at Saks 34th Street along with the older salesmen: Mr. Gold, Mr. Diamond, Mr. Silver, and Mr. Seltzer. Both grandmothers contribute cuisine that I have neither the talent nor patience to prepare: cucumber salad, pot roast, mandelbrot, and Ukrainian roasted eggplant appetizer. My husband and I request these dishes, both for our own pleasure and to show our children how much we appreciate the special talents of our mothers.

Before you think about ways in which you can encourage your children to treat you more respectfully, take a few moments to reflect on the way you behave toward your parents and in-laws. Honoring them now is an investment in how you'll be treated when it's time for your children to decide whether to seat you at the dining table or hand you the wooden bowl.

One caveat, for those who are choking. In the *Mishneh Torah*, physician and philosopher Moses Maimonides provides guidance to people whose parents are cruel, crazy, or criminal. If an adult child is unable to endure the strain of an insane parent, he should leave the parent and appoint others to care for him properly. A child should turn his back completely on an abusive parent, because such a parent will be a bad influence on the grandchildren. If the parents' physical needs are so great that the child cannot care for them, Torah tells us to hire someone to do the job and to pay for it with the parents' money if they have enough. If they don't have the funds, the adult children must provide it. Nowhere is martyrdom even suggested, but everywhere in Jewish literature we are reminded that thoughtfulness, dignity, and compassion for those who brought us into the world is a divine mandate.

BUT WE ARE NOT WORTHY!

Most of you will agree that your parents deserve respect. But how well are you teaching your children about honoring *you*?

- Do you allow them to interrupt you unnecessarily when you are on the phone in a conversation with another adult?
- Do you have a designated place at the table? Do they sit in your place?
- Do they consistently contradict your words in the name of lobbying for their own point of view?
- Do they talk back to you in public? How often?
- Do you give your children enough opportunities to help out? To demonstrate thoughtfulness? To take care of you?
- Do your children ask if you want a glass of juice, a banana, a bowl of ice cream when they are getting one for themselves?

- Do they respect your privacy? Do they enter your room or take your things without asking?
- Do your older children commandeer the remote? Tie up the phone line? Forget to give you phone messages that they have taken?
- Do they talk too loudly at home? In public?

Are you squirming? Don't bother. You are not alone. Many intelligent, goodhearted, sensitive parents have trouble in this area. They have bred disrespectful children in large part because they don't demand respect from them. Why? Deep down, the parents don't believe they deserve it or that they can master the struggle. In my practice and parenting classes, I've encountered many of these "unworthy" parents. Let me introduce you to a few of them.

The Ideological Parent

Peter, a freelance graphic artist, and Lynn, an attorney, were having problems with their ten-year-old daughter, Sasha. More often than not, when they asked her a question, she would roll her eyes or ignore them. Sasha borrowed Lynn's clothes without permission and consistently interrupted Peter when he was on the phone. When Peter's parents came to visit, Sasha continued whatever she was doing and refused to go to the door to greet them.

"How do you feel when she does these things?" I asked Peter.

"We feel sad for her that she doesn't want to be closer to us," he said.

"Sad?" I repeated. "Don't you feel annoyed? I do, just listening to this. Have you thought about telling Sasha that she needs to speak respectfully to the exalted rulers in her home?"

"We want equality and mutual respect in our home," Peter

replied. "I don't believe in authority that is given and not earned."

And there it was, the source of the problem. My thoughts went back to the "Question Authority" buttons and the T-shirts from the late '60s and early '70s that said, "Never trust anyone over 30." Here were two parents, well over thirty, whose political philosophy was sabotaging their home life. Peter and Lynn rationalized away their feelings of irritation, indignation, and hurt by defending Sasha's right to self-expression and the value of a nonhierarchical family power structure. After all, they reasoned, this was Sasha's house too.

The Guilty, Overwhelmed Parent

Tamara, a single mom, was tongue-tied when her six-year-old son, Jake, acted like a critical husband, expressing displeasure at her choice of nail polish, radio station, or dinner menu, or when her older son, Ryan, ignored his curfew. When Tamara felt indignant about her sons' behavior, she told herself that it was typical for boys their age or she shifted into pitying mode, feeling sorry for them because their dad wasn't very involved in their lives. Guilt over her divorce made Tamara feel as if she owed her children an enormous debt and led her to repress any notion that they might owe her something too, such as respect.

The "As Long as Your Grades Are Good You Can Treat Me Like Dirt" Parent

Heather and Robert's sixth-grade son, Gavin, was an excellent student and athlete. He strode rather than walked through the house, giving orders and expecting service. His parents didn't confront him with his discourteous behavior because they felt great pride about his many achievements and took the attitude, "If it's not broken, don't fix it."

The "Children Know Best" Parent

Irina and Alexander, recent émigrés from Russia, were struggling to assimilate. Although both parents were highly accomplished—Irina was a biologist and Alexander an engineer—they had ceded much of their authority as parents because they saw their two preteen children as more "American" than they were. The children watched a lot of television and spoke in a sassy way. When they responded to their parents' questions by saying, "Whatever," or "And I need to know this because?" Irina and Alexander acted as if they didn't understand the demeaning tone and words the children were using. This was America, they reminded me. Didn't all children speak this way?

The Hyperattuned Parent

David, the father of twelve-year-old Grant, described his own father as the old-fashioned "children should be seen and not heard" type. When David asked, "Why?" his father would shoot back, "Because I said so." As a dad, David was careful to listen respectfully to his son's feelings. Yet Grant was rude, moody, and uncooperative, and seemed to have little appreciation for his father's efforts to understand him. Late at night, David ruminated about Grant's future. He realized that unless things changed, Grant would find himself facing troubles with teachers, coaches, and bosses throughout his life.

BECAUSE I'M YOUR MOTHER:
ESTABLISHING YOUR AUTHORITY

Today parents work hard to honor their children's ideas and feelings, and that is good. But the world is starting to turn upside down, as children become the power elite while their parents are squashed beneath them. Peter and Lynn, Tamara, Heather and Robert, Irina and Alexander, and David all shared a common belief that their children were their equals (or, in the case of Irina and Alexander, their cultural superiors). They came to my parenting classes because this egalitarian philosophy was not working.

Children are not our equals, and they don't want to be. In class discussions, besides teaching Jewish wisdom, I often quote another set of sages: dog trainers. These experts know how important it is to establish dominance over a dog when it first enters a family's home. The trainers teach new owners to constantly reinforce their "alpha" status by not letting the dog sit at a higher level than the owner and not letting it go through a door first. If the dogs could talk, the trainers certainly wouldn't let them talk back. They have found that when dogs are allowed to be dominant over their owners, they become both timid and bossy. It's the same with kids.

A democratic system doesn't work very well for dogs or children; it just makes them feel insecure. Parents get fooled because their kids are such skilled debaters, but children are not psychologically equipped to handle winning those debates. They don't have the maturity to regulate their own television viewing, monitor their own language, or teach themselves good manners. We read in Proverbs, "Train a child in the way that he should go, and when he is old he will not depart from it." It's important to start teaching children that you are The Boss when they are very young, and to keep reminding them until they're old enough to leave home.

The First Commandment, "I the Lord am your God. . . . You

shall have no other gods besides me," contains no rule about behavior. It's not like "Keep the Sabbath," or "Don't steal," or "Don't commit adultery." "I am the Lord" functions only as a preamble, establishing God's authority so that people will pay attention to the rest of the commandments. God is saying, "I'm the boss" like a parent might say, "I'm your mother."

For many parents, any tautological phrase such as this evokes the old "because I said so" line that they despised as children. Like David in the previous section, they fear insulting the dignity of their child, a dignity they are far more attuned to than their own. If we look closely at the reasons behind the First Commandment, we can gain a lot of insight about establishing authority. As it turns out, there are plenty of instances when a respectfully delivered "Because I said so" is a perfectly justifiable response.

Let's contemplate why God would bother to make such a big issue out of his authority if the commandments are inherently reasonable and ethical. Wouldn't people naturally want to obey the commandments if they made such good sense? Wanting may not be enough. God knew that some people would try to slide around the laws even if they understood and agreed with them. God realized, too, that there would be certain people who didn't understand the laws. Without a threat of almighty retribution, both of these groups might ignore the commandments.

The same reasoning applies when you go about establishing your authority in the home. First, even children who understand that four straight hours of Nintendo is probably not healthy will play that long if they can get away with it. It's human nature, and only a stronger power will dissuade them from the temptation. But equally important, there are certain edicts you cannot explain and others that your child will stubbornly refuse to understand. "Why does Kirk always have to play at my house? Why can't I go to his?" your son might question. (Because you know that Kirk's dad keeps guns in the house and is a drinker, and you'd rather your son not be aware of those facts just yet.) The persistent child will plead every afternoon, "Why can't I watch 'Bill Nye the Science Guy' before my homework? It's educational!" (Because pulling your child away from the TV puts her in a sour, uncooperative mood.)

From the serious to the tedious, the questions keep coming. You can spend hours trying to explain and rationalize every decision, or you can reply, "Because I said so," or a less flippant version of it. Your children's right to know does not supersede all other concerns. Your word, not your reasoning, is what matters.

Doing things "because God said so" is built into the Jewish tradition. Jewish laws are broken into two groups: *mishpatim* and *chukim*. Mishpatim are the group of Jewish laws that, although divinely ordained, clearly have logic behind them. For example, observance of the Sabbath falls in the category of mishpatim, because taking one day of the week as a day of rest has obvious practical and logical benefits. Another of the mishpatim is the requirement to pay a hired person his wages on the same day that he worked. Makes sense. Good labor relations.

Chukim (singular, *chok*) are those statutes for which there is no logical rationale. They are beyond our understanding, and we observe them out of deference and service to God. The laws of being kosher are commonly misconceived to be legislated by the ancient rabbis for health reasons, but they are considered chukim, divine commands to eat in a special and holy way.

The laws requiring us to respect our elders are technically mishpatim, and there are many pragmatic advantages to teaching children respect. But the sages consider it best to treat the Fifth Commandment as a chok rather than one of the mishpatim, both for the children's sake and for yours. This way, there is no question about the commandment's relevance, no arguments about whether or not a parent's request makes sense. The issues of practicality and logic don't come into play. If "honor your father and mother" is a chok, we do it simply because God commands it.

WHAT ARE THE RULES?

Having acknowledged that you should wear the mantle of authority in your home even if it feels awkward at first, you are now ready to lay down the law. But what exactly is the law? Our society is a casual one, and while we need to set boundaries for our children, trying to buck this casualness altogether isn't appropriate.

Judaism is a great help here, giving us a set of basic standards—a "bottom line" of respect—that applies to children of all ages. Jewish law requires adults to care for their elderly parents by providing them with food and drink, clothing, and shelter, and by escorting them in and out of the room; in other words, by not neglecting or abandoning them. When children are young, Jewish law states that they must:

- Always address their parents in a gentle manner.
- Not contradict their parents' words in front of others.
- Respect their parents' privacy and the privacy of others.
- Not sit in their parents' place at the table.
- Honor their stepparents.

Interesting how, two thousand years ago, the rabbis managed to identify exactly the behaviors that still matter to us (and aggravate us) the most. The first two items alone represent a monumental challenge. Polite, well-mannered children who address you in a gentle tone of voice and don't contradict you in front of others? Seems like a fantasy. But with enough commitment to riding out your child's initial shock and resistance, and faith that the end result will be worth the effort, we really can teach our children to improve their behavior and treat us more respectfully.

THE WORDS THEY SAY,
THE TONE THEY USE

"I hate this dinner!"

  "Grandma stinks. I'm not going to her house, no way."

  "The play date's not over. Go away!"

  "But why? Tell me whhhyyyy?"

Tone and language are inextricably linked. A child doesn't necessarily need language to telegraph a negative attitude—clicking the tongue, sneering, and looking exasperated will work just fine—but the words a child speaks do affect the tone he or she uses. Just as it's awfully difficult to say "Duh" nicely, it's hard, though, of course, not impossible, to say, "Mom, thank you for dinner," in a nasty tone each and every evening. In psychology, the theory of cognitive behaviorism holds that feelings follow behavior. In other words, rather than wait for your children to feel like being agreeable, you can teach them habits of politeness. If you and they use polite phrases every day, feelings of gratitude and respect can grow out of your behavior.

In addition to instilling good manners, the phrases and actions below will focus your children's attention on their blessings, their responsibility, and the efforts of others. Requiring them to say these words is a fine starting point for teaching respect.

- Greetings and questions should include a parental title: "Dad, may I be excused from the table?" "Thanks for driving us to the mall, Mom."
- When a child is offered something, he or she should say, "Yes, please," or "No, thank you." Discourage children from silently nodding or shaking their head.
- Upon entering and leaving the house, rather than darting past you to the GameBoy, basketball hoop, refrigerator, or answering machine, children should offer a salutation: "Hi, Mom, I'm home." "See you later, Dad."

- When taking food and eating it in the presence of a parent, friend, or sibling, your child should make an automatic habit of offering either to share or to get some for the other person. "I'm getting myself a glass of orange juice. Would you like one too?" "Would you like some of these chips?"
- Children should ask parents if they are finished eating and automatically clear their own, and their parents', place from the table at the conclusion of a meal. If this seems extreme, think of it as a gesture in the direction of a fair equalization of labor. After all, they can't drive you to the mall.
- Children should knock on the door of your room and say, "Hi, it's me [Jamie]. May I please come in?" whenever the door is closed, even if it is unlocked.

A caveat: As critically important as it is to teach your children honor, it is also important to pick your targets carefully and avoid becoming a drill sergeant. If you are constantly criticizing, you'll lose their goodwill and end up defeating the honor project. Here are a few sample acts of dishonor you would be wise to let pass:

- Silly bathroom talk or sad, angry talk in preschoolers: "You're a poo-poo, Mommy." Or, as Emma once said to me, "I wish I could hit you with a hundred stones."
- Smiling in response to your reprimand. Often this reflects embarrassment, not impudence.
- Requests from children older than ten for you (parent) not to sing, be too friendly in public, or wear your plaid backpack in front of her friends.
- Eyeball-rolling at any age.

It may seem tedious or priggish to insist on lots of potentially phony politeness, but this is how we build habits for a lifetime. Judaism stresses the power of our words as tools to express respect for God's creations. And as always in Jewish theology, the smallest things count.

Curing Sitcom Mouth

Many children spend more hours watching television each day than they do talking to their parents. Unfortunately, the young-sters in sitcoms talk back to adults, make nonstop wisecracks, and rarely converse with their parents in a civilized way. Although many parents find it hard to believe, children who watch a lot of TV are often completely unaware of the sassy tone of voice or rude language they're using. They think it's normal.

My husband is a writer, and in our home the children hear talk of scripts and dialogue. If they answer a question by saying, "Whatever," or "Duh," we ask them to rewrite the line. If they whine or speak in baby talk, we say, "Can you try that in a different tone of voice?" or "Could you read that line again so I can understand it?" If they answer us in a wise-guy way we might respond, "Uh-oh, you're talking in TV talk. Maybe you've been watching too much television."

Our point with our children is not to humiliate them or preach to them. We want to raise their consciousness and make sure they know when they're being rude. I've found that the most effective way to do this is with a light touch and without delivering a lecture. It's not necessary to discover why children are sarcastic or sulky; the point is to get them to change their behavior, not to improve their mood. Children need to learn to be polite regardless of how they are feeling.

When teaching your kids about respectful language, be clear about your standards. If your child talks back to you, take his or her hand in yours and in a calm voice say, "You are not allowed to talk to me this way." Just as important, be consistent. Otherwise, your child won't take you seriously and the whole program will fizzle.

SHORT-CIRCUITING THE ARGUMENTS

The Jewish edict that children are not to contradict their parents in front of others is deceptively simple. Even the word *contradict* implies a civilized disagreement ("Father, I beg to differ with you") as opposed to the humiliating public showdowns many of us have experienced. As in so many other areas of child-rearing, accepting the concept that parents are in charge and children don't need to understand or agree with our rules goes a long way toward resolving the problems.

Not that it's easy. You may need to change many of the ploys you now rely on to cajole your child into compliance in public settings. To demonstrate the nuances, let's listen to seven-year-old Ruby and her mom, Ann, as they prepare to leave a party. First I'll deconstruct the message each is giving the other, then I'll provide some suggestions for rewriting this script with Mom instead of Ruby in the lead.

Ann: Ruby, it's time to go home.

Ruby: No, Mom, I don't want to go now.

Ann: We have to leave. Maria *[the baby-sitter, at home with Ruby's baby sister]* is expecting us at five. She has to go home to her house.

Ruby: Call her and ask her if she can stay later.

Ann: Ruubyyy? We need to go.

Ruby: C'mon, why can't you call her? I don't want to go home now!

Ann: It's time to get supper ready, and you've been here long enough.

Ruby: No I haven't. I'm still having fun. You could call Maria. Mom, please?

Ann: *(Annoyed, bored, and exasperated by now.)* Ruby, it's time to go! *(Takes her arm and pulls her away.)*

The emphasis in this parent-child interchange is on Ruby's unwillingness to leave the party. But offering her daughter logical reasons to depart is a waste of Ann's time. At this moment, Ruby doesn't care about the baby-sitter's family, nor does she agree that she has been at the party long enough—she'd like to stay all night! By waiting for Ruby's "permission" to leave, Ann is giving her daughter room to refuse. Ruby's defiance is disrespectful, but Ann opened the door for it.

What could Ann have done instead? With a shift in the goal from getting Ruby to be willing to leave the party to the importance of listening to Ann and respecting her decisions, the dialogue might go differently.

Ann: Ruby, we'll need to leave the party in ten minutes, so you should start saying your good-byes now.

Ruby: No, Mom, I don't want to go now.

Ann: I know it's hard to go when you are having fun. But you need to listen to me now. We will be leaving in ten minutes.

Ruby: Why do we have to go?

Ann: I'll be glad to explain the reasons to you in the car on the way home.

Ruby: Tell me now.

Ann: Ruby, part of being grown up enough to go to parties is remembering how to listen when I tell you it's time to leave.

Ruby: OK, but let's find out where the party favors are.

Or . . .

Ruby: I'm not going. *(Ann waits ten minutes, then takes Ruby's arm and firmly leads her out of the party to the car.)*

In this version, Ann is fair and firm. She warns her daughter ten minutes ahead of time that they will be leaving, and she briefly acknowledges Ruby's feelings. She lets her daughter know that she'll answer her questions in the car, but for the moment Mother has spoken and her word is law. When Ruby resists, Ann issues an implied threat that if she doesn't behave, she won't go to the next party. Ann must be willing to follow through on this threat or it won't work next time.

You, the parent, are the most important adult in your child's world. When it's time to leave a party, begin or end a play date, do homework, go to sleep, or get up, your child has a chance to demonstrate how much she honors you by cooperating promptly and without a fuss. If you are always casual and friendly, you'll unwittingly turn these moments into opportunities for her to hone her negotiation skills rather than her parent-honoring skills.

This doesn't mean that you won't tell your child the reasons for your demands. For example, in the car Ann could explain some rules of party etiquette to Ruby: "You generally leave a party when the invitation says the party is supposed to end or when most of the other people are leaving." But your main focus should be on short-circuiting arguments, letting go of your wish to reach consensus, and taking advantage of opportunities to let your child practice honoring you.

TEACHING YOUR CHILDREN TO RESPECT YOUR PRIVACY

In Genesis, God remained outside the Garden of Eden and called out to Adam before entering, saying, "Where are you?"

even though, being God, he certainly knew exactly where Adam was. This story is used as the basis for the prohibition against startling another person. Respecting the privacy of others is a deeply held value in Judaism. We are taught, "One must never enter a friend's house unexpectedly." Because it is considered so important not to surprise or disturb others, we are even taught to knock on the door of our own house!

While children are unconstrained and forthright about demanding privacy for themselves—"Mom! We are having a meeting of the Speedo Barbie Club. It's private!"—I find that parents are quite inhibited in this area. They tell me that their master bedrooms are littered with toys, shin guards, and dirty socks. And children march right into parents' rooms without knocking at all times of the day and night.

Two clients of mine, Jon and Elizabeth, were having this type of problem with their five-year-old-daughter, Hannah. For about three months, Hannah had been climbing into their bed every night between midnight and 2 A.M. When I questioned them about this routine, they admitted that it had all started when Jon had been out of town on business and Elizabeth, feeling lonely, had allowed Hannah to sleep in her bed one night. Seeing a break in the usual set of house rules, Hannah came back night after night, complaining of sleeplessness and general misery. Now, months later, the parents had convinced themselves that Hannah was suffering from an emotional disorder. They kept their bedroom door open at night, "so Hannah won't have to knock."

"You're not worried about her interrupting you while you're having sex?" I asked.

"Well, frankly, we've been so concerned about Hannah's sleeping problem that we haven't been focusing on that aspect of things too much," confessed Elizabeth.

"Three months. Hmmm. What's it like having your sleep disturbed every night?"

"I'm really tired all the time, but I'm more worried about Hannah. I think she must be having nightmares. Why else would she wake up like this every single night?"

"I think she wakes herself up. She's got a sweet deal. I'm not very worried about Hannah, but I'm starting to worry about your lack of privacy. If you let this go on too long we may all need to start worrying about your marriage."

At first Elizabeth tried the "reasonable" tactic and told Hannah that she would get a better night's sleep in her own bed. Hannah assured her mother that she actually slept better with Mommy and Daddy. Then Elizabeth took an approach that felt unnatural because she was so used to focusing on what was best for Hannah as opposed to what was best for her and Jon. She told her daughter, "You'll have to start sleeping in your own bed so that Daddy and I can have our privacy." Later Elizabeth realized that this was better for Hannah as well. Once she and Jonathan were well rested, they became calmer, more patient parents, and Hannah learned a lesson about the dignity and rights of adults.

You can do it too. You can make your bedroom a sanctuary that is off-limits to children who haven't knocked and been invited in. Your children can learn to keep their toys in their own rooms. They can learn not to interrupt you while you are on the phone. They can learn these things if you begin to believe in the value of your own privacy and that teaching children to respect others' territory is a worthwhile investment of your time and energy.

HOLDING YOUR PLACE AT THE FAMILY TABLE

Earlier in this chapter I wrote about Peter and Lynn, whose daughter Sasha was competing with them for use of the phone, borrowing her mother's clothes without asking, and seemed not to understand the difference between her parents' belongings and her own. Metaphorically and in reality, no one had a special place at the family table. Sasha sat anywhere she liked and took anything she wanted.

Peter and Lynn were unhappy with the way their daughter was treating them but didn't know how to change the situation without becoming autocratic or rigid. I suggested that the three of them have a family meeting to discuss the problem and make general rules for respectful communication among all family members.

"But what if Sasha doesn't agree that there's a problem?" Peter asked. "What if she doesn't change?"

"If you recast many of the things that Sasha feels entitled to as privileges, you'll discover a world of consequences for non-compliance," I replied.

We started with a major point of contention: the telephone. Sasha was in the habit of getting on-line the minute she came home from school, but 3 to 5 P.M. was still part of Peter's business day, and he needed to keep the phone free. Prior to the family meeting, Sasha rarely complied with Peter's requests to get off the line, saying, "In a minute," but staying on for a half hour or more. After the meeting, Peter and Lynn introduced a new set of rules: As a parent and breadwinner, Peter had control of the phone. Going on-line became a privilege for Sasha, to be earned with respectful behavior. Time spent on-line (fifteen minutes to check e-mail or do research when she first arrived home from school) had to be monitored by Sasha herself without Dad watching the clock, reminding, and getting exasperated.

Your place at the head of the family table, literally and symbolically, should be sacrosanct. This means that a parent's possessions, control of the remote, need for peace and quiet, and the right to a free telephone or modem line must be respected by children. In order to do this, your expectations must be clear, you must be calm, firm, and convinced, and your commitment to following through must be evident to your children.

STEPPARENTS
DESERVE RESPECT TOO

The *Shulhan Aruch* (the sixteenth century code of Jewish law) states that a person must honor his stepparents and adds that honor for stepparents must continue even after the death of one's own parents. This is for the sake both of honoring elders and for the maintenance of *shalom bayit* (peace in the home). If you feel guilty about your divorce or fear losing your children's loyalty and affection, you may be reluctant to demand respect for your new mate. The child's full parent should remain in the role of the boss, but honor for the new partner or stepparent—regardless of how the child feels about him or her—is an essential ingredient of shalom bayit and must be actively taught. If you are struggling with pre- or postdivorce parenting issues, I highly recommend Anthony Wolf's practical, sensible, and humorous book *Why Did You Have to Get a Divorce? And When Can I Get a Hamster?*

Teaching children to honor adults in difficult situations is good preparation for learning to remain calm with the overwrought classroom teacher or the boorish boss who may show up down the line. When an elderly grandparent repeats himself or squeezes a cheek too hard, or when a stepparent moves into your home and sits in the chair that used to be Dad's, your child needs to learn how to handle the discomfort. The family is the laboratory, and you are teaching the science of living.

TEACHING HONOR
BEYOND THE FAMILY

Derech eretz (the way of the land) means etiquette and good manners in its narrowest sense, and standards for honorable, dignified behavior in its broadest. The sages taught that if the Jewish people demonstrate the virtue of derech eretz yet don't fulfill any other Torah principle, they will still receive merit from God. Derech eretz teaches us to always be sensitive to the feelings of others. Opportunities to practice derech eretz include greeting people, inviting them into our homes, and speaking about other people in a respectful way whether or not they are within earshot.

Judaism is very big on social niceties because they are considered an essential element of a stable and wholesome community. We are taught to greet another person first even if it means crossing the street to catch him, so that he will not for a moment think we are trying to avoid him. We are even permitted to interrupt the recital of the *Shema,* a central prayer in the Jewish service, in order to return someone's greeting. Greetings can be seen as a polite gesture or as something larger, a symbol of our desire to honor each of God's human creations every chance we get. Teaching children how to give and receive greetings then becomes a lesson not just in manners but also in spiritual generosity.

Both adults and children often feel awkward when meeting new people, but adults have learned strategies for overcoming their awkwardness. Young children who bury their head in your leg and refuse to utter a word are not insulting anyone, but children six and up need to learn strategies for handling the natural bashfulness they feel. Otherwise, their downcast eyes and silence will be read as rudeness. With some children these social skills come easily, especially if they see you practicing them regularly. For other boys and girls, overcoming shyness can be quite difficult.

You can teach your child how to greet others by using a few

tips from the etiquette books. There are just four basic rules. Tell your child to:

- Make eye contact. A trick is to look to see the color of the other person's eyes.
- Begin a greeting with the person's name: "Hi, Sara," "Hello, Rabbi Nachman."
- Smile.
- Tolerate small talk with grace. People often ask children they've just met rather impertinent or personal questions. "What's your favorite TV show? Do you like your little sister? Your teacher? Do you have a boyfriend?" Tell your child that she can answer these questions very briefly or change the subject if she doesn't want to answer, but that she has to say something.

Teaching children about the proper way to greet others begins at home, like everything else. If Benjamin blows in the front door, nearly knocking you over with his backpack as he heads for his room, he has much to learn. Stop him and smile, greet him by name, and hold on to him for a moment. He is likely to remember what to do.

Honoring Guests

Torah puts great emphasis on the importance of welcoming people into your home, making sure they feel comfortable, and giving them your full attention—it's a mitzvah called *hakhnasat orchim* (hospitality to guests). According to the teachings of the Talmud, we are required to:

- Greet guests at the door and escort them inside.
- Make an effort to remain cheerful during the visit.

- Offer food and drink.
- Ask our guests questions about their interests and activities.
- Escort them to the door when they leave.

If children are to follow these rules, it means that when the play date arrives your four-year-old does not have the luxury of staying in her room playing with Duplo but must come to the door to greet her friend. If your child is very absorbed when the friend is due to arrive, give advance warning.

Young children ages two to five often end a play date with a fight. It seems to make it easier to say good-bye if you're convinced that your friend is really an enemy. Give warning here, too, by telling both children, "It's time to start cleaning up. Sammy's mom will be here soon and you will need to see him to the door."

Some parents worry that the formal play date agenda that fits well with our tight schedules doesn't match the ebb and flow of young children's moods. That is true, but most children can learn to adjust to our schedules and be polite about it. This is another example of why Jewish teachings are so useful for parents: you know what you're working toward. The rules of hakhnasat orchim can be taught to children of any age, even those who aren't yet able to master each rule each time.

Speaking Respectfully About Others

"Are you going to tell the principal that you think Mrs. Hart should be fired?"

"Why did you say that Uncle Jack is a moron?"

"Why don't you want Evan to join our carpool?"

Many intelligent, discerning parents who are troubled by the injustice or laxity in the world unwittingly offer their children a critical or cynical running commentary on current events.

"Mrs. Hart is incompetent to teach third-grade math" . . . "That TV show is for idiots" . . . "I don't know why Fiona stays with Martin." But making negative statements without taking action demoralizes children and crushes their need to have something to believe in. It's up to us to bolster our children's enthusiasm and optimism, not undermine it.

Just like adults, children love to hear the dirt and will listen intently when you're bad-mouthing people or places that are important in their lives. What are the consequences of hearing their parents dishonor others through words? Often children take our careless observations quite literally. If they learn to see the world as a place where others are judged behind their backs, they may become inhibited, fearing that their own actions and words are not safe from ridicule.

The Torah takes dishonorable words very seriously—gossip and murder are mentioned in the same breath: "You shall not go up and down as a talebearer among your people, and you shall not stand forth against the life of your neighbor." God went out of his way to punish Moses' sister, Miriam, when she gossiped about Moses' wife. According to the sages, gossip harms three people: the one who is gossiping, the one who is listening, and the victim.

One mother in a parenting class likened gossip to spiritual pollution because it fouls the air we breathe, even though we can't see it. I believe that is a fair description. And the sages make it clear that "gossip" doesn't just mean falsehoods—the definition of gossip specifically includes loose talk that is true. Within the family and beyond it, one of the wisest things we can teach and practice is the wisdom of holding back if we cannot say something positive. Unless, of course, you plan to do something to remedy the situation, in which case you should involve your children or at least make them aware of the action you're taking.

THE TOUGHEST COMMANDMENT

The full text of the Fifth Commandment reads, "Honor your father and mother that your days may be long upon the land that your Lord God is giving to you." The deal God promised— "that your days may be long upon the land"—encompasses more than just you and your spouse. Raise responsible, respectful children, and not only will they care for you in your old age, they'll extend that care to their society. Your most lasting legacy, the only one that really matters, is how your children will treat their fellow creatures and the world you're leaving them. It begins and ends with honor.

CHAPTER 4

The Blessing of a Skinned Knee:

Why God Doesn't Want You to Overprotect Your Child

Several years ago, I stood before an auditorium at a top private school in northern California. I love speaking at this campus, where the parents always get my jokes and grasp the nuances of my message. I even love the bathroom decoration—beautiful tiles hand-painted by the children, and sinks mounted so low that even the youngest can wash up with dignity. I was lecturing on one of my favorite topics, "Raising Strong Children in a Complex World." During the question-and-answer period, a smiling, stylish woman in her late thirties raised her hand.

"Ever since her friend got hurt in the big earthquake, my daughter can't sleep alone," she said. "How can I get her to be braver at night?"

"Does she sleep in your bed?" I asked.

"No."

"How do you know she's afraid? Does she call out to you?"

"She doesn't call out. She's not alone. She sleeps with the housekeeper in the housekeeper's bed."

In all my years of counseling, I'd never heard of such an arrangement. Impressed that the mother was willing to expose this setup in public, I probed a little further.

"Does the housekeeper mind?"

"No. It was a condition of hiring her."

"A human teddy bear!" I exclaimed. "Your daughter has a human teddy bear!"

I was afraid I'd gone too far, but the mother laughed in a good-natured way and seemed to get the point. When I suggested that this cozy solution to her daughter's sleeping problem could be depriving the girl of an opportunity to overcome her fears and to mature, the mother agreed.

Flying home, I wondered about this mother. Was she the daughter of Holocaust survivors? Did she survive a childhood terror of another sort that she was projecting onto her daughter? Was there something else going on in the family that she had not revealed? And then I realized that there was probably nothing especially traumatic taking place in the family. This level of fearfulness in children and intense protectiveness in parents was something I saw all the time.

RAISING HARDY CHILDREN

The Talmud sums up the Jewish perspective on child-rearing in a single sentence: "A father is obligated to teach his son how to swim." Jewish wisdom holds that our children don't belong to us. They are both a loan and a gift from God, and the gift has strings attached. Our job is to raise our children to leave us. The children's job is to find their own path in life. If they stay carefully protected in the nest of the family, children will become weak and fearful or feel too comfortable to want to leave.

For twenty years now, I have watched as well-meaning, dedicated parents become ever more deeply enmeshed in their children's lives. No matter how busy these parents are, the child's problems remain a central preoccupation. Instead of enjoying their time with their children, they're busy fretting and fixing. The housekeeper who was required to sleep in her charge's bed was an extreme but natural extension of the sort of parental hovering that was typical of my clients. Little Kayla is overtaxed, so her mom is off to the library to do research for the Hopi Indian social studies project while Kayla is at her dance class. Zack's dad is hiring a softball tutor so Zack will feel more secure about playing on the teams the boys form at recess. These are the same parents who refuse to let their children walk to the corner alone or don't permit their children to hand in a homework assignment without a parental edit.

I'm not against helping with homework and building skills in sports, but what these parents are trying to do goes far beyond standard support and encouragement. They are trying to inoculate their children against the pain of life. There is a Hebrew phrase, *tzar gidul banim,* that refers to the ubiquitous pain of raising children. We parents go through years of emotional anguish as we raise our kids, but tzar gidol banim also refers to our children's pain. Without it they cannot grow strong. They won't learn to swim. And the message communicated by all this loving parental protection is that the child doesn't have what it takes to swim alone.

When Dustin's teacher won't allow him to be in the school play because of his C grade in English and his mother promises to go talk to the principal, telling Dustin, "I don't see why she's making such a big deal out of one C," she's giving him an unrealistic impression of the world. Dustin's college professors, colleagues, and employers won't be creating special rules just for him. When Ellie's feelings are hurt about not getting invited to Mimi's birthday party and her dad offers to call up Mimi's mom to try to find out why, he's teaching her that missing out on a party is a catastrophe that deserves special intervention. When we treat our children's lives like we're cruise ship directors who must get them to their destination—adulthood—smoothly, without their feeling even the slightest bump or wave, we're depriving them. Those bumps are part of God's plan.

Mitzrayim, the Hebrew word for Egypt, means "straits," "narrow place," or "blockages." Most of the Hebrew slaves in Pharaoh's Egypt could not imagine that they might successfully escape to freedom. Commentators on the biblical book of Exodus tell us that only 20 percent left to follow Moses. The rest stayed behind, enslaved by their fear of the unknown. The world in which we are raising our children challenges them with many straits and narrow places. We want them to have faith that they can make it through and leave the familiarity and safety of home. If we overprotect them, we enslave them with our fears. If we give them the freedom to develop strength through overcoming difficulties, they'll be out in front with the courageous 20 percent.

WITHDRAW YOUR POWER
IF YOU WANT YOUR CHILD TO GROW

In the Jewish mystical principle of *tsimtsum* we can find a lovely spiritual model for slowly relinquishing control over our children. *Tsimtsum* means "contraction of divine energy." Originally, everything was God; God filled up the entire universe. But in order for one thing to exist, something else has to withdraw. So in order to make a place for the world, God had to withdraw a bit.

At first God stayed close by us, his new and vulnerable creations, to provide help as needed. When we were trapped by the Egyptians, God provided plagues; when we needed to escape quickly, God parted the Red Sea; when we were hungry in the desert, there was the miracle of manna from heaven; when we were thirsty, God provided water from a rock. God was a day-by-day, sometimes minute-by-minute miracle maker. Later, as we matured and were able to manage on our own, God withdrew further and made fewer miracles. Left to our own devices, we humans took lots of false steps. But we learned from our mistakes and became a resilient people, strong enough to endure for more than three thousand years.

Like God, new parents are miracle makers. When children are tiny babies, we vigilantly monitor everything that goes into their mouths and comes out their bottoms. We make sure they aren't hungry or thirsty, and we provide constant protection and care. But as our children mature, we need to withdraw from smoothing their path and satisfying all their wishes. By giving them a chance to survive some danger and letting them make some reckless or thoughtless choices, we teach them how to withstand the bumps and knocks of life. This is the only way children will mature into resilient, self-reliant adults. By continuing to make miracles on demand, we are unwittingly slowing down the development of our children's strength.

FEAR AND FREEDOM, COMPASSION AND COWARDICE

Parents' urge to overprotect their children is based on fear. Fear of strangers, the streets, the Internet, the mall. Fear of the child's not being invited to the right parties or accepted by the right schools. Fear about safety, sex, disease, and drugs. In my parenting classes there are always lots of questions about fear and its flip side, freedom:

"At what age can the children stay home alone? I'm still getting baby-sitters for my thirteen-year-old."

"How do I explain to my eight-year-old why I won't let him go to the bathroom in a restaurant by himself? I don't even want to tell him what I'm afraid of."

"My daughter wants to take gymnastics, but I don't think it's safe. I heard about an Olympic gymnast who lost the use of one eye in a balance-beam injury."

Few stories illustrate the level of fear we are passing along to our children as well as the one told by my twelve-year-old client Rebecca. Home alone on a weekday afternoon, Rebecca heard the doorbell ring and saw an unfamiliar man and woman at the door. Terror-stricken at the sight of the strangers, she slithered across the floor for ten minutes, making herself as flat as possible so she could get to the phone to beep her mother without being seen through the window. By the time her mother called her back, she was exhausted.

"Mom said they were landscapers who had dropped by to give an estimate," Rebecca recalled. "She hadn't told me they were coming because she thought she'd be home to let them in. But they came two hours early! I'll never forget how scared I was."

Rebecca's reaction was understandable in light of how often her parents had warned her about potentially dangerous strangers. But a twelve-year-old can safely inquire from behind a locked door about the reason for the visit. Rebecca was too panicked to think clearly. Overwhelmed by the vision of well-publicized child-abduction victims, we train our children to fear everyone outside our immediate circle and to expect the worst in any unusual situation. We are teaching our children to slither rather than to roll with the punches.

Parents are determined to keep children safe not only from physical dangers but also from emotional pain. Recently a local girls' school faxed me a document called "Why Students Can Only Learn in a Safe School." As it turned out, this bulletin had nothing to do with violence. It was about protecting students from discrimination. Specifically, it called on parents, teachers, and students to protect "glbtq" (gay, lesbian, bisexual, transgendered, or questioning) students from feeling "minimized, unseen, unimportant, or worst of all, 'bad.'" To this end, the school held a consciousness-raising workshop for all students, including kindergartners. The children learned about the importance of maintaining a safe environment for everyone, including children who have gay or lesbian parents or siblings or who will, at some point, figure out that they are gay or lesbian themselves.

The goals of the glbtq policy and lots of other "safe" behavior policies are ethical—the administrators are trying to create a well-rounded child, one who is not only skilled in athletics, sports, and the arts but who also has an ability to be tolerant and kind. The policies can be effective ways to raise awareness of the pain of discrimination, but in order to build character, time spent on consciousness-raising should be balanced with time spent developing tolerance for the inevitable unfairness and messiness of life, an enterprise in which most of us "feel bad" at least some portion of every day.

If this seems harsh, consider Ruby Bridges. In 1960, when she was six years old, Ruby initiated desegregation in New Orleans by walking into her school building escorted by federal marshals while murderous, heckling mobs threatened her life. Her mother said that Ruby smiled at the hecklers and prayed for them every night before she went to sleep. When I took my daughters to meet Ms. Bridges at a book signing near our home, I was as excited as they were to meet the woman who had shown such courage as a young girl. Her courage had inspired me when I was a child, and she inspired me even more as an adult.

Real protection means teaching children to manage risks on their own, not shielding them from every hazard. Worrying excessively about discrimination while not letting your children walk around the block on their own can create highly conscious cripples. If pressed to stand up for what they have been taught to believe, I fear that most of the children we are raising wouldn't behave like Ruby Bridges. They wouldn't have the will to be courageous, and perhaps more important, they wouldn't have the support of their parents.

Freud said that the goal of psychoanalysis was modest: to convert neurotic misery into ordinary unhappiness. Judaism teaches that all people should be on a lifelong quest to build *middot* (literally, "measures," or good character traits). One of those traits is the ability to tolerate emotional distress. But most of the parents I speak with believe that their children should be spared "ordinary unhappiness" and should be protected from feeling sad, angry, afraid, frustrated, or disappointed. According to Orthodox psychologist and parent educator Miriam Adahan, children need an opportunity to learn about the "wave pattern" of emotions. If parents rush in to rescue them from distress, children don't get an opportunity to learn that they can suffer and recover on their own.

TURNING DOWN THE WORRY: THE TWENTY-MINUTES RULE

The fears that cause our overprotective parenting style seep out every day in the form of worries. The fear of a child being abducted gets translated into a continuous hum of worry anytime the child steps out of the house. Is there any way to turn down the worry so we can give our children more of the freedom they need to grow?

The first step is to try, as much as possible, to put common sense and faith before emotion. The parents I listen to worry a lot, and not just about the big scares like illness, abduction, or car accidents. They are highly creative in coming up with things to worry about and loyal to the worries once they've birthed them. Some real-life examples:

"What if sending Eva to a developmental preschool isn't really preparing her for an academic kindergarten?"

"What if Daniel gets influenced by those two wild boys in the class?"

"What if Alexa and Julie become best friends and leave Claire out?"

"What if Josh can't handle both Hebrew School and homework on Wednesdays?"

Well, what if one of those things did happen? You would size up the problem and make some changes. It is all part of *tzar gidul banim*, the pain of raising children. If you believe you can wipe all the tzar gidul banim from your life and your child's, you'll spend a lot of time trying to run interference and in the end you won't succeed anyway. If, on the other hand, you can use common sense (we've overcome challenges before and we'll overcome this one) and *bitachon* (trust in God), you can relax a little. The spiritual discipline of bitachon requires us to make our best efforts on behalf of our children, use our best judgment, and leave the rest in God's hands.

Judaism requires us to be happy. We are supposed to enjoy performing *mitzvot*, commandments. If we've been fruitful and multiplied, we've fulfilled a commandment. To contaminate the job of parenting with worry violates the joyous spirit of the mitzvah. I once heard a Jewish educator say that parents should spend twenty minutes a day thinking about their child's education. This is both a lower and an upper limit! This wise woman was asking parents to reflect and be thoughtful, but not to obsess. If you are spending more than twenty minutes a day worrying about your child, you are not performing the mitzvah of raising children in the proper spirit. Judaism requires us not only to be fruitful and multiply but to enjoy the ride.

How to know if you're spending too much time worrying about your children? If you notice that even during seemingly perfect moments you're thinking about potential troubles ahead, you're worrying too much. Another sign: your children seem overly cautious or anxious. A group of second graders I know recently went on a horseback ride. One little girl wouldn't put on a helmet since her mother told her never to wear anyone else's hat because she might get lice. Another complained that the flies on the horses might bite. Frequently, worrier parents raise worrying children who see the world as overwhelming and threatening. Finally, if your spouse or your child's teacher or adult friends tell you, "I don't see what you're so worried about.

Connor seems just fine to me," you might want to lighten up and start adhering to the twenty-minutes-a-day rule.

Some parents seem to have a worry vacuum that must be filled as soon as it starts to get empty. I learned about this phenomenon early in life, because my grandmother was a professional. Grammy could set herself up with a good worry and turn it this way and that in her mind for great spans of time. The moment the worrisome situation resolved itself, she would search around for a new one to replace it. She was blessed with three generations to worry about. When her daughter and grandchildren were fine, she would start in on the baby great-grandchildren. If they appeared to be properly nourished and appropriately dressed for the weather, she would worry about the cat. If she judged the cat robust and content, she would worry about the health of the plants or the neighbor's children. If we teased her about her constant worrying, she would smile indulgently and then set right back in again.

I've since decided that Grammy was a prophylactic worrier. The idea that you can prevent a bad event by worrying about it turns up in Jewish folktales, like the one about the chimney sweep Yossel, who, in exchange for a salary of one ruble a week, was appointed the official Worrier of Chelm. One resident of Chelm complained, "If Yossel gets a nice salary of one ruble a week, what has he got to worry about?" Grammy was carrying on the grand old tradition. I was reminded of her when I treated a highly intelligent woman who suffered from fear of flying. She told me that she feared the plane would stay in the sky only by the force of her grip on the armrest. It's not obvious, but one of the problems with this perspective is its lack of humility. It's arrogant to think we are in charge of everything. That's why, when some traditional Jews speak about something that will happen in the future, they always append "God willing" to the end of the sentence. This serves as a reminder that we aren't fully in control of our destiny.

SEPARATING LEGITIMATE CONCERNS
FROM NEUROTIC OVERPROTECTION

Of course, there are aspects of modern life that parents are justified in worrying about. Among the families I work with, the fears center around the big three: crime, safety, and the media (TV, music, film, and the Internet). These worries stand out in bold relief against the rosy memories of their own childhoods. Robin, a client in her late forties, waxed nostalgic one day:

> It's a shame our kids can't live the way we did. The summer I was seven, I had an adventure a day. I rode my bike everywhere. Marcia, Susan, and I had our club meetings in a vacant lot littered with broken glass. I don't remember anyone ever getting cut. I do remember teaching my four-year-old sister how to get across a stream by walking on logs and rocks. That summer we sold our homemade paste door-to-door. When it got dark, one of my parents would call out from the front door for us to come home. Our safety in the neighborhood was a given.
>
> Things are so different now! There are so many problems to be fearful of. When I found out that there was a registry of convicted child molesters by zip code, I checked out our neighborhood and found out that there were fourteen! We have since moved to a neighborhood with six.

You no doubt have your own enchanted-summer memories. You, too, probably wish your kids could experience some of the intense joy and freedom you did the summer you were seven. If so, consider the possibility that your overprotection, as much as the real world, is clouding your children's summers. While there are dangers, bad influences, and risks you must protect them from, you should think very carefully about how much protection they actually need.

It's a Jungle out There—Isn't It?

While it's indisputable that the world today is more dangerous than the one we grew up in and that none of us can let a seven-year-old roam the neighborhood unsupervised for an entire summer, it may not be as dangerous as we imagine.

Part of what fuels our fear of letting children out on their own is media scare-mongering. In order to compete for viewers, the most disturbing stories are given the most attention and our sense of impending danger becomes exaggerated. When violent crimes involving children occur, the whole country is quickly inundated with details of the story. For example, because it was broadcast constantly, the whole country knew about the abduction of Polly Klaas in 1993, and parents had one more justification to fear strangers. After the murders at Columbine High we are even afraid when our children are at school.

The broadcasters who exaggerate danger are like the biblical spies fearful of venturing toward an unknown land. After traveling in the desert, Moses and the Israelites neared Canaan, and Moses sent a scouting party of twelve spies to check out the territory ahead. The spies returned and reported that although the land was flowing with milk and honey, it was surrounded on one side by enemies in the mountains and on the other side by the sea. Caleb, one of the twelve spies, was ready to move ahead in spite of the risks. "Let's go," he said. "We're strong, we can handle it." But other spies panicked and warned the people, "He is wrong, we can't fight these people, they are stronger than we are and the land is a land that eats the people who live there. . . . They are giants there! We looked like grasshoppers to ourselves and so we must have looked like grasshoppers to them!" All the people lifted up their voices and cried. They turned against Moses and Aaron: "We want to go back to Egypt!"

When media broadcasters are effective, parents start to feel like grasshoppers unable to defend their children against being swallowed up by the land. But are such fears warranted? Statistics show that violent crimes rarely occur randomly or without warning and that while many children are abducted by family members in child custody disputes, very few children get abducted by strangers. One of the oldest urban myths—that evil strangers periodically lace Halloween candy with poison and apples with razor blades—was debunked in 1985 by sociologist Joel Best, who traced the rumor to a misleading *New York Times* article first printed in 1970. Best examined every reported incident of tampered treats from 1958 through 1985. He found that there had not been a single death or serious injury from Halloween candy or goodies in all that time.

You owe it to your children to use good judgment and caution without overreacting to distorted threats. If you don't allow your children the freedom other parents in the neighborhood give their kids, you're probably being overly protective. We need to let our children go and show them that even though it is different than it used to be, the land where we are raising them is a good place that can nourish and support them.

The View from the Safety Seat

My adult friend Kathy told me that she likes to ski but hates to fall, and that after skiing for two seasons she has never fallen once. She is also still skiing on the bunny slope. Overly protective parents who are zealous about keeping their children safe are encouraging them to be timid bunnies rather than strong and healthy adults who can zoom down the steeper, more exciting slopes of life.

You'd think that these cautious parents had led very sheltered lives as children, yet typically the opposite is true. When I ask adults about the dangerous things they did when they were young, I'm often struck by how quickly they respond. It's so immediate that it feels like a coincidence, as if they've been recollecting their most thrilling childhood caper just at the moment I've asked them to tell me about it. Said one mother: "In the summer my sister and I put bunched-up pillows under the covers. Then we climbed out on the roof at night with no clothes on. We looked at the moon and stars and felt the breeze. My parents never knew."

A sage once said that we may freely take "commonly accepted risks" and that God "will take care of the fools." This means that sometimes our decisions will land us in perilous situations but that we must proceed using our best judgment rather than hang back in order to keep safe at all costs. Securing babies in car seats and requiring children to wear helmets while bicycling makes sense. But going too far in the direction of protecting children can backfire, leaving them fearful of stepping out into the world on their own.

Fear of the Media

I was speaking to a small group of parents in a *havurah* (friendship group), when Deborah spoke up.

> I don't want my children to be exposed to the extreme junk that kids watch on TV and in the movies. I have three children, ages three, six, and eight. I took the two older ones to see *Tarzan* last week. It was the first movie they had ever seen. There is no television watching in our house either. My elderly aunt, whom I have a lot of respect for, recently told me that I am wrong to shield them this way. She said, "Deborah, you have to let go. You're going to turn these children into freaks." Is she right?

In my work with parents I encounter two general schools of parenting media philosophy: the What the Hell, Everybody Else

Is Doing It School and the School of Total Abstinence. Both are a form of cheating. The first cheats your children out of protection against grim, overly sexual or violent images that bathe them with experiences they can't put into perspective. The second school cheats them out of fun and fellowship because so much of grade school social currency is based on knowing what is going on in the media. Certainly there are things to fear about letting our children trawl around in the modern media, but it's also easy to become paranoid. In his wise and useful book *The Culture of Fear: Why Americans Are Afraid of the Wrong Things*, sociologist Barry Glassner debunks one juicy parental worry after another, including the danger to children from cyberpredators and pedophiles. It's a worthwhile read if you'd like to gain some sensible perspective on the risks of the media.

The principles of moderation, celebration, and sanctification can guide you in setting up a TV/film/music/software/Internet rating and rationing system for your family. Let's start with celebration. The media offers our children a stunning abundance of cultural riches, silly delights, and cathartic gross-outs. Once you decide what you'll let your children watch or log on to or play with, don't make fun of the form or content. It's not fair to unburden yourself of ambivalence by letting them watch *Kenan & Kel* while you sit on the couch delivering pious little lessons about art, feminism, or politics. This will only make your children ashamed of their naturally childlike taste, diminish their pleasure, and lead them to resent you.

If you decide to let them watch, log on, or play computer games, take the role of an enchanted spectator from Mars. "What show are you watching? Is it new? Is that girl the other one's sister?" Don't overdo this either or you'll get annoying. The point is to try to appreciate what your children love through their eyes and to add your own (positive) observations. Notice the charming way the animators draw the characters' mouths on *The*

Wild Thornberrys, ask about the attributes of the various characters on Dragon Ball Z, laugh along with the jokes on Ace Ventura, Pet Detective, join in a round of Where in the World is Carmen San Diego? If this is impossible for you, leave the room when they are consuming their dose of media and keep your mouth shut.

Moderation applies to both the amount and type of media exposure you allow. Some movies, TV shows, and Internet sites contain disturbing images that will be indelibly etched on your child's innocent mind. Once they've been viewed there is no way to retrieve them. There's no SPF for movies or television, no safe way to let your children bask freely for two hours without risking a burn. Unlike the "what-the-hell" parent, you have to supervise media consumption and limit both content and time.

In her book Failure to Connect: How Computers Affect Our Children's Minds for Better or Worse, Jane M. Healy writes eloquently about the hyping of computer use for young children, arguing that the academic benefits are largely overrated. Books and hands-on learning trump even the most sophisticated software. Like the allegedly "bad" foods I'll talk about in Chapter 7, computer games are mostly for fun. It's crucial that parents enforce limits on these games, because children can and do become addicted to them. I was once at a Shabbat dinner table with three very bright eleven-year-old boys. When we went around the table to say what we had been grateful for in the past week, each one proudly announced how many days he had been able to abstain from Ultima Online, a computer role-playing game. Parents of younger boys tell me that they are in a constant battle with their sons over Game Boy usage.

Sanctification applies to cosmic moments of media experience: a family viewing of The Wizard of Oz with lots of popcorn and no interruptions, your child's first Power Point–enhanced book report complete with snappy technical bells and whistles that you have no idea how to use, watching the announcement of a presidential election on the news. At these times, you can consider saying the *shehecheyanu,* the blessing of gratitude for "bringing us to this moment." Appreciate the power of what people have created using God's gifts.

The late Lubavitcher rebbe Menachem Mendel Schneerson said that we should not fear the Internet: "It can knit the world together." If parents aren't protective enough, children become overstimulated and reckless, but if they try too hard to protect their children from the outside world and all forms of progress, the children won't get street smart—or the modern version thereof, cyber smart—by learning what's useful and exciting and what to stay away from.

LEARN THE *MINHAG* OF YOUR COMMUNITY

In the Talmud there are numerous stories of students who hid under the bed of the great rabbis to see how they made love to their wives or hid in the bathroom to study how they conducted themselves before, during, and after relieving themselves. Were the students incurable voyeurs? Not exactly. Judaism advises us to learn from those we respect, and the eager students were trying to acquire knowledge from the masters. Likewise, parents who are concerned about overprotecting their children can learn from those whom they respect in the community. Pick parents who have kids you like, kids who seem to be turning out well. Study their actions and ask their advice.

When I let my nine-year-old walk to our local shopping boulevard alone, Belinda, my sensible and forthright Scottish neighbor (mother of five children, including two teenagers), intervened without my asking. "I saw Susanna walking to the boulevard alone. She's too young," she told me matter-of-factly. "At nine they have to go in pairs." With Belinda's help I figured out the *minhag* of my neighborhood. (*Minhag* is a useful Hebrew word meaning the local custom or practice of a community or a particular congregation.) On my block, the hierarchy of freedom works roughly like this:

- Seven-year-olds can walk a few blocks in pairs but need to call when they arrive.
- Eight-year-olds also go in pairs with no call necessary.
- Nine-year-olds can walk alone to each other's houses but must still walk in pairs or threesomes to the local shopping street.
- Eleven-year-olds can go alone to the boulevard.
- After dark, children go no farther than a scamper home from a friend's house on their own block.

Your neighborhood will have different customs than mine, but it's useful to spend some time determining what those customs are and push yourself, if necessary, to give your child appropriate, sensible freedom. In general, physical protectiveness means you are safeguarding your child from serious threat or injury. Physical overprotectiveness means you are guarding your child against life. It's worthwhile to talk to friends and neighbors whose opinions on such things you respect and to figure out the distinction between the two.

FIVE KEYS TO A STRONG CHARACTER

"*Lech lecha*—Go forth, move!" God told Abraham when it was time for him to leave the land of his father to venture out into the unknown Promised Land. The phrase literally means "go to yourself." Unless your child ventures forth into the world he won't get a chance to learn how to master it and to find his place. Having a clear goal in raising your child—"I want this young person to learn to swim"—can help you figure out what to do when your child prefers to remain on the shore, or when your own fears threaten to stall his growth.

Know When to Insist on Independence

Moses, Noah, Ruth, and Naomi. Almost every biblical and mythical hero was afraid before venturing out on a great journey. Your little hero will be too. If you believe that fear is always a reliable indicator of danger, your child will believe this as well. A mother and daughter, Mina and Lily, offered me a powerful lesson about why the fear-danger connection should not always be trusted.

A few years ago, my daughter Susanna asked her ten-year-old friend Lily to spend the night. When I asked Lily the usual Solicitous Mother questions—"Is the cot comfortable? Do you need another blanket?"— her reply impressed me: "Oh, thanks, I'm fine. I can sleep anywhere." When Lily woke up in the morning before anyone else, she made her bed, toasted a frozen waffle for breakfast, rinsed her plate, and put it in the dishwasher.

I wondered what had helped Lily become so independent. The answer came as her mother, Mina, and I chatted about Lily's first experience at a sleepaway summer camp. Mina said, "Of course Lily was pretty nervous and threw up the usual few times the night before, but I just put her on the bus in the morning."

The usual few times? Had I heard this right? In my community a child who became physically sick from fear of going away to camp would be kept home or might even be taken to a therapist to be evaluated for separation anxiety disorder.

For some children, this degree of fear would be a legitimate red flag for a miserable camp experience, but Mina felt confident about sending Lily off despite her daughter's genuine anxiety. Mina took a risk because she knew that her daughter needed to learn how to swim, both literally and in a psychological or spiritual sense.

"How did Lily like camp?" I asked.

"She had a wonderful time. Can't wait to go back next summer," replied Mina.

Having the courage not to pamper and overprotect your child means that sometimes she will be uncomfortable, unhappy, or even in peril, but that you are willing to take a chance because of your commitment to her growth and development.

Get Children in the Habit of Solving Their Own Problems

Chloe Eichenlaub, the former head of the Oaks School in Los Angeles, talked to me about parents' desire to protect their children from having to tolerate a difficult child in the classroom: "'Get him out!' the parents cry. 'He takes up too much of the teacher's time!'"

Many good parents don't realize the value of having such a child around. When the behavior is not extreme or dangerous, the potential for social learning is enormous all around. A difficult child gives the rest of the children a chance to build up their conflict-resolution muscles, to learn how to manage with a distraction, to grow strong as an inclusive group.

American researchers Dana Davidson and Joseph Tobin, while studying cultural differences in the socialization of young children, observed a classroom of four-year-olds in a Buddhist preschool in Kyoto, Japan. Here's how they described the behavior of Hiroki, one of the students:

> Hiroki started things off with a flourish by pulling his penis out from under the leg of his shorts and waving it at the class during the morning welcome song. During the workbook session that followed, Hiroki called out answers to every question

the teacher asked and to many she did not ask. When not volunteering answers, Hiroki gave a loud running commentary on his workbook progress: "Now I'm coloring the badger, now the pig." He alternated his play-by-play announcing with occasional songs, entertaining the class with loud, accurate renditions of their favorite cartoon themes, complete with accompanying dancing, gestures, and occasional instrumental flourishes. . . .

During the course of the day, Hiroki started many fights, stepped on a girl's hand and disrupted a game by throwing flash cards over the railing to the ground below.

While the Americans felt ready to stop the video camera, drop all scholarly neutrality, and tell Hiroki to cut it out, the Japanese teacher, Fukui-sensei, remained composed and impartial about Hiroki's transgressions. She didn't chastise Hiroki and did almost nothing to intervene or even to redirect his behavior. When questioned about her unusual reaction, the teacher explained that rather than seeing Hiroki as a problem, she valued his presence in the classroom because she believed that Hiroki provided the other children with opportunities to learn many important things about life: how to concentrate when there are distractions, how to defend yourself, and how to manage conflicts and difficulties without the intervention of the teacher.

Fukui-sensei gave up her own control in order to put control in the hands of her students. Are you ready to challenge your own child to courageously solve his or her own problems?

Give Children a Chance to Exercise the Divine Gift of Free Will

On the sixth day of creation God said, "Let us make man." To whom was He speaking? There weren't any people yet. Moses

Hayyim Luzzatto, an eighteenth-century kabbalist, explains that the "us" in this phrase refers to God's ministering angels. God made the angels on the second day of creation to help him forge the world. But why would the ruler of the universe include the angels in the task of creating people? Why not just plow right ahead? Luzzatto explains that God brought the angels in on his decision because he wanted to make sure they wouldn't become jealous of humans. Although angels are holy beings, they cannot create holiness because they have no free will. Human beings have the ability to choose, and our good choices—the ethical, mature, reasoned ones—are more precious to God and have more world-changing power than the angels' automatic fulfillment of divine instructions. God knew that the angels would recognize free will as humans' most unique and valuable trait, and that is why he wanted to protect them from feeling jealous.

Free will is indeed the attribute that will define your child's life. How she makes decisions and chooses between right and wrong will directly influence everything else. Letting your child learn to exercise free will doesn't mean being permissive. It means allowing her to choose badly and to learn from the choices she makes. How to start? She can't learn to make choices unless she has some. Begin by giving her a chance to mess up. As parent educator Barbara Colorosa says, "Let kids make cheap mistakes. If your ten-year-old daughter feels cold because she forgot her sweater, she's learned more than if you reminded her one more time to bring one along." For a child, the best lesson in remembering to check to see if her lunch bag is in the backpack is a few hunger pangs at noon.

Let Them Experience the World, Warts and All

There's a Jewish blessing that is said when one sees exceptionally beautiful people or things: "Blessed are you, Lord our God, who has such in his universe." And there is one to say when noticing strange-looking people or animals: "Blessed are you, Lord our God, who varies creation."

When my family and I were studying at a Hebrew language institute in Israel one summer, we were housed at a hotel with a large group of what the Israelis called "special people" (mentally retarded and physically handicapped adults) enjoying their government-sponsored beach holiday. My children had never before seen people as peculiar looking and oddly behaved as these. One had a large knobby growth protruding from her ear, one had legs two inches in diameter, and there was Moti, a friendly young man of very limited intelligence. Moti spent much of his time vigorously greeting every passerby with a hearty "Good morning!" and a nonstop handshake whatever the hour, day or night.

Every evening the special people were provided with costumes—curly rainbow-colored wigs, prince costumes with golden swords and shields, and metallic hula skirts—and were entertained by a DJ and a loud, live stage show. Each day the children from the language institute would watch the special people and their activities. They weren't all happy or wholesome scenes. One special person pulled a child's hair, a man hid in the women's bathroom, and two were stopped just short of having sex in the crowded swimming pool.

In America, we often keep such people separate. Although we let children see horror movies, we protect them from seeing real people who look scary and act inappropriately. In Israel, these people were being honored with a beach holiday, costumes, and nightly celebrations. The first time ten-year-old language student Peter got caught in Moti's nonstop handshake, he didn't know how to break away and stood paralyzed and mildly panicked for many minutes. By the end of the summer, however, Peter calmly and effectively instructed Moti, "Let go now," after the briefest handshake.

If someone had asked me beforehand, I'm sure I would have said that I wished to protect my children from being exposed to these people whom God had made so very different. Ultimately, I felt grateful that my daughters had an opportunity to learn more about the variety of life than they ever could at home. When we protect our children from people who are different, inappropriate, and even frightening, they'll be too easily shocked and frightened as adults.

Teach Your Child Not to Panic over Pain

Medical doctors use the term *titration* to describe the process of adjusting the standard dosage of a medication up or down based on an individual patient's reactions. Young children titrate their own level of upset up or down depending on their parents' facial expression or gestures. If a child is distressed and sees Mom react with panic, he knows he should wail; if she's compassionate but calm, he tends to recover quickly.

The scene: afternoon in the playground. The players: four-year-old Katelyn, her mom, and Katelyn's friend Taylor. The action: Katelyn bumps her chin on the seesaw. She looks up at Mom, who rushes in with concern, her voice pinched and solicitous. "Katelyn, are you all right?" Katelyn grabs her chin and begins to wail. Grabs Mom by the skirt. Looks up at her mournfully.

Take Two: Katelyn bumps her chin on the seesaw. She looks up at Mom, who shakes her head in acknowledgment and looks Katelyn in the eyes. "I see you bumped your chin." Mom does not move in to inspect the injury. Katelyn, realizing that this is not turning into an opportunity for much attention, rubs her chin once, hops on the seesaw, and calls to Taylor to join her. Katelyn has taken the cue from Mom: a bump on the chin is no big deal.

Treating children's daily distresses as an expected and unalarming part of life is an effective way to discourage them from turning small difficulties into big dramas. Building *middot*, good character traits, is a lifelong process. We can help children become calmer and more resilient by staying calm ourselves.

RAISING YOUR CHILDREN TO LEAVE YOU

In the book of Leviticus, God warns us not to put a stumbling block before the blind. Keeping too close an eye on children is a stumbling block. If they don't have the chance to be bad, they can't choose to be good. If they don't have the chance to fail, they can't learn. And if they aren't allowed to face scary situations, they'll grow up to be frightened of life's simplest challenges.

When horticulturists want to prepare hothouse plants for replanting outdoors, they subject them to stress to strengthen them. Gently and progressively deprived of food and water and exposed to greater extremes of heat and cold than they've been accustomed to, the plants grow stronger root systems and thicker stems. While parents don't need to deprive their children of life-sustaining essentials, they do need to prepare them for rough conditions by teaching them to tolerate some stresses and extremes.

Every child is different. Some have better judgment than their peers or even their older siblings and can be trusted with freedom that is typically granted to older children. An agile child can and should climb a taller tree than her less able brother. An adventurous teenager may desire to spread her wings early, while her more cautious sister may prefer to stay closer to the nest for a longer time. Look at the particular person God has given you and use your best judgment, but never assume that any child is too fragile to fly.

CHAPTER 5

The Blessing of Longing:

Teaching Your Child an Attitude of Gratitude

"He who has one hundred wants two hundred," an ancient sage observed. He was probably a parent. Two thousand years ago, the rabbis realized that gratitude, a most essential character trait, does not come naturally but must be taught to children. They knew it was a tough one.

Here's a story that's happened to you. When my daughter Emma was nearing seven, her grandparents sent her a birthday check. Emma wanted a Pound Puppy Playhouse for her birthday. It was the only thing she wanted and she talked about it with a swooning passion. They didn't have one at our local toy store, so she convinced me to take her to Kmart. The toy aisles were a mess. There were toys on the floor, toys out of the boxes, G.I. Joes in the section with the Barbies. No Pound Puppy Playhouses. We asked for help. An unconcerned clerk shrugged and said, "If it isn't on the shelf . . ."

I felt a missionary zeal rising in me. I suggested that we ignore the fast-approaching dinner hour, brave the traffic, and head out to Toys "R" Us. Emma looked at me with both awe and great tenderness. When we arrived I felt hope rise in me. Nice and neat. An alert salesperson directed us to the Pound Puppy section. I saw the Playhouse right away and wanted it to be the only one. I wanted to have found the Holy Grail. Emma sensibly didn't care how many there were as long as there was one for her. For three days, she and the Pound Puppy Playhouse were never apart. She slept with it perched on the foot of her bed. She took it to her dental appointment. But then it was over. The pink plastic case sat on the floor. She now longed for a Backstreet Boys CD.

CAN LONGING FOR BAD THINGS BE GOOD?

Nancy and Paul, a couple in one of my parenting classes, neatly summed up our concern about our children's seemingly endless lust for stuff: "We just want Molly not to want so much." Seven-year-old Molly, they declared, was basically a good girl, but "she's driving us crazy asking for things! She wants a moon bounce *and* a petting zoo at her birthday party. She hounds us for a new Beanie Baby every week. She begs for clothes and shoes and jewelry. What's going to happen when she's a teenager?"

Nancy and Paul had no idea where or how to draw the line with their daughter. When they said no to Molly, she complained that they were mean and unfair. When they said yes she immediately wanted more.

"Sometimes, when I look at her, I see this spoiled little princess—the kind of child I always swore I'd never raise. How can we get Molly not to want so much stuff that she doesn't need?" Paul asked.

"You probably can't," I replied. "But maybe you don't need to." According to the sages, longing isn't all bad. It's how we deal with our longing that counts.

The dynamics of desire were carefully studied by the rabbis of the period of the Talmud. They concluded that everyone is endowed at birth with both a *yetzer tov* (impulse for good) and a *yetzer hara* (impulse for evil). The yetzer hara, an aggressive, potentially destructive inclination, is of distinct value. The Talmud says that the evil impulse is *tov meod* (very good) because it is made up of some of our most robust traits. Curiosity, ambition, and passionate desire all derive their energy from the yetzer hara. Without it, there would be no marriages, no children conceived, no homes built, no businesses.

To make the point, I like to tell parents a story from the Talmud. The men of the Great Synagogue wanted to get rid of the yetzer hara once and for all. The yetzer hara warned them not to wipe it out: "If you kill me the world will come to an end!" Not sure whether or not the yetzer spoke the truth, the men captured it and locked it up for three days. Alas, they discovered that even this was too great a harness on the evil inclination. Searching the land for a newly laid egg during the time of the yetzer's imprisonment, they could find not a one. So they let the yetzer free and with this action gave the world back its passion and fruitfulness, leaving each one of us the responsibility of controlling and channeling our own yetzer hara.

While the yetzer hara should be treated with extreme watchfulness, it must not be eliminated, because it is necessary for human survival. It's our juice, our spark, our zip. We live fully by balancing two forces: our burning passions and our ability to exercise self-restraint. The rabbis firmly believed that we should worship God with both our yetzer tov and our yetzer hara.

If desire is neither bad nor "curable," how should we curb our greed? The Jewish philosophy of deed over creed provides a solution. Doing the right thing is more important than feeling the correct feelings, so while it is perfectly acceptable to desire things that aren't necessary, we must discipline ourselves and direct our actions away from them. Talmudic teaching and modern child psychology share a common principle here. Behavioral therapy is founded on the belief that changed behavior can lead to changed feelings. The Talmud teaches that if parents put limits on their children's whining and begging and require them to perform good deeds, the children will eventually become less greedy and more grateful—the feelings will follow the actions.

Where do Emma and her Pound Puppy Playhouse and Molly and her Beanie Babies fit into all of this? Nancy and Paul and I might have better luck dealing with our children's materialistic cravings if we could say to ourselves, "Witness this spirited, impassioned, forceful young being. She is magnificent in the intensity of her desires and the brilliant locutions of her argument. As her parent I accept my dual responsibilities: one is to respect her zeal, her yetzer hara, and the other is to help her develop a strong yetzer tov. So I will say a calm and emphatic no to the Beanie Babies and the moon bounce, but I will not criticize her for desiring them, for that is her right."

Parents cannot and should not try to eliminate longing in a child. Instead, we must teach our children how to redirect their longings, accept "no" graciously, and appreciate the blessings they do have.

IT'S ABOUT GUIDANCE, NOT CONSENSUS

Earlier, I talked about Peter and Lynn, parents who believed in a "democratic" family and treated their surly daughter, Sasha, as an equal participant in the family power structure. Peter and Lynn were far more honest with themselves than many of the parents I meet, who have the same egalitarian attitude but aren't as aware of it. A child's cry of "It's not fair!" will hit these parents right in the conscience, prompting at least a few moments of serious reflection: "Is she right? Am I being too rigid? Do I have a good reason for denying her the Beanie Baby?"

Judaism clarifies some of these issues. Your reasons for denying your child's myriad requests have a larger context: you are teaching self-control, giving her practice in redirecting her yetzer hara, and strengthening her capacity for gratitude. The biggest shift you'll need to make is the one away from child-size logic— "Give me one reason why I can't have the Beanie Baby! You got me one last week, why not this week?"—to the grander logic of balancing yetzer hara and yetzer tov. This shift will occur slowly, as you revise the way you respond to your child's demands. Let's look at the mistakes we most commonly make when trying to deal democratically with our children's requests. When we're aware of the power of the yetzer hara, we can see why these methods don't work.

Rhetorical Questions

Although they didn't try the old-fashioned ploy, "Think of all the starving children in China who would be grateful to have what you have," Nancy and Paul did use an equally hopeful and ineffective modern version: "Molly, don't you think you already have enough Beanie Babies?" Molly's standard response was to roll her eyes or issue a frank rebuttal: "No, Mom, fifteen is not enough if I don't have Stinky or Snort." And when Nancy tried a slightly different angle—"This Barbie Dreamhouse with all the stuff you want costs sixty dollars. Do you have any idea how much money that is?"—she simply gave Molly the opportunity to come back with a perfect straight line: "Yes. Just the right amount to buy the Barbie Dreamhouse with all the stuff."

By using rhetorical questions, Nancy and Paul hoped that their efforts would lead Molly to what psychologists call an "aha" experience: "Gee, Mom, you're right. I didn't realize how many Beanie Babies I already have. And come to think of it, some kids probably don't have many at all because their parents, unlike you, need to spend all their money on rent and food. I really should be grateful. What was I thinking?"

But the "aha" reaction doesn't come because the yetzer hara is too strong and focused. Molly wasn't looking for insight, she simply wanted more Beanie Babies.

Logic and Reason

Samuel Butler said, "Logic is like a sword—those who appeal to it shall die by it." Today's parents tend to have a great deal of respect for verbal acuity and logical arguments. The great majority of them prefer to try to reason with their children rather than punish them. Typically, the parents attempt to talk their kids out of excessive desires by patiently explaining cause and effect. An earnest father might say, "Let's just think this through together. If five boys sleep over you will probably be up all night and too tired the next day to enjoy the Space Museum." To which his son will reply, "No we won't. We'll just have fun at night and then have more fun the next day."

Explaining cause and effect rarely works with children, because their passion and sense of omnipotence overwhelm their capacity for logic. The rational reason for not spending $120 on a pair of shoes that one will outgrow in three months is generally lost on them. And, of course, parents can't win with strict logic because the yetzer hara, even in a seven-year-old, is much more forceful than any line of reasoning.

Pious Lectures

Most pious lectures are a waste of everybody's time. Rather than change your child's opinion, they prompt an internal dialogue that alienates him from you. Here is a typical interchange. Jesse's remarks are unspoken.

Dad: Jesse, I won't want you to watch *South Park* even if it's still around when you're a teenager. It's a dumb, mean-spirited show.

Jesse: *That's what you think. My friends all love it. Even the smart, nice ones.*

Dad: You wouldn't get the jokes, the animation is terrible, and you wouldn't really like it.

Jesse: *Wrong, wrong, and wrong.*

Dad: Stuff like that makes you stupid, and I want you to be smart. Let's rent a *National Geographic* video instead.

Jesse: *No thanks. Stuff like that makes you bored.*

Thus we reasonable parents waste our breath trying to convince our children to take the high road. No matter how psychologically insightful or profound the lecture, it's likely to have little impact on the strength of your child's desires. Don't bother talking to the yetzer hara—it doesn't speak "parent."

Deep in the trenches of a typical day, every parent encounters children afflicted with the gimmes, whining, and ingratitude. Rhetorical questions, logic and reason, and pious lectures only reinforce children's excessive demands by giving them lots of attention. Inspired by the wisdom of the rabbis—evil inclinations have potential for good, action is what's important, and gratitude is tough to come by—you can use a different approach to teach your children moderation and gratitude.

CHANGING YOUR CHILD'S UNGRATEFUL BEHAVIOR WITH THE YETZER HARA IN MIND

Before you can start teaching an attitude of gratitude, you must be very clear about what your child is entitled to. Children (and adults) frequently confuse what they *want* with what they *need*.

In children, the yetzer hara is easily inflamed by the allure of seeing something enticing on a television commercial, a supermarket shelf, or in a friend's toy chest. "I must have cargo pants from Old Navy by Thursday or I can't go to school!" your child may cry in genuine anguish. Sensitive to peer pressure and not wanting to see her left out of the crowd, you may be tempted to slide the cargo pants from their obvious "wants" position into the "needs" column.

Let's look at a short list of things that children are fully entitled to: respectful treatment, healthful food, shelter from the weather, practical and comfortable clothing, yearly checkups at the pediatrician and the dentist, and a good education. Everything else is a privilege. It's an adult's job to remember that ultrabaggy shorts, Game Boys, and the latest CDs are not necessary for human survival. Your child need not understand or agree with this point of view.

Once you embrace this premise—and it may take a while, because it's drastically different from what we're used to—you can begin the practice of saying no. Your goal is to respect your child's desire for stuff without caving in to his demands. Remember, just because he wants a pair of Air Jordans or a TV in his room doesn't mean that he is a bad person, greedy, or already ruined.

The basic game plan for saying no goes like this:

1 Describe the child's dilemma using a compassionate tone: "Terry, I know you would really like me to buy you a pair of Air Jordans."
2 Explain briefly and clearly why you're saying no: "You already have a pair of sneakers that we bought last month. You don't need another pair."
3 Don't go overboard naming feelings and don't try to be overly understanding ("Honey, I know you are very frustrated—I know this is hard for you—I know you're longing for Air Jordans"). This patronizing attitude merely irritates

children or comes across as weakness on your part. A gentle, firm no and short explanation will do.

Naturally, your child will rail against you with vehemence and fire when you deny his requests. He'll tell you you're heartless, dumb, and mean. He'll tell you he's been born into the wrong family. Try not to respond to these protests. It's your child's yetzer hara speaking, and you can be respectful of his passion without taking his complaints too seriously. He is entitled to believe that you are misguided or even evil. He is entitled to feel enraged. But he is not entitled to say whatever he pleases about the situation.

Putting the Jewish deed-versus-creed principle to work helps remind us that the creed (belief) is his business but certain deeds, such as verbal abuse of parents, are unacceptable. When your child's complaints cross your line of tolerance you should take action. Gratuitously criticizing adults is the beginning of a bad habit, one that can get your child into trouble with other adults later in his life. Randy didn't mind when her six-year-old son, Luke, said she was mean, but she drew the line when after she refused to buy him bubble gum, he said, "You suck." Luke didn't know what the word meant, but Randy wanted to teach him not to say it anyway. A stern look, a rebuke, and the loss of Rollerblading privileges for the afternoon sent an effective message.

Part of the strategy of the yetzer hara is to overcome all obstacles to its satisfaction. Parents often admire verbal prowess in their children and are tempted to see just how good an argument their little attorney can present. Then, seduced by their child's intellect, they'll offer their reasoned response. This is a big mistake. Just because your articulate, passionate child can come up with an excellent argument, you don't need to counter it with an equally thoughtful rebuttal. If you do, your child will never really listen to your point of view anyway, because he'll be too busy preparing counterarguments. The back-and-forth can drag on for a long time, leaving both parent and child irritable. If you do go down this path and then cave in, you are teaching your child that wearing you down through lawyerly debate is an excellent strategy for getting what he wants.

Should you listen to your child's point of view at all? Yes, because listening is respectful, because he might provide you with information that will change your mind, and because you want to set the example of being a good listener. But listen briefly! If you are tempted to reason with your child, resist. Remember that a healthy capacity for appreciation will help him more in the long run than a pair of Air Jordans. By calmly ignoring his arguments, both you and he will gain in the end.

If your child continues to beg, whine, and demand, be resolute. Try starting your sentences with the word *nevertheless*. Although you accept his desire without condemnation, at some point you'll need to say, "I know you want the sneakers but the case is closed. We are not going to discuss this anymore." Let him know exactly what will happen if he doesn't quiet down: "If you continue to bring up the subject of Air Jordans, you will lose your television privileges."

CULTIVATING AN ATTITUDE OF GRATITUDE

The problem of taking for granted what we already have, wanting more than we need, and forgetting to count our blessings comes up frequently in Torah teachings. In Deuteronomy, God reminds us that he will punish us for feeling deprived when we "have plenty of everything" but "will not serve God with happiness and a glad heart." Consciousness-raising on this subject comes up anew each year when on Rosh Hashanah we are required to say, "Let us (not) be consumed by desire for what we lack or grow unmindful of the blessings which are already ours." And, of course, covetousness makes it to the list of the top ten commandments.

The rabbis respect our passions but require us to refrain from overindulgence. What, then, are we to do with our natural desires? We are to convert them into good impulses via prayers of gratitude called "blessings." Jewish tradition encourages adults to say 100 blessings of gratitude a day. To fill a blessing quota this huge, you have to be vigilant about looking for things to be thankful for. Ritually observant Jews don't waste any time. The moment after awakening, they begin with the morning blessings: "Thank you, God, for returning my soul to me." The next blessing is said after going to the bathroom because, wondrously, "the tubes and passages that should be open are open and those that should be closed are closed." They say another prayer before eating breakfast, to thank God for the food. Throughout the day, they continue to give thanks at every possible opportunity. There's even a blessing for when bad things happen: "Thank you, God, the true judge, for this test of my spiritual elevation." The obvious purpose of all these prayers is to increase our awareness of good fortune.

The rabbis knew how easily we slip from counting our blessings to coveting things, money, and neighbors' spouses. That's why they treated gratitude as a character trait that needed constant vigilance. For the Orthodox this heightened awareness is built into the structure of daily life, but we can all cultivate gratitude in ourselves and our children. It requires doing two things: appreciating what we have and redirecting our desires.

In order to effectively teach children gratitude, we parents must start with ourselves. If you lift your mood by a trip to the mall or try to maintain your status by keeping up with the Ornsteins, your children will pick up the not-very-hidden message that acquiring things is a way to reward yourself, feel important, or cheer yourself up. Even if we manage to get our children to stop asking for so many things, they still won't learn how to be grateful unless they see us practicing gratitude. No one is born feeling grateful; it's an acquired skill. That's why traditional Jewish law forbids spending money on the Sabbath. God commands us to stop shopping and count our blessings on that one day because he knows that left on our own, we wouldn't be so inclined.

Most non-Orthodox Jews don't observe the no-spending rule on Saturdays, but if you want to nurture appreciation and downplay desire in yourself and your children, here are a few behaviors that might help:

- Try not to let a visit to the mall become your most frequent family outing. Consider visiting friends; taking a trip to the park, museum, or library; or going for a walk around the neighborhood instead.
- Avoid frequent conversations about how much you want to own things you see advertised on television.
- Don't use the word *need* when you really mean *want*.
- Notice how much you verbalize your envy for other people's things in front of the children.
- Don't let mail-order catalogs pile up; try not to let your children see you spending lots of time reading catalogs or shopping online.
- Teach your child nonmonetary ways to delay gratification. For instance, instead of doing a lot of shopping for a forthcoming vacation, you might say, "I'm really excited about going to Arizona next month. Let's go to the library and check out some books on the Grand Canyon."

LEARNING TO SEE OUR BLESSINGS

One way to turn our focus to our many blessings is to learn from the pros—the very same children who we claim are too fixated on stuff. While at times they seem to take all their cues from TV commercials and shopping mall culture, they are also masters at appreciating the little things. The sages say that God is in the details. Children are specialists in the holy details. Just as the yetzer hara leads them to pester you about toys and clothes, the same source also provides natural exuberance and appreciation of life in all its limitless glory:

"Watch this, Dad! When the wind blows in one direction all the grass lies down flat, then when it blows the other way, the grass flips over! I'm not kidding. Come see this!"

"Can we stay here at the zoo all day and come back tomorrow?"

"I hope I can see Elana today. I miss her so much. I think I have best friend fever."

"I can have rainbow and chocolate sprinkles on my ice cream? This is the best day of my life!"

You may have to slow down to appreciate what enthralls, astonishes, charms, and tickles your child. Go out back to see the teeny red worm. Sit down with the class picture and let your daughter tell you every single name. Save time when your son visits your office to let him make five photocopies of his hand in slightly different positions. Listen and ask questions when he tells you about the refrigerator the size of a room that he saw on his class trip to the supermarket.

Susanna and I were riding bikes in our neighborhood when we passed a dead animal on the street. She wanted to circle back to see it. I agreed. We studied the squirrel and its innards for a little while. "Not a lot of moms would do this, you know," my grateful child said. Children can be cheap dates if you know where to take them. Show them how to make egg whites and sugar explode into satiny billows, teach them how to use an old-fashioned handheld drill. When you're tucking them in the night before the school play, offer a real back rub with massage oil. Their gratitude and uninhibited enthusiasm can be contagious, but you have to slow down and make these moments a priority or else you'll both miss out.

Formalizing the ritual of blessings so that it becomes a habit is another way to teach children to remember what they've been given. We tend to want to send God "wish lists" of the things we want, rather than remembering to thank him for what we already have. In our house we go around the table each week at Shabbat dinner and say our "gratitudes." This ritual has multiple benefits. It's often a chance to catch up with one another on the goings-on of the week, and it teaches the children what their father and I value. I might tell Emma: "I'm grateful that you got dressed and ready for breakfast all week long without any reminding," and continue to the rest of the group, "I'm grateful that Uncle Sol is feeling better. I'm grateful that Josie is here to join us for dinner. I'm grateful that I finished another chapter of my book this week." A friend told me that shortly before her birthday, her four-year-old said, "I'm grateful that I don't have any homework this weekend. I'm grateful that Dina said I can keep her scooter all day tomorrow. I'm grateful that I got to help Daddy pick out a pearl necklace for Mommy's birthday."

Stopping before eating in order to bless food is a ubiquitous religious practice because it's a natural—every time we eat we have a choice between gluttony or gratitude to God. The rabbis really refined this one. There are special blessings for different occasions and different kinds of food. All of these prayers can help build an attitude of gratitude throughout the day. You'll know you've made an impact when you overhear your young child saying a blessing over her dolls' party: "Josephina, don't forget to say thank you to God for the cupcakes and tea."

GIVING AS A WAY TO SAY THANK YOU

Giving to others can also be a way to acknowledge one's blessings. In Judaism everyone is supposed to think of themselves as having more than they need. Even the poorest person is obligated to find someone in greater need and to share what he has with him.

tikkun olam (healing or repairing the world) conveys the idea that if we are blessed with abundance, it's because God wants us to figure out how to use it to help others.

Judaism teaches that we have been given the gift of life in order to use it to make the world better. If your child is disappointed about a canceled play date, you can take him to the toy store to cheer him up *or* you can give him an opportunity to make things better. Instead of buying the toy you might say, "Jonah's mom called to say he can't play with you today because he's sick. Let's figure out what kind of get-well card we could make to help him get better faster."

Note that this is not a yes-or-no question but a sentence that starts with the magical parenting word *let's*. It also focuses the child on the blessing of his good health and his responsibility to help a friend who is not, at that moment, similarly blessed. *Bikkur holim* (the mitzvah of visiting the sick) is commanded, not simply encouraged, precisely because the rabbis knew that people would rather avoid sick people. In a situation like this you have the chance to help your child transform his disappointment into an act of kindness and generosity.

Twelve-step programs teach the participants to "act themselves into right thinking." Children love all the appreciation they get from doing something nice, even if they have to be prodded to do it. Teaching them to become aware of the different ways they can receive love and thanks from others gets them into the habit of service. These experiences grow into an adult understanding of the spiritual value of community involvement and volunteering.

Words alone rarely teach children much about the good of giving rather than receiving. The key to getting this message across is letting your child use his leadership ability and judgment in the process of helping others. For example, you might say to him, "There are a lot of children in this city who don't have enough warm clothes for the winter. We have a big pile of stuff you've outgrown. Let's fold the clothes and put them in bags and then you can choose where you think we should take them. Three different shelters have written me letters asking for donations. You read the letters [or for the little ones, "I'll read the letters to you"] and you decide which shelter sounds the best." During the Thanksgiving holidays (or anytime), you might say, "Let's go to the food bank and help fill the bags. I know you'll be good at picking out stuff for families with children your age."

More and more synagogues sponsor a mitzvah day. Heeding the call at our temple, our family volunteered to help serve a Passover seder dinner to three hundred elderly Russian immigrants at a local community center. Emma asked the Four Questions and Susanna, Michael, and I served the food. We all helped to clean up. The trays were heavy, the soup spilled, and when the kitchen ran out of chicken the unfed guests were understandably testy with the waiters—us. It was hard, tiring work, but we had a fulfilling day and were grateful to have the chance to be of service. If your child's school or your synagogue doesn't offer a community service program, look in the newspaper for "involvement opportunities" or go on-line to check out the Web sites—Kids Care Clubs and Family Cares (kidscares.org and familycares.org) are two—that offer ideas for teaching children compassion through involvement in community service projects.

LONGING IS ALSO A BLESSING

Children who get most of their desires satisfied right away don't have a chance to appreciate what they've already got. Deprived of opportunities to wait and dream and long for something, they never learn to value their possessions or experiences. Everything carries the same weight, and none of it weighs very much. The sooner a child gets what she wants, the sooner she'll use it up and move on to the next desire. I only have to think of the Pound Puppy Playhouse to remind myself of this fact. Getting one's wishes granted immediately doesn't make a child more grateful or content. On the contrary, it makes her less appreciative and more acquisitive. This is what our grandmothers meant when they talked about "spoiled" children—what got spoiled was the child's capacity for waiting, satisfaction, and gratitude.

Lisa, a seventeen-year-old who baby-sat our daughter at the mountain resort where we vacationed one summer, demonstrated how adults can teach children gratitude and help them understand the value of work. When Lisa arrived at our room, I recognized her from the reception desk. I later learned that she was working days and baby-sitting in the evenings because she was saving for a car. She told me that she would need it in the fall when she entered parole officer training school. Lisa planned to start at school A, which had the right basic courses, and then transfer after a year to school B, which charged higher tuition and was farther from home but offered a specialty she wanted to study. Recently, Lisa's grandmother had offered to match any money she earned that summer. This would mean that Lisa would be able to buy the car and start school one semester sooner than she had expected. She was deeply grateful. I was impressed with this young woman's focus and dedication to her goals and couldn't help comparing her with my young friends Matthew and Spencer.

As soon as Matthew learned to ride a bike, his parents bought him a top-of-the-line children's bike complete with an electronic horn. When he left the bike in front of his friend's house and it got stolen, his parents replaced it right away. Matthew's parents were equally determined to keep his brother, Spencer, stimulated and happy. When the boy expressed an interest in collecting stamps shortly before his eighth birthday, his present from Mom and Dad was a leather album filled with beautiful stamps from all over the world. While the parents had generous, loving intentions, neither Matthew nor Spencer appreciated their fine gifts as much as our baby-sitter appreciated her grandmother's contribution to her car fund.

The Jewish concept of *shmirat ha-adamah* means "saving or caring for the earth." In developing children's character we always want to "think global, act local." Helping them to fix things when they are broken instead of just replacing them or throwing them away is good insurance that when they're adults they'll do their part to take care of the community and the planet. When things come too easily to children they not only get spoiled but also can become "spoilers" when they grow up, because they haven't learned to value what they've been given.

At Hanukkah we celebrate the miracle of the oil lasting eight days. Perhaps the real miracle was that there was already enough oil, but that under the stress of war and adversity, we panicked and forgot about our resources. The modern version of this miracle is the recognition that what we already have may be all that we need, and that there's even enough to share with others. It takes determination and self-discipline to teach these lessons to children, but when you do, they'll reward you by counting their blessings instead of counting what they want and don't have.

CHAPTER 6

The Blessing of Work:

Finding the Holy Sparks in Ordinary Chores

In the strange and magical P. L. Travers story "Mrs. Corry," Mary Poppins and her friend Mrs. Corry acquire a pile of star-shaped gold paper decorations peeled from the tops of ordinary pieces of gingerbread. They climb up on a tall ladder with a bucket of glue and a paintbrush. Once at the top they glue the stars, one by one, straight onto the sky. As each star is placed into position it glitters furiously, sending out rays of sparkling golden light. Watching this scene through her bedroom window, eight-year-old Jane says to her younger brother, "What I want to know is this: Are the stars gold paper or is the gold paper stars?" This is a good description of what life is like at the core of Judaism. Things that seem as ordinary as paper or as simple as climbing a ladder with a bucket have the potential to repair the rip in the cosmos. The key is to take advantage of these everyday holy opportunities, of the sparkling rays waiting to be released.

LEARNING BY DOING

In Judaism, the path to holiness lies in human activity, or what the modern philosopher Abraham Heschel calls "right action." Judaism values deed over creed and learning by doing. The

sages believed that life should be a work-study program—we
have to apply our knowledge. In fact, intellectual study alone is
suspect. The first-century priest Eleazar ben Azariah said, "Anyone whose wisdom exceeds his good deeds—to what can he be
compared? To a tree whose branches are numerous, but whose
roots are few. The wind will come and uproot it and turn it
upside down."

The ancient rabbis all had day jobs. They worked as wood-
cutters and cabinetmakers and blacksmiths. Rav Huna, a wealthy
fourth-century rabbi and businessman who is frequently quoted
in the Talmud, worked his own fields and picked his fruit himself.
He taught, "Whoever occupies himself with Torah only is like
one who has no God." We get acquainted with God, we make our
presence known to him and his presence is known to us, not only
through prayer and acts of heavy-duty, obvious-to-bystanders
goodness, but also through the mundane tasks of everyday
domestic life: clearing the table, brushing our teeth in the morning, feeding the children, loading the dishwasher, taking out the
trash. No task is too simple or too menial to be elevated by our
awareness of its potential connection to holiness.

In his book *Jewish Spiritual Practices*, Yitzhak Buxbaum tells
about the time the great eighteenth-century Hasidic rabbi
known as the Baal Shem Tov traveled with Rabbi Yitzhak of
Drobitch in the role of his personal assistant. The Baal Shem Tov
brought Rabbi Yitzhak his coffee in a pot and served it to him.
After Rabbi Yitzhak drank the coffee, the Baal Shem Tov
removed the coffeepot, the cup, and the spoon from the table and
brought them into the kitchen. Rabbi Yitzhak's young son
observed all this and questioned the Baal Shem Tov: "Holy
Rabbi, I can understand why you want to offer personal service
to my holy father. But why did you also trouble yourself to
carry out the empty dishes?" The Baal Shem Tov answered him
by explaining that carrying the spoon out from the Holy of
Holies (in the Temple) was part of the service of the high priest

on the Day of Atonement. Then and now, clearing the table can be a great act of devotion to God.

SWEATING THE SMALL STUFF

The core of Jewish theology, then, lies in sweating the small stuff—life's prose—and the cosmic importance of teamwork. Children can be taught these principles in Sunday school or through Bible stories at home, but learning them intellectually is not enough, just as reading the Torah is not enough for adults. In order to practice "right action," children need both skills (competence to do what is good) and motivation (the will to take on responsibility). Doing chores—looking after themselves and helping the family—are their first good deeds.

In addition to giving children a sense of their obligation to other people, doing chores gives them survival skills. By teaching our children a habit of responsibility at an early age, we give them the confidence to take on ever-more complex challenges as they grow older. And helping out at home raises self-esteem: when parents insist that children do their chores, they are letting them know that they're not just loved, they are needed. Ordinary chores are the foundation of our children's character and spiritual well-being.

The sages say that the answer to the question, "Where does God live?" is "Wherever you look for him." As I mentioned in Chapter 1, a traditional Jewish word for *home* is the same as the word for a house of worship: *mikdash me'at,* or "little holy place." If God's presence rests in our homes, our schools, and our places of business, when we work together to build a peaceful, well-run community, we are giving God a welcoming place to come and visit. By teaching our children to see chores as more than just drudgery but as their way of honoring their parents and welcoming God into their home, we elevate the tasks they have to do.

MEANWHILE,
IN YOUR HOUSE AND MINE . . .

How lovely, how noble, how inventive of the rabbis, this concept of the cosmic potential of the everyday and the connection between chores and holiness. But what about your house? The place where the children don't want to do chores? The place where the parents aren't sure whether it's worth the trouble anyway? Children have always resisted chores, but the current generation has somehow managed to gain an extraordinary edge over their parents in this age-old contest.

I recall the toothbrushing wars my husband and I waged with our younger daughter, Emma, when she was three and a half. On the battlefield were one naked sprite running from room to room and a parent, sometimes two, chasing behind her waving a toothbrush and pleading. The scene is still vivid in my mind: the humiliated adults; the exhilarated child; the unbrushed teeth and the bacteria having their own little festivities. I'll confess that in the beginning Emma's independence charmed me a bit, but as the same scene was replayed night after night, I grew tired and annoyed. We tried a star chart and praise. Nothing worked. I turned for advice to my friend, a child development specialist. "You just have to come up with some form of positive reinforcement that will capture her imagination," he said soothingly. "You aren't trying hard enough." What did Emma need? Fife and drum players to precede her into the bathroom? Fireworks? A dollar rebate per brushed tooth? It didn't make sense to me.

We eventually found a solution, which I will reveal later in this chapter. But that drama and my friend's suggestion helped me understand why I and most of the parents I knew were losing these battles. Self-care responsibilities and chores require parental commitment and strong enforcement. Most of us want to stick with praise and enthusiasm—"Jack! What a good helper you are!"—as our tools for reinforcing good behavior. These approaches work just fine when your child is in the mood to fling his socks across the room for a slam-dunk into the hamper or when he feels like a big boy if he's allowed to carry breakable plates from the table to the kitchen, but young children lose interest when the novelty wears off.

When we're in need of unpleasant consequences for chronic noncompliance, many of us are stuck. In most households today, spanking has been replaced by "time-outs," which, unfortunately, require time—the one commodity we don't have. So we keep aiming for the positive spin my friend recommended: use your imagination, make chores fun, keep the children entertained. Then we pay. We discover that by constantly jollying our kids into doing their chores, we give them the impression that chores have no value beyond the immediate payoff of being entertained or bribed. Parents get exhausted, bored, or resentful trying to delight their children into compliance, so they give up.

If each small act is part of a larger effort to honor God, toothbrushing is placed in a different context. Taking care of oneself is not just a personal responsibility, it is also a communal and cosmic responsibility. It's bigger than the chore itself. Your three-year-old may not need to hear a long sermon on this topic from you, but you may need to give yourself a little pep talk before you once again give up and take over responsibility for him.

In our grandparents' day, chores didn't require so much creativity or so many justifications. Modern parents, however, are plagued by uncertainty. How important are chores? Is caring for a younger sibling after school as important as cello lessons? Which chores are right at which age? Above all, how will we find the time?

Our ambivalence about the value of children's chores is at the heart of our difficulties. If we aren't sure chores are necessary to our children's growth, why go to all the trouble of assigning them? The fewer chores we require of our children, the more free time and peace we'll all have. And indeed, I've heard every possible argument about why little Gordon or Marissa simply cannot be held responsible for household duties. In order to win the chore wars, you need to think about these arguments and become aware of the psychological struggles beneath them. For until you believe in the value of chores, you won't have the resolve or patience it takes to assign them and make sure your children follow through.

WHY WE DON'T WANT OUR CHILDREN TO DO CHORES

In many homes parents have two categories of domestic responsibilities for children: true chore demands that the children intuitively know they must remember and comply with and "chore gestures," those parental dicta that look authentic only on the surface. The chore gestures start with a grand proclamation, "From now on . . ." and end with, "Is that clear?" The children always look serious and nod in agreement and the parent invariably falls for it, naively anticipating a future filled with made beds, neat rooms, and well-flossed teeth, all with no nagging or reminding.

Why don't these assignments take? In part because your children and mine have highly functional ambivalence barometers. They know when we are serious and intend to follow through and when we are just spouting. But why are we ambivalent? Don't we want them to be responsible and helpful without reminding them every step of the way? Maybe not.

The sources of our ambivalence about chores are varied and deep. Some of the mixed feelings come from simple time pressure. I once spoke at a school where the parents, only slightly exaggerating, told me that their children had so much homework each night that they had to start in immediately after arriving home from school. The mothers served the children dinner on a tray so they could keep working while they ate. The children worked until late in the evening. Before bed the mothers would dip the children in the bathtub, slip them into their pajamas, and tell them to hurry and get to sleep so that they would be rested for school the next day. In the morning they would wake the sleepy little children and help them get dressed. No time for everyday chores for these young scholars. Even without this heavy homework load, most of us are so harried that if we take care of domestic responsibilities ourselves, things get done faster and with less mess and bother than if we let them get taken care of child style.

There are other, more psychological reasons for lack of follow-through on chores. We may fear that because we are working or occupied with activities outside of home, we do too little for our children. Wanting to demonstrate our love and commitment, we smooth their path by picking up after them and by not requiring them to do tasks they aren't in the mood to do. Some of us even pity our children, for a variety of reasons: they live in a congested, pressured, polluted world; their parents are divorced; their parents aren't divorced but should be and they suffer from the tension in the house; younger sister Jasmine is in the 70th percentile of height while poor Parker is only in the 10th percentile.

Paradoxically, effective parenting can cause parental separation anxiety. If we really expect and demand that children take responsibility, we may no longer need to nag them. But if we are suffering from a sense of loneliness in marriage or feelings of insecurity in our fragmented world, we may unconsciously seek the involvement and intimate connection with our children that nagging and reminding bring. And there's yet another hidden advantage to having irresponsible children—if we keep them dependent on us we won't have to face our own mortality. We'll always be a helpless someone's mommy or daddy.

CONQUERING YOUR AMBIVALENCE

I mentioned earlier that according to the Talmud, "teaching your child to swim" is a primary parental responsibility. Swimming is required because the goal of parenting is to raise our children to leave us. Parents who insist that their children are too busy to waste time on chores might want to contemplate how their kids will fare in the future, when Mom isn't around to wash every shirt and butter every bagel. I meet many children with lots of fancy technical skills who lack practical, ordinary survival skills, and I'm not alone in this observation. An art teacher told me about an incident that occurred when she was working with some second graders on a papier-mâché sculpture project:

> The children needed to pour water from a large pitcher into a bowl. None of the kids volunteered to do the pouring. "Do you guys know how to pour? Have you ever done it before?" I asked. It turned out that none of them had! It's so modern. They can't pour, but I'll bet they all knew how to load software on the computer by the time they were in kindergarten.

I'll also bet some of the children had learned how to pour in preschool but were out of practice because they no longer got the chance to do it. They get poured for at home. I've seen many parents who complain that their children are too prissy, lazy, overscheduled, or clueless to pitch in and help, but when we dig below the surface we discover that it's the parents, not the children, who are causing the problem. They find it easier to do the chores themselves than to take the time to teach their child to master them. It's true that many of the tasks very young children can do won't really save you any time, but if you view them in terms of your child's future self-reliance, it may help you slow down and encourage their early efforts.

The parent who avoids assigning household tasks because she feels guilty for working or takes pity on her children is doing them no favor. Instead, she is buying their immediate goodwill with their future well-being. By shielding them from the real world, which is filled with repetitive tasks and tedious paperwork as well as bonuses and accolades, she is making them weaker. Take, for example, a job you are well acquainted with: parenting. It requires us to do a wide range of tasks, from the heavenly, like kissing a silken head and cheek good night or applauding at a first clarinet recital, to the less delightful, like changing crib sheets covered with vomit two or three times in a row, or drilling the multiplication tables with flash cards at the end of an already long day. All of these chores are essential parts of our job as parents, just as taking care of themselves and helping the family are essential parts of the children's jobs as members of the family team.

According to psychologists Donald Akutagawa and Terry Whitman, "Humans are the only creatures that devote energy to making their offspring 'happy.' The rest of the animal kingdom is devoted to fostering competence to survive in the world." Children deserve more than our love and devotion. They deserve to be taught how to fend for themselves and eventually contribute to society. Seen this way, chores are not extracurricular activities, they are the basics. When your children realize you are serious about them, they will get serious about them too.

MAKING CHORES MATTER:
LESSONS FROM THE FARM

Once you are convinced of the genuine value of household chores, you can shed your guilt and ambivalence and assign table-cleaning and pot-washing duties as confidently as your grandmother did. In our hearts, of course, we know that chores are good for us. I recall a conversation in one of my parenting classes that brought to light just how hungry mothers are for meaningful chores to give their kids.

It all started when one of the moms began describing her sister Liza's life. Liza lived on a small dairy farm that was the family business. Each week she, her husband, and their four children would hold a family business meeting to assign a set of rotating chores that included feeding the animals, supervising some of the milking, and working on the books. When the profits from the farm came in, they were divided among the group. The youngest children got a tiny percentage. The older ones got more. The money the children received was their discretionary income. For the little ones it covered extras like candy bars, hair accessories, and computer games. The older ones used the money as their clothing budget, for their phone bill, and for gas money. Parents covered all necessities, such as school supplies, doctor visits, and warm sweaters, but the extras rose and fell with the bottom line. During a quarter when there was less profit from the farm, there was less money for extras.

Talk about meaningful chores and logical consequences! Clearing the table or putting clothes in the hamper can seem mundane compared with barnyard chores. The urban mothers in my parenting class imagined that Liza's children gained a great sense of dignity along with their paychecks. This kind of pride and competence was something they wanted to confer on their own children, but how?

YOU HAVE TO START SOMEWHERE: CHOOSING THE CHORES

When it comes to assigning tasks, a major stumbling block for parents is lack of basic knowledge about which chores should begin when. Because we don't live with an extended family of seasoned parents to provide child-rearing advice, we may be unsure about what is appropriate to expect from our children. And because the world is changing so quickly, the old rules may not apply. You can't send a six-year-old to the market by herself to pick up some bread and milk anymore, but you can teach her how to sweep the kitchen floor, feed the dog, and put away her clean clothes. Children learn responsibility in phases. The important thing is that your child continue to add more tasks as the years go by.

In general, children start with self-care, which includes toileting, their own grooming, and feeding themselves. A two-year-old can wipe up the high-chair tray with a big industrial-sized sponge and can dust big sturdy objects like chairs with a feather duster. By three, children can begin to be given responsibility for dressing themselves. Older preschoolers can water plants, wipe the table, and help to sort the laundry by color. By four they can wash hands and brush teeth with some supervision.

By four and five, children can learn how to care for their own belongings: putting their toys away, straightening their bed, putting their clothes in the hamper. The next stage is care for the family and the household. Here your child contributes to the smooth running of the ship by helping to set and clear the table, loading and unloading the dishwasher, bandaging a sister's skinned knee. Older children and teenagers graduate to cooking, ironing, washing the car, and earning their own spending money. The family is the little laboratory for what Judaism sees as the most mature stage of responsibility, where we treat our community as family, give charity, and provide service to others.

Shabbat and the Jewish holidays create plenty of opportunities for children to do useful work. On these occasions, you don't even have to dig for the holy purpose. A preschooler can sprinkle seeds on the challah, put candles in the candle holders, and bring a pile of napkins to the table. We use a little tin of sticky wax called "licht magic" on the bottom of each candle. The child twirls the candle in the wax, places the candle in the holder, and—magic—it stands perfectly upright without listing to one side. I've yet to meet a child who doesn't feel empowered by this effect. We also use long fireplace matches for lighting Shabbat candles. This way even the youngest children get to play with fire for a moment and to kindle the special lights. A two-year-old can carry two unbreakable things to help clear or set the table. Young children love to decorate cookies. They also like both the concept and the shining outcome of polishing silver with tooth-paste. An eight-year-old can be trusted to carry eight things to or from the table, including fragile, thin-stemmed wineglasses. Everyone can help pitch the sukkah with a hammer and nails, hang the garlands, and decorate the walls with drawings and cards. Everyone can make *mishloach manot* (small holiday food baskets) for friends, neighbors, and needy families on Purim.

Assigning tasks is an ongoing process. A child's duties will evolve as she evolves, and sometimes you'll need to take into account more than age. Occasionally the chores will depend on your relationship. For instance, when a parent asks if a five-year-old should be washing her own hair, I always (in good psychologist fashion) respond to the question with a question: "Do you mind doing it for her?"

One parent might say, "Actually, I love washing Eva's hair. It's long and copper-colored and looks so beautiful when it's wet. We always make up stories and sing together when she's in the bathtub. That's when I have a chance to teach her new songs." To this mother I would say, "Please don't stop washing Eva's hair. Find another chore or big girl job for her to do, but don't give up this lovely time for both of you."

Another parent will answer differently: "Yes, I do mind. I think Shira is old enough to wash her own hair but I'm afraid that if I let her do it she won't rinse properly, or remember to spray on No More Tangles, or hang up the towel." To this mother I might respond, "There's only one way to find out. What if she doesn't do it just exactly the way you think she should? What is gained and what is lost? When you wash her hair for her while feeling frustrated and resentful, she knows it. It isn't good for either of you. It's time to step back and give her a chance to learn by doing."

DON'T UNDERESTIMATE YOUR CHILD

Just as you don't want to ask your child to do something at which he can't succeed, neither do you want to underestimate him. A mother in a parenting class, sounding demoralized and overwhelmed, told the following tale. Her tone was that of a participant in a twelve-step meeting testifying about hitting bottom:

> My name is Naomi. I'm a single mother. I have nine-year-old twin boys. I work full-time. This week I really felt that I failed my children. Last Thursday, after preparing dinner and helping the boys with their homework, I fell asleep on the couch. It was no later than seven-thirty. The boys covered me with a blanket, turned off the lights, and put themselves to bed. When I woke up in the morning I was still in the den and they had made their lunches and snacks and gotten themselves dressed for school.

I should hope so! I'm not advocating letting all nine-year-olds put themselves to bed each night, but these boys were clearly able to do things such as making lunch that Naomi was accustomed to doing for them.

Parents are sometimes amazed at how much their kids are capable of accomplishing on their own. For anyone lucky enough to have grandparents who are still alive, a reality check is just a phone call away. Ask them what responsibilities they had when they were seven or ten or twelve years old. When I queried the oldest generation in our family about this, the women, now ranging in age from seventy-five to past ninety, reported that when they were in elementary school they "polished the floor by putting down wax and then skating around with rags on my shoes," "dusted," "ironed," "bathed, fed, and diapered my little brother Lenny," and "helped to kosher the pots." Several men reported that in addition to schoolwork, religious training, and taking care of younger siblings, they helped their fathers with their jobs.

GRANT AUTHORITY WITH RESPONSIBILITY

Along with acknowledging your children's capabilities, you'll need to grant them more authority as they take on more chores. The psychoanalyst Wilfred Bion defined slavery as responsibility without authority. When you give children a job to do, let them, as much as is reasonable, decide how to get it done. Don't insist that they do it precisely the way you would or you risk being like Pharaoh. They are learning, and you're an expert. Equally important, they are not miniature versions of you. They will develop their own unique style of dressing, cleaning their room, or preparing food. If you demand that they do it exactly your way, you'll take the creativity out of the task and increase their resistance to it.

When Emma made her first sandwich, she carried it proudly to the table on a thin, unfolded paper napkin (no plate). The sandwich was composed of a large piece of matzo covered with layers of margarine, peanut butter, and jelly, with two slices of sandwich pickle crisscrossed in the center and four small red roasted potatoes balanced precariously on each corner. As soon as I saw it, I sussed out the flaws—nutritional and architectural—and was ready to fire a line of questions about whether or not she had left a mess in the kitchen. Instead, I kept quiet except to say, "Emma, I see that you made your own lunch. May I join you at the table with mine?"

MOTIVATING YOUR CHILDREN

In Jewish philosophy, there are two basic views about how to motivate children to take responsibility. One is that positive reinforcement works and the sweeter the deal, the higher the compliance rate. Moses Maimonides, the twelfth-century Jewish physician and philosopher, believed that children were not naturally motivated to study Torah. In his famous code of law and ethics, the *Mishneh Torah*, he explains that the best method for getting children in the habit of doing what is good is to entice them with rewards when they are young. To entice little children to study Torah, he said, they should be coaxed with "nuts and figs and honey." For teenagers he recommended using "splendid shoes and magnificent shirts."

At our synagogue this practice still holds. Rabbinical students lead the Saturday morning services for children. Any child who volunteers an answer to a question during the Torah discussion is rewarded with a small candy treat. Intuitively grasping the efficacy of this six-hundred-year-old tradition, few parents complain that the children are being fed sweets in the morning.

Positive reinforcement is different from entertaining children into compliance. The reinforcements you use don't necessarily have to be sweet, expensive, or time-consuming. Children can be rewarded with honors or privileges such as the chance to choose the family dinner menu for three days straight or to pick which restaurant the family will go to next weekend, or the privilege of staying up late to watch a special video. For preschoolers the glory of a star chart may be sufficient.

The other Jewish view regarding motivation is that chronic noncompliance requires strong discipline. It is said that Rabbi

Joshua told his students, "The child may be compared to a heifer—if he is not taught to plow when young, it will be difficult for him to do so in the end; or to a wine branch—if you do not bend it when it is full of sap, once it hardens, you can do nothing with it."

How do we teach and bend? In Proverbs we read several versions of "spare the rod and spoil the child": "For he whom God loves God admonishes" (13:12), "Who spares the rod it is as if he hates his child" (13:24), and "Correct your child and he will provide you rest" (29:17). But Torah teaches us to administer discipline with a light hand. The weight of Jewish tradition forbids humiliating, threatening, or physically harming a child and advises us to follow the example of God, who never punishes without previous warning and without telling the transgressor what to expect if he continues to misbehave. In Chapter 8 I'll discuss the Jewish perspective on punishment in greater detail and share with you the Torah's suggestions for effectively disciplining your child.

At the beginning of this chapter I related the story of Emma and her toothbrushing antics. When we finally solved that problem, we didn't use the Maimonides method, a star chart, or pure encouragement. Instead, we realized that if this tiny heifer was ever going to plow, we'd have to get tough.

One night I simply got fed up and said, "Emma, you have a job to do. It is your responsibility to go to bed with your teeth brushed. You can brush your teeth yourself or I will be glad to do it for you. This house is a place for people who are doing their jobs. If you are not willing to do your job, you'll have to go outside in the backyard. Do you understand what I said? I want to make sure. Can you say it back to me please? What are your choices?"

Emma twinkled, she smiled, she darted out of the room. I found her, took her hand, and said, "You made a choice, Emma. You'll have to go outside now."

I caught her, picked her up, and started walking calmly downstairs. Emma looked sober and curious. We live in southern California, where October nights are dark, but balmy. Emma did not want to be outside alone. We got to the back door. She looked nervous. "Mom," she said, like it was something she had just thought of, "let's go back upstairs and I'll brush my teeth right now."

"You're sure?"

"I'm sure."

I put her down and she walked upstairs solemn as a soldier. She brushed her teeth, climbed into bed, and went to sleep. Next night she cooperated perfectly. On the third night she started to twinkle, dance, and squirm again. I reminded her about the backyard. She knew that I meant it. She brushed her teeth. It was never a problem again.

STOP NAGGING, START FOLLOWING THROUGH

Our goal as parents is to get children to take responsibility without having to remind them all the time. Ultimately, we want them not only to do their chores without being prompted but also to volunteer their services. We want them to ask, "What can I do to help?" rather than, "Do I have to?" To encourage this attitude, you must present chores as an inevitable but honorable element in their lives.

When instructing your children about the chores you want them to do, be friendly, matter-of-fact, brisk, and specific. You can avoid misunderstandings by having your children repeat back to you, in their own words, what you've asked of them. "It's time to get supper ready," you might announce. "I need Caroline to set the table. Derek, you can peel the carrots and chop the celery. I'll chop the onions and the garlic. Adam, you can fill the water glasses and put in the ice as soon as your homework is done but no later than six-fifteen. Everybody understand? Any questions?"

Such an announcement will probably be met with a long silence or the inevitable protestation, "That is not fair!" In response to silence, you will carry on: "Let's make sure everybody knows what they are supposed to do. Tell me what you heard me say. Caroline, you start." In response to the complaint that the system is unfair, you can do an instant examination of your conscience. If you determine that the job apportionment is basically fair, treat the protest as a canny stall and say, "I hear that you feel strongly about the injustice of this system." Or to the younger child, "I heard you say that you don't think this is fair." Then make it clear that fair or not, these are their duties.

If you are speaking to two or more children, you might say, "I offer you this option. You guys can set up a chart system to rotate the chores and I'll help you organize it if you need some help. If you don't want to rotate the chores, then we'll sit down and talk about how to devise a fair system at our family meeting on Sunday night. But for tonight these jobs need to get done and I'm not willing to talk about it any further. Do you understand? If there are any more complaints about this, there will be consequences that you will not like." (See Chapter 8 for suggestions about appropriate consequences.)

You should not have to say this every night! Tell them once that you will tell them only once. Constant reminding, nagging, or screaming leads to death—of your child's sense of accountability. Pretend that your child or children are members of a troop of soldiers, a pack of wild donkeys, a litter of sleepy kittens. Use whatever image you need to remove yourself from the personal aspect of the situation. There is a job. It needs to be completed. You delegate, they do. You do not do everything and then simmer in frustration and resentment. God wants them to learn how to do these things promptly and efficiently. They do not have to like it, and it's not your responsibility to try to talk them into understanding the ultimate benefit of helping around the house.

When the job is done, acknowledge good work without hopping up and down with excitement. If you put on too big a show your child may come to expect effusive praise each time he pitches in. Catch them being good. Say thank you. Praise effort: "Thank you, girls. You and Natalie were both thinking ahead. I can see how hard you both worked at cleaning up your room before her mom came to pick her up. It looks great."

AN ACTION PLAN FOR ASSIGNING CHORES

Assigning your children household chores and seeing that they follow through is one of the most tiresome jobs you'll ever have. The sheer endlessness of it is enough to undermine the most noble of parents. A client of mine named Marguerite was a living example of how a well-meaning parent could be worn down by a determined child. "Sara, my six-year-old, rarely remembers to make her bed," Marguerite told my parenting class one day.

When I ask her why she hasn't done it, she always has an excuse ready: "My arm was hurting," or "It's too hard for me to do by myself," or "I forgot." She wants me to help her with things that she could easily do herself, like putting her toys away or pouring a glass of milk. If I ask her to take out the garbage she says she's afraid to go outside by herself—she'll do it if I would please, please come with her. At that point it's easier to do it by myself.

Getting a recalcitrant child to accept responsibility comes down to a battle of wills. The hardest part is at the beginning, when the child is first introduced to the new routine and the newly resolved parents. To make the transition easier, here's an action plan for assigning chores and helping your child follow through. Marguerite and Sara will serve as our guides.

Imagine Your Child
as Part of a Larger Family

To view the chore options objectively, start by thinking about the kinds of jobs your child might have to do if he were one of a family of six children, where without everyone's contribution the whole operation would falter. Marguerite realized that if Sara left her shoes, socks, and toys all over the house in a bigger, busier household, she wouldn't be able to find them. She also realized that Sara would have to help with table setting and clearing and perhaps even help take care of younger children.

Make a Wish List
of Child-Appropriate Chores

Write down all the responsibilities you think your child is capable of performing. Try to match the jobs with your child's interests, temperament, and level of maturity. Marguerite came up with a long list of unexciting but essential jobs that Sara was old enough to do, including hanging up her backpack and jacket, unpacking her lunch box when she came home from school, setting the table, and clearing the table after dinner.

But Sara also had some special jobs to perform, which grew out of a discussion her parents had about their daughter's nature. From birth Sara had been attuned to her senses. She loved bright colors, the smells of cooking, and listening to music. She also loved to eat. Marguerite invited Sara to bring a CD player into the kitchen so the family could listen to music while they cooked dinner. Sara was put in charge of loading the CD player and adjusting the volume.

Introduce Responsibilities Gradually

Grand proclamations—"There are going to be some changes around here!"—don't work. Judaism teaches us not to dive in all at once, but to take on *mitzvot* (ritual or ethical obligations) one at a time. For Sara's first new chore, Marguerite chose the "hanging up of the backpack and jacket upon entering the house" because finding these items on the floor by the front door irritated Marguerite daily. When Sara forgot the first day, Marguerite warned her that the privilege of computer time was contingent on remembering to hang up her things without being reminded.

"What do you think could help you remember, Sara?" Marguerite asked.

"If you remind me" was Sara's first suggestion. Marguerite rejected that idea. Sara then came up with a new suggestion.

"We could tie a red ribbon around the doorknob."

"Hmm, interesting. Let's try it." It worked.

Marguerite spaced her introduction of new chores a few weeks apart. The hardest to implement was table clearing. Sara didn't mind setting the table because that meant dinner was on the way, but clearing held no interest for her. A star chart didn't help. After a few weeks with no stars, no *Reader Rabbit,* and no improvement, I suggested that Marguerite change tactics. She offered Sara the job of clearing only the silverware, rinsing it under the faucet, and putting it in the dishwasher. This job appealed to Sara because of its start-to-finish nature, and she did it without being reminded.

Do Not Tell Them How to Do the Job
Unless They Are Thoroughly Clueless

Give authority with responsibility. Authority includes the opportunity to do a job badly the first time or two. Leave lots of extra time for spills and cleanup; let children make mistakes and learn from them. Sara learned through trial and error that when she forgot to put glasses of ice water on the table, she was the one who would have to get up from her meal and retrieve the items during dinner. (If your child can't figure out what to do, you probably haven't chosen the right job for her.)

Give Them What They Need to Succeed

Parents need to make sure that children are given whatever they need to perform their job, such as a lightweight tray for clearing dishes from the table, a carpet sweeper for a child who isn't yet ready for a vacuum, a clothing rod and drawers placed at a height that they can reach. Also match your expectations with the moment. Most children are a "mixed multitude" all by themselves and you'll find them helpful and responsible one day or week and great sluggards the next. Aim for a broad pattern of helpfulness rather than punctilious compliance every time.

Devise a System of Rewards, Privileges, and Consequences

Make the punishments and privileges fit the crimes or triumphs. Obviously you won't take the children to Disneyland for remembering to change the toilet paper roll, but do remember that too many external rewards can reduce internal motivation. Sometimes a pat and smile are sufficient reward, and I've observed enough talented classroom teachers to know that a stern glance, aimed right, can be a potent punishment.

Sara's parents chose a one-hour-later bedtime on weekends and the privilege of watching a favorite TV program as Sara's reward for completing her chores each week. She also got some new authority. Marguerite divided Sara's closet and drawers into two categories—school and party clothes—and let Sara choose her outfits herself each day. In addition, Sara got to be the boss of the family menu a few nights per week and earned the privilege of helping her parents with the cooking. When Sara's level of responsibility increased a few more notches, Marguerite let her ride her bike on her own to her best friend's house down the block.

Follow Through!

Parent educator Barbara Colorosa says it's not the severity of a consequence that has an impact on children but the certainty. Same goes for rewards. If you say you're going to take your child to see the new *Star Wars* movie as a reward for a week of compliance with chores and responsibilities, do it. Sara's parents learned that consistency was the key to compliance. They were surprised to see that when they stopped cajoling and started tracking Sara's fulfillment of her responsibilities on a chart, she quickly shaped up. Sara knew that if she didn't do her chores, she would be denied her precious computer time.

HOW MY FAMILY WISED UP ABOUT CHORES

Few chores are as loaded with life lessons as animal husbandry. I learned this when we failed miserably with our first dog. When the girls were four and eight they begged for a puppy and we ended up with a Visla, a Hungarian hunting dog whose beautiful russet coat coordinated nicely with our dining room walls. We justified getting the puppy by saying that caring for it would provide the children with an opportunity to learn responsibility. We named him Bo, the Hebrew word for "come."

We didn't know it then, but getting Bo was clearly violating the prohibition in Leviticus 19: "Do not put a stumbling block before the blind." Everything went wrong. Vislas are an unusually friendly, exuberant breed. They are also large, rambunctious, and difficult to train. Bo knocked four-year-old Emma over every time he greeted her. She spent a lot of time looking for places to hide. I spent a lot of time comforting the children after the dog had chewed up another one of their shoes or drawings or stuffed animals. I was also on the phone a lot, making play dates for the dog (this is true) with other big, energetic neighborhood dogs in hopes of tiring Bo out so we could have some moments of peace at home.

Did the children learn responsibility? Not one bit. But their parents learned many useful things. For starters, our desire to make the children happy was misguided. As much as they beg, children are not expert on what they need. Our timing was wrong, because the girls were not mature enough to take care of a high-spirited puppy. And we forgot to consider the mood and nature of the participants: this breed was not a good match for our family because we're not rough-and-tumble country-living people who could properly train and play with a big hunting dog. We ended up giving the dog away to a family that, as hard as I found it to believe, loves Vislas.

When the girls were eight and twelve, we tried again. This time we acquired Mila, a super-low-maintenance, year-and-a-half-old, fourteen-pound, calm, sturdy Border terrier. At twelve, Susanna is mature enough to take full charge of this relaxed little dog. She feeds her every morning and expertly washes her in the sink on weekends. Emma walks Mila down the block, dresses her up in aprons and pipe cleaner hats, and puts her in little musicals.

Both children work every day to help love and care for this new member of our family. Mila and the girls are a match because all the elements necessary for performing chores well are present: the task is physically manageable for the children, they possess the maturity and judgment necessary to do their dog care jobs without adult supervision, and the tasks are rewarding—the dog plays dressmaker's dummy for Emma and follows her master, Susanna, everywhere. One day Emma parlayed her dog care expertise into a new entrepreneurial venture. She and her neighborhood friend Rose, armed with a pooper scooper and plastic bags, offered to clean up the neighbors' backyards—for 15 cents a poop.

Despite all the frustrations and setbacks, chores give us a unique opportunity to teach our children family citizenship, self-reliance, responsibility, and a sense of the holy potential in every action. The sages teach us to turn some of our priorities upside down. The lessons we instill by insisting that our children do mundane tasks may very well be the ones that stay with them longest, helping them to become self-reliant adults, responsible community members, and loving parents.

CHAPTER 7

The Blessing of Food:

Bringing Moderation, Celebration,
and Sanctification to Your Table

In the beginning God was hospitable and generous to Adam and Eve. He said, "Welcome to Eden. Since I created you with hearty appetites, I know you'll be getting hungry soon. Please don't hesitate, help yourselves to whatever you like. There's only one thing I don't want you to eat. See that apple tree in the middle of the garden? Stay away from it." God then made the consequences of not listening very, very clear: "If you eat from that tree you shall die." Did this stop Adam and Eve? Of course not. The forbidden apple was just what the first children had to have.

Among many of the families I know, love, power, and food have been bound together for as far back as anyone can remember. Certainly in America the stereotype of the overenthusiastic Jewish mother urging just one more slice of brisket on her already full child has some truth to it. A 1923 article in the *Froyen Zhurnal*, a Yiddish advice magazine for newly arrived immigrants, noted that "the Jewish mother betrays an unusual amount of concern about the problem of feeding her children. In general, she should stop worrying so much about how much they eat and what they wear."

Perhaps Jewish parents place so much importance on food

because at its core Judaism is a table-centered religion. With the destruction of the ancient Holy Temple, each family's dining table serves to replace the original holy altar: the table belongs to us and to God. Demographers report that today, fewer than 50 percent of American Jews belong to a synagogue, but more than 90 percent attend a yearly ritual meal, the Passover seder. For many Jews, "kitchen Judaism" is their primary connection to their faith. Judaism recognizes that it is possible to use food as a potent vehicle for holiness and family unity. Through the proper attitude toward food and the proper environment for eating, spiritual ideals can be transmitted into daily living.

FROM YOUR PARENTS' TABLE TO YOURS

When parents come to see me about their children's eating problems—or perceived eating problems—I get a fascinating portrait not only of their family but of one or two generations back. I frequently see reflections of the Depression and the post–World War II era in modern parents' battles with their children over food.

One such parent, Marny, came to me because her five-year-old son, Asher, had an eating fetish. He would eat only white foods. Before offering my advice, I asked Marny about her own family background regarding meals. While Marny's parents were more extreme than most, many of the clients I counsel were raised by parents who had similar attitudes toward eating. "Both my parents were martinets about food," Marny told me.

> They were terrifying, really. It was the worst thing in my childhood. Mom made us finish everything on our plates and eat the foods in a certain order, vegetables first. She was a smart, capable woman who could have run a business, been a lawyer, done anything. But it was the fifties so she stayed at home and

cared for us full-time. I think she funneled [...]
trol into us. She studied every bite we ate or didn't [...]

My dad was worse. If we didn't finish a meal, he told [...]
to put it in the fridge. She would then serve it again and again
until we ate it. He had this Depression-era mentality about not
wasting anything. I hated it.

With a background like this, it wasn't surprising to learn
that Marny abhorred fighting with Asher about food. Some parents, wanting to respect their children's dignity, are especially
sensitive about honoring the child's right to refuse food. At
the same time, these parents are acutely health-conscious and
concerned (and sometimes even unconsciously competitive
with other parents) about their children's weight, height, and
strength. They want their sons and daughters to excel and to be
healthy, but it's more complicated than that: they want their
children to prefer healthy food so the parents don't have to be
the bad guys. Children, of course, rarely comply with this mix
of parental desires.

Making the whole process even more frustrating is the fact
that the definition of "healthy" keeps shifting. One day 2 percent milk is fine; the next it's got too much fat; the day after that
children should drink whole milk because they need the fat to
grow and the fat content helps them absorb more calcium. The
four food groups seem like primitive cave drawings compared
to the elaborate nutritional tables we're supposed to memorize
these days. In comparison, Mom and Grandma had it easy.

THE POWER OF FOOD

In today's world, teaching children to eat in a healthy way and to
demonstrate self-control and good judgment about food is like
having an AA meeting in a bar. No, it's worse. We can't abstain

...cohol and drugs. Because food
...d in as a driving force in our lives.
...d is an extremely attractive com-
...uing profits over health, target the
...mers, our children. Advertisers pursue
...the flavors, colors, and slogans that they
...em. Children, seeking pleasure and satis-
... vulnerable to the allure of advertising and
beg u... n the things they see on TV. Too much Cocoa
Puffs, Lun... es, and macaroni and cheese, and they end up eating more calories, sugar, and fat than their bodies need.

Good health, not to mention current social fashion, favors thinness, so parents are frantic. The children lobby tirelessly for unhealthy foods. They don't get enough exercise. Some grow fat. The parents become very involved in what their children are and are not eating. Intuitively, children recognize this as the perfect place to seize power. When it comes to food, few modern parents are clear, calm, and authoritative. Put all this together and food becomes a battlefield.

While some parents are busy arguing with their children at the dinner table, others are engaged in a different type of conflict: the food itself is seen as an enemy. In these households, overzealous concern about health and weight sets the tone for every morsel that passes the lips of parents or children.

Eating disorders are in part spiritual disorders, because the sufferer is battling with the source of life. Women in particular often harbor a deep, private love-hate relationship with food. Many distrust a substance they must rely on to stay alive but fear will lead them to lose control, overeat, and gain weight. More of us make a daily ritual of visiting the bathroom scale than of taking time for prayer. This ambivalence about food and eating and the resulting tension over self-control, guilt, and sensual pleasure get passed along to children, even if we don't voice our worries aloud.

It's not unusual for parents who are overly concerned about food to put their children on an ideal *adult* diet. Sociologist Sheila Kitzinger writes wryly about "muesli-belt malnutrition," a condition that occurs when children are fed the low-fat, high-fiber diets their parents need to stay slim and healthy. This diet leaves the children undernourished, because they feel full before they've gotten the protein they need to grow. If food is a dark and dangerous force in your life, it is likely to be so in your child's life as well. Better to wrestle with both the gluttonous and the guilty aspects of your own yetzer hara than to try to tame it vicariously through your child.

Viewing food as a battlefield or an enemy is not a new dilemma, but today's parents raise these struggles to the level of "food theology." In a society without clear and specific moral anchors, many families have turned beliefs about what constitutes a healthy diet into a substitute for religion. By giving moral weight to food choices (low-fat foods and thinness equal virtue, junk food and being overweight equal sin), they substitute food theology for deeper spiritual values. This approach can make the power plays even more emotionally charged.

Why do parents turn food into a moral crucible? At the beginning of the twenty-first century, we find that few aspects of life are within our control. The only thing we can be sure of—if we're very vigilant—is the food that goes into our mouths and the mouths of our children. If we feed our sons and daughters a healthy diet, we feel as though we are good parents. If they learn to control their desires for junk food and to love baby carrots instead, they are being good children. I frequently hear stories that provide evidence of my theory: eight-year-old Emily, when offered 2 percent low-fat milk on her school camping trip, refused to drink anything. She explained to her teachers with a sense of holy rectitude, "In our house, we only drink one percent milk." Emily was trying to be good.

Jewish wisdom can help us develop a more dignified and reasonable attitude toward food. By applying Jewish principles to our powerful hunger drive, we can learn how to use food and eating as a path to nutritional balance, holiness, and harmony within the family.

WE'RE NO ANGELS:
WHY GOD WANTS US TO ENJOY OUR FOOD

God purposely made us different from the angels. As noncorporeal beings, angels have no physical needs or free will. They never have to read a menu and make choices. Despite appearances, this is not an advantage. Unlike humans, angels don't have the ability to turn an instinct into a sacred act, because they are already there. Every act is sacred, so it's no big deal.

If humans attempt to emulate the angels through asceticism and strict self-denial, we're cheating. God wants us to get into the fray, to struggle with desire and self-restraint, with what Yitzhak Buxbaum, author of *Jewish Spiritual Practices,* calls "food lust." Judaism teaches us that in order to be fully ourselves we need to play up our human part, not deny it. However, this doesn't mean we should indulge in pagan-style worship of food for its own sake. If we go too far in the direction of pure sensuality, we enter the realm of hedonism. We are commanded to worship God, not chanterelles or a perfect tarte tatin.

We are not to deny ourselves the joy of eating or to make an idol of food. There's a third possibility we must also avoid: consuming food without any thought at all, like beasts. Animals eat alone and on the run; they eat to survive, not to savor. They don't cook, or arrange the food on the plate, or set a nice table. Animals have no ability to stop and count their blessings; they eat without conscious gratitude.

No asceticism, no gluttony, no tearing at a juicy carcass alone on the veldt. What's left? The Talmud instructs us to find a balance between eating to live and living to eat. We are to elevate the act of eating by being conscious about when, what, where, and why we eat. In other words, we must make our table an altar.

MODERATION, CELEBRATION, SANCTIFICATION

Perhaps nowhere in life do the principles of moderation, celebration, and sanctification apply so well as in the realm of food. Here, where so many of our human concerns are brought into sharp relief—self-image, health, "goodness," self-control—these three principles offer a safe harbor from contemporary pressures and unrealistic expectations.

If we diet excessively or forbid our children any white sugar or a single artificially colored Popsicle, we are emulating the angels. If we give up entirely and heave a bag of burgers from McDonald's into the backseat of the minivan and let the children dive at it, we place ourselves at the level of the zookeeper. We need to approach food in a conscious way so we can take full advantage of our human capacity for self-control and enjoyment.

One way to encourage your family to eat moderately and with maximum pleasure is to sanctify mealtime. Sitting with other people around a table, as Jewish tradition encourages, assures that we'll spend at least part of our meal conversing instead of consuming. The blessings we say before we eat can also help. These prayers of thanks force us to slow down and reflect on the meal set before us. In pursuit of moderation, we can use these moments to think about how many people are at the table, how much food there is, and how much of it we'll need to feel satisfied.

Eating in moderation and sanctifying mealtime are two concepts that most of us can feel comfortable with. We're used to chiding ourselves for overindulging, so moderation sounds attractive. The idea of sanctifying a meal is appealing, too—we all wish we could slow down and appreciate things a bit more.

Where most people have trouble is in cultivating a guilt-free celebration of food. It's not that we don't love to eat, it's just that so many of us believe that if food is not nutritious it is inherently bad. Any pleasure we derive from "bad" food must be guilty pleasure; there's no room here for a carefree celebration of chocolate éclairs. If we spend our mealtimes counting nutrients and assessing our food on the good-bad scale, our food theology is in conflict with the Jewish principle of celebration.

One of my favorite lecture props is a candy wrapper designed by the underground cartoonist R. Crumb. It reads: "Devil Girl Choco-Bar—It's BAD for You! Seven Evils in One!" The wrapper goes on to list the seven sins contained in the candy bar, including "delicious taste," "quick, cheap buzz," and "bad for your health." Everyone in class can relate to the enchanting sins of "bad" foods. They're usually surprised when I tell them that, according to the rabbis, in the world to come, we humans will have to give an account to God for all the pleasing foods that our eyes beheld and we refused to taste. In Judaism, the purpose of eating is partly to fuel ourselves to serve God and partly to force us to enjoy what God has provided. This means that if you eat a chocolate bar or allow your children to have one, you must say a blessing before you eat it to remind yourself to celebrate its worth. If you eat too many candy bars, you can't celebrate, because they are no longer special. If you eat and feel guilty at the same time, you demean the experience of pleasure and misspend the blessing. It's not a celebration anymore.

Childhood memories of scents and tastes stand out more vividly than other memories. I have a feeling that now, much more than a generation ago, we tarnish our children's experiences of food with joyless food theology. Yes, cake is bad for their teeth, packed with calories, and isn't "growing food" like the virtuous carrot or celery stick. But the pure pleasure derived from a slice of coconut cake occupies holy ground all its own. In Judaism, there is a place for both nutrition and delight.

Judaism offers plenty of special times for celebrating food. There is the yearly cycle of holidays, each with its own representative foods: honey, symbolizing the sweetness of a New Year; jelly doughnuts, symbolizing the miracle of the oil on Hanukkah; chopped apples, nuts, and wine, symbolizing the mortar we used as slaves in Egypt at the Passover seder. Then there is the food-focused holiday that occurs each week—Shabbat, with its wine, braided challah, and bountiful dinner.

In moderation, celebration, and sanctification we have reference points to which we can turn when challenged by our own food fears or the national obsession with eating, health, and physical perfection. Taking the emphasis off ourselves and putting it on God can lead to a healthier, more appreciative approach toward food.

A CHILD'S-EYE VIEW OF FOOD

Before embarking on a plan to make your table an altar, it's useful to know what food looks like from your child's perspective. Children tend to take the short view about eating. They pursue the delightful and immediately satisfying. It's easier to get a Popsicle out of the freezer than to peel a carrot. If the Popsicle is shaped like a rocket ship and has rainbow stripes, they have no doubt about the superior choice. This is normal and appropriate.

It is your child's rightful job to try to get you to feed him from the food groups that children find most alluring:

- sweet
- crispy / crunchy
- creamy
- salty
- amusingly packaged

It's your job as parent to provide these foods—in moderation only—as the ornament, the treat that makes an occasion special. As you go about introducing your children to the concepts of moderation, sanctification, and celebration, keep in mind that these are principles they will absorb unconsciously at first. They'll still want the ring pops and chips. However, you might be surprised at how well your children take to new rituals and more structured mealtimes. They'll eventually understand that the time and care you put into these meals are expressions of your love for your family.

BEFORE YOU SET THE TABLE, SET A GOOD EXAMPLE

Eating is such an intimate and constant part of our lives that it can be hard to step back and identify the aspects of mealtime that are causing us and our children stress. Parents tend to get so focused on their children's psychological well-being that they ignore their own role in the drama. That's why, when people in my parenting classes bring up problems about feeding their children, the first thing I do is ask the group about their own eating habits:

- Do you eat leftovers from your children's plates?
- Do you eat standing up in front of the pantry where the crackers and cookies are kept?
- Do you frequently eat in the car?
- Do you carefully monitor your children's food intake throughout the day and then unwind by overeating ice cream and cookies, drinking wine, or snacking on peanut butter and crackers once the children are asleep?

More times than not, the answer is yes. I then tell the parents about my own neurotic eating problem: nutrient osmosis. I overanalyze my children at dinner. With the seriousness of a Food and Drug Administration scientist, I calculate the vitamin, mineral, antioxidant, and fiber quotient of each morsel they eat. I find myself thinking, *The meal went well. Each child consumed at least half a sweet potato. Rah! This heavy hitter covers beta-carotene, vitamin A, antioxidants, and fiber. Tomatoes in the salad. Good, good. vitamin C to make up for no orange juice at breakfast. Fish sticks for protein, B_{12}, omega-3! Ice cream for dessert. Could be worse. Lots of sugar but calcium too. We've got this chunk of the day covered.* I tick off the list of nutrients and sigh. If I can make sure they stave off unhealthy snacks before bed we will have made it through one more day. The hidden meaning of this sigh is that because my children have eaten healthful foods I now believe that I'm properly nourished too, as though a cosmic nutrient osmosis could vicariously benefit my bones and nervous system along with my children's.

In psychology, the process of separating yourself from your children so that they can grow up to be self-sufficient is called differentiation. When it comes to eating, parents—especially mothers—sometimes have a very hard time with differentiation. I don't think I'm alone when I unconsciously assume that I can benefit from my children's diet. Consciously or unconsciously, many parents believe that as long as our children eat what's good for them, that's all we have to worry about.

We and our children are separate entities, however, and if we sometimes forget it, they do not. In the kitchen as elsewhere, our children closely scrutinize our actions and are quick to point out hypocrisy. If you eat in the car, in front of the TV, or standing at the counter, they'll want to do it too. If you eat food off their plates, they'll grab it off yours. So when you decide to make changes and elevate eating from survival mode to a vehicle for civility and consciousness, start with yourself. Changing your own behavior will make your children much more receptive to the rituals and blessings you teach them.

CHANGES YOU CAN MAKE AT MEALTIME

Jewish eating rituals are designed to train a person to be more disciplined and to sublimate some of his or her appetites and desires. The rituals are part of a holy way of life because they elevate the physical act of eating to a spiritual discipline. This sounds wonderful in theory, but how can such ambitious goals be transmitted to boisterous six-year-olds or sulky teenagers? The answer is similar to the one I gave in Chapter 3, "The Blessing of Having Someone to Look Up To." You'll recall that I set down a few courteous phrases that children were to use whether or not they felt like it. The idea is that if they behave like polite, appreciative children, eventually they will start to feel like polite, appreciative children. The same holds true for eating. As your children watch you change your attitude toward food, as they say the blessings and follow the rituals, it can begin to sink in. You can rewire the family's whole approach toward eating, but it's not going to happen overnight.

Create a Peaceful Environment for Eating

Jewish mysticism teaches us that food starts out full of holy sparks and that we have the opportunity to transform it and elevate it further. How? By applying our humanness to it—by preparing it with care and arranging it attractively.

When you work hard at something it means more to you. Convenience foods, although useful and practical, may undermine your family's effort to make your table an altar. Children learn best from hands-on activities that involve many senses, so cooking and setting the table are excellent ways to transmit values. Since we have to eat anyway, cooking together, even infrequently, covers two bases: quality time and getting a necessary job done.

Judaism commands us to perform *hiddur mitzvot,* to beautify the commandments, to go the extra mile. By preparing special foods and setting the table with special care for Shabbat dinner, the mystics say that we get a taste of the world to come. At our house, everybody gets involved in the Shabbat dinner preparations. My husband, Michael, does the cooking. I cut flowers from the garden, and the children arrange them and set the table with the ritual objects: kiddush cup, candles, and challah. We don't have exciting desserts during the week but for Shabbat dinner I take down an etched glass cake stand with a pedestal and put on a paper doily. It's my younger daughter Emma's job to arrange the bakery cookies or rugalah or fruit tart on the stand. Shabbat dinner is a big production that I would never consider doing on a daily basis. But it caps our week, slows us down, and draws us together in a powerful way.

Mark Twain said, "Grief can take care of itself, but to get the full value of a joy you must have somebody to divide it with." Eating with your family can enhance the delight you take in your food. Shabbat dinner is a good place to start, and so are family birthday dinners (separate from the actual party) or leisurely Sunday breakfasts with "ritual" foods your family loves. My older daughter, Susanna, makes us fruit smoothies in the blender using prefrozen banana chunks, frozen raspberries, and orange juice. It is beautiful, pink, and creamy. The point is not elaborate preparation or effort but the effect of preparing food and breaking bread together, and eating it in a peaceful environment.

Sit Down and Take Your Time

Is your dinner table a sanctuary or bedlam? Do you eat on the run? Bobby Calder, a marketing professor at Northwestern University, writes, "Everybody wants to save time by multi-tasking.

So you don't just sit down and eat. You eat while you work, while you're watching TV, while you drive."

The rabbis who wrote the Talmud placed great value on the manner in which we eat our meals. They ruled that a person who eats in public is disqualified from testifying in court since he is considered to lack the fear of public ridicule that is a natural barrier against giving false testimony. The Talmud says that a person who eats in the street resembles a dog. The focus here is on dignity and self-respect. Applying these teachings to our homes means questioning whether it is possible to have a fully human meal if the television set is on, if we are trying to take care of family business at the table, if we are arguing or silent.

The Talmud recommended that one should eat slowly and chew the food well; the *Shulhan Aruch* (sixteenth-century code of Jewish law) states that children should not be fed when they are nervous or upset. A college-age Frenchwoman told me that her American friends get annoyed with her about the way she eats pizza. "You're not supposed to take little tastes," they said. "It takes too long. You're supposed to eat as many pieces as you can as quickly as you can."

For the sake of good digestion, to heighten the possibility of gratitude, and to enjoy time with your family enhanced by the pleasure of eating, monitor yourself to see how often you or your children eat standing up, or straight out of the package. Start sitting down for as many meals as possible. See what a table as altar brings.

Remember That Not Everyone Has Enough to Eat

Food is necessary for survival. Most children are anxious to rectify things when they first learn that some people are poor and hungry. They ask, "Why can't that man come live in our house?

We have an extra bed and he could take a shower so he wouldn't be so dirty."

Mazon, the Jewish food relief organization, recommends giving 3 percent of the cost of your grocery shopping to a charity that fights hunger. Before Shabbat dinner at my house we put money in the *tzedaka* (charity) box at least equivalent to the cost of feeding a needy person the meal we are about to eat. Consider connecting eating with giving. Which charities appeal to your children most?

Use a Blessing as a Consciousness-Raising Tool

The rabbis designed a system to counterbalance the natural tendency to gluttony and to help remind us to be grateful: saying a blessing before every meal. The blessing creates a little window of consciousness about what you are eating.

First you have to stop and figure out which blessing to say. It is a traditional practice to bless the specific food about to be eaten (bread, wine, a full meal) and to use the proper hierarchy of blessings (bread, the staff of life, supersedes other blessings). As you size up what you are eating, you open the window of consciousness a crack further. Remembering these blessings brings dignity to the individual food itself, to its cosmic soul. You are calling the food by name and giving each food its proper recognition. If you then eat with guilt, in an angry mood, or in a hurried manner, you are misspending the blessing.

USING JEWISH THEOLOGY TO OVERCOME COMMON MEALTIME TRAUMAS

Parent-child food struggles often start early. Some parents spend the first eight years of a child's life urging their son or daughter to eat and the second eight urging them not to. In many households mealtime is a tense soap opera that never ends, just lurches along at four- or five-hour intervals. Merely instigating rituals won't solve all your problems, but I have helped families use Jewish principles to deal with some of the most common mealtime conflicts: picky eaters, food refusal, snacking and missing meals, and the resentful cook/ungrateful family syndrome.

The Picky Eater

Remember Marny, whose parents forced her to eat the same dish meal after meal until she finished it all? She had come to see me because her son, Asher, was small for his age and an extremely picky eater. "He's an air fern," Marny told me.

> He eats almost nothing, and the few things he will eat have to be white: pasta, bread, Monterey Jack cheese, cream cheese, cream of wheat, Rice Krispies, peeled cucumbers, peeled apples, and milk. He also doesn't like it if the foods touch each other on the plate. And he won't eat any foods with a few ingredients mixed together, like chicken soup or cereal with banana. He also smells his food before he eats it. It's very weird, and the whole situation is getting worse.

"Is your pediatrician concerned about Asher's health?" I asked. "No. She says that he's growing and his health is fine. But I'm worried. He's in the tenth percentile of weight. He's very skinny."

Marny tried to get Asher to eat a variety of foods by coaxing him, imploring him to "try one bite of everything," or using dessert as a reward. If he refused to eat what the rest of the family was eating, she worried that he wouldn't eat at all and rushed to prepare his white foods for him. This routine convinced

Asher of the very special status of his appetite and left Marny frustrated and tired.

In bending over backward to cater to Asher, Marny was trying to avoid subjecting him to the childhood misery she had suffered. But her strategy wasn't working, and Asher was taking advantage of her goodwill. I've met plenty of Ashers: children who couldn't tolerate whole categories of food such as meat, fish, vegetables, or eggs; one girl who went on a food strike and would eat only bananas; one who would eat no breakfast other than frozen waffles eaten frozen. And plenty of Marnys: moms who, wishing to spare their children the agonies of their own childhood food experiences, ended up enslaved by their children's mealtime demands. Children naturally look for opportunities to exercise their will, and refusing to eat vegetables or eating only white foods is an attractive target.

You can help your children eat well and use self-discipline without being coercive or humiliating them. Feeding children is a situation that calls for a balance of power. If you don't use yours, your child will use his. Marny realized that in this situation Asher had a tremendous amount of control over her. To change the dynamics, she needed to stop believing that her son's food consumption was a yardstick of his well-being. If Asher's doctor was satisfied that he was healthy, Marny was free to stop worrying so much and change a few of the mealtime rules.

Judaism teaches that the dinner table is a place where a family come together to appreciate the blessings in their lives and to enjoy one another's company. If Marny is anxiously monitoring Asher's every bite and allowing his eating habits to ruin every meal, she is not creating a pleasurable environment for eating. I suggested that instead of getting upset by Asher's refusal of foods, Marny change her perspective and view the opportunity to eat together as a privilege. "Have zero ambition," I advised her. "Don't bribe him or try to persuade him; treat him just like any other member of the family."

I told Marny that no matter how long Asher lived, he would never respond to the question, "Aren't you going to eat this lovely piece of chicken?" with "Come to think of it, Mom, I will. I didn't realize just how delicious it looks and didn't think about how much trouble you went to buy it, brown it so nicely before braising it, and arrange it on this platter. Would you mind if I had a breast *and* a leg?"

I then advised Marny to limit herself to six words: "Would you like some X?" She was to require of Asher only a two- or three-word answer: "Yes, please" or "No, thank you." Better yet, she could place foods on the table in platters and let Asher serve himself a portion of any size he'd like.

"Be neutral," I told Marny. This is very, very difficult, but it is the key to maintaining the balance of power. "Don't share your anguish with Asher. Take acting lessons if you need to, rehearse with your husband or a friend. Just don't pass along your anxiety."

Marny had to clarify with Asher that if he didn't eat this meal, no food would be served until the next one. She had to steel herself to let him be hungry and perhaps regretful. There is no other way for a child to learn what mealtime means. "Don't confuse Asher's food rejection with personal rejection," I said. "Remain calm, casual, firm, and matter-of-fact."

"What about dessert?" Marny asked. "Should I encourage him to eat by offering dessert?"

The question of whether to use dessert as a reward causes parents much confusion. Let's look at three scenarios.

If Asher clearly is not hungry or is revolted by the offering at the table, you don't want him to stuff the food down just to get dessert. These are the times when you will say, "I can see you aren't hungry. Any suggestions for what would appeal to you for supper tomorrow?" Case closed. Do not offer him dessert even if other family members are eating it.

In the second scenario, Asher is testing the limits of his power. He tauntingly refuses all the healthy parts of the meal.

He wants to see how much he can get away with; it's a battle of wills. In this situation, too, he should not be forced to eat, nor should he be given dessert.

But if Asher resists his main course because it is less enticing than a Klondike bar, he can be encouraged to push himself a bit, to stretch his taste buds and demonstrate his willingness to cooperate by eating a part of his meal. He can then be rewarded with the part of dinner that is the most delightful to his palate— dessert. This is a good business practice. You are rewarding a good customer.

I concluded my session with Marny with the same advice I offer all parents who are engaged in eating battles with their children: "Light a few candles, pour a little wine if you like, relax, and enjoy your meal. Concentrate on your blessings and invite your child to do the same." He may catch the spirit.

Food Refusal

Even good eaters will turn their noses up at certain foods. Earlier I mentioned the importance of setting a good example for your children by eating meals at the table without multitasking, arguing, or rushing. Setting a good example also extends to the sorts of foods you require your children to eat. Don't ask them to do things you aren't able to discipline yourself to do, such as abstaining from sugar entirely, consuming either broccoli or spinach every night, or drinking large glasses of milk down to the last drop. If we focus too intently on the nutritional content of each meal, we miss out on the celebratory aspect of eating.

The code of Jewish law states that it is forbidden "to partake of any food or drink which we find revolting." Forcing children to eat foods that don't appeal to them creates resentment and increases their dislike of the foods. At the same time, don't allow your children to go on and on about how disgusting they find any particular food. This demonstrates a lack of gratitude for what God provides. If they are confident that they will not be forced to eat anything they don't want to, they won't need to vociferously label it disgusting to bolster their argument. It should be sufficient for them to say that they simply don't wish to eat it.

Too Many Snacks, Too Few Meals

Clients Scott and Joyce complained that their eight-year-old daughter, Dakota, refused to eat at mealtime. Here's what I learned by putting together details provided by Mom, Dad, and Dakota.

Dakota resisted going to sleep at her designated bedtime and was always difficult to rouse in the morning. Only half conscious during the morning rush to get dressed for school, she never wanted to eat more than a few bites of a granola bar and take a sip of juice. These were usually consumed in her bedroom or standing at the kitchen counter. By the midmorning snack time at school, Dakota was very hungry. She frequently traded her turkey sandwich for a friend's Pizza Lunchable or other treat. Dakota ate everything in the Lunchables kit, including the Snickers bar, the Capri Sun, and chips. Joyce never knew that Dakota didn't eat the sandwich because when Dakota got home, her lunch box was reassuringly empty.

During lunchtime the school cafeteria was noisy and bustling, not conducive to eating. Dakota, full of Lunchable, wasn't hungry anyway. Sometimes she would eat the peach or strawberries that Joyce packed for her snack. At 5:45, when Dakota arrived home from afterschool care, she was starving and her body craved calories and bulk. She often drank milk and ate cookies and leftover pizza. This snack seemed nutritionally reasonable since Joyce assumed that Dakota had eaten a turkey sandwich for lunch.

This scenario is not much different from the one that takes place in many households: a rushed, inadequate breakfast followed by who-knows-what at school. If dinner at Dakota's house was served at 6 or 6:30, she might have had a chance to recover from her bad food day. But, like many working parents, Scott and Joyce didn't get dinner on the table until 7 or 7:30. Dakota couldn't hold out that long, so she filled up on snacks when she got home from school. She wasn't hungry at 7 or 7:30, but by 8 her tummy started to rumble. A late snack would fill her up so that she was not hungry for breakfast the next morning, and the cycle would begin anew.

The whole approach to mealtime at Scott and Joyce's was well intentioned but misguided. If we begin with the Jewish premise that it's important to sit down at the table to eat a meal, we can see that breakfast should be more than a granola bar on the run. In order to give Dakota a chance to get hungry for breakfast, I advised her parents to eliminate her late-night snack. Heading into her school day with a full belly would increase the odds that she would not gobble her lunch at snacktime and not arrive home from school ravenous.

There is only so much control any parent can have over what her child eats during the school day, but Joyce did take some constructive action. When she called Dakota's teacher to find out about the rules regarding trading food, she learned that second graders were not allowed to trade, and the teacher assured her that she would keep an eye on Dakota and remind her of the rules.

The final link in the chain was dinnertime. I told Scott and Joyce that, after hearing too many stories about young children having dinner at 7:30 or later, I've started discouraging parents from trying to have a family dinner every night. Despite the study that showed a correlation between winning National Merit Scholarships and having a family dinner, eating at this late hour does not match the rhythms of children's natural hunger cycles. After children are fed an early supper (at the table—not in front of the television or at their desk), they may join their parents at the later dinner hour to socialize and catch up on the day. Shabbat dinner can be the leisurely, special, festive family meal each week.

For some families two seatings won't work because there is no one home to prepare the early-shift supper for the children. Consider preparing ahead on weekends, letting the children help with the cooking, or making extra portions of simple adult suppers (chicken, pasta) and reheating them for the children's early supper.

Resentful Cooks and Ungrateful Families

Preparing the family meal is a tangible offering of love. Tom, a writer, was married to Polly, a chiropractor who worked late most weekdays. When Tom came home at 5:30, he cooked dinner for the whole family. When the food was ready Tom got impatient if the children didn't come to the table right away or if Polly was later than expected arriving home. He wanted everyone to enjoy the food he had made "before it got cold" and to appreciate his effort on their behalf. Although he denied feeling rejected, he looked unhappy if the children and Polly didn't eat heartily or compliment him on the dinner.

When Tom told me about his feelings of resentment, I thought about the principles of celebration and sanctification. As I questioned him further, I learned that what he most resented was being left by himself in the kitchen to prepare everything while other family members went about their solitary business. "I feel like a hired hand," he said. "When we do sit down to eat, it's all over in ten minutes. Why should I bother? But somebody has to cook, and I actually like to do it. I just wish they'd appreciate it a little more." This is a complaint I hear from lots of parents who do the cooking. They put forty-five minutes of labor into a meal and the family tear at it like a pack of hyenas, maybe offering a garbled "Thanks!" as they rush from the table.

Celebrating and sanctifying a meal requires that we take the time to appreciate the cook's work and creativity. The ideal way to go about doing this is to have each family member help out, even if it's just for the fifteen minutes prior to the meal. Children can set the table while the parent who isn't cooking can pour the drinks and help pull the final details together. Once everyone is seated, the family can say a blessing that includes a thank-you to the chef. These seemingly small changes will help everyone focus on their blessings and encourage them to think about the fact that they are a family, not just random individuals who happen to collide at the dinner table.

KASHRUT, THE JEWISH DIETARY LAWS

Should you follow dietary laws in your family? Most faith traditions—Moslems, Catholics, Hindus—prescribe rules for holy eating. Many Jews find that keeping kosher is a practical and effective way to keep their Jewish identity at the forefront of their awareness. In the very simplest form, these laws prohibit mixing milk and meat products at the same meal, require abstention from eating pork and shellfish, and require eating only meat that has been ritually slaughtered in a prescribed and humane fashion.

These laws are a consciousness-raising tool. We separate meat and milk to tune up our awareness of what we are eating and to exercise self-discipline. At every meal, we monitor our food choices to remind us of our commitment to God and to our faith. The rules of kashrut combined with the rules for blessings—for example, there is a different blessing for bread than for cake—make it hard to eat unconsciously. The perceptive rabbis picked an urgent and pleasurable instinct and turned it into a vehicle for holiness. They even applied special rules to slaughtering and to eating meat so that we would acknowledge the significance of taking a life.

The health and moral benefits underlying the laws of kashrut have been debated by rabbinic authorities and Jewish philosophers for thousands of years. Most modern thinkers agree with the sentiments of a medieval scholar who said, "The dietary laws are not, as some have suggested, motivated by therapeutic considerations, God forbid! Were it so, the Torah would be denigrated to the status of a minor medical treatise and worse. . . . What does the Holy One care whether one kills an animal by the throat or by the nape of the neck? The purpose [of kashrut] is to refine humanity."

Most people who haven't grown up in a kosher home but choose to "take on the mitzvah" of kashrut do so in phases. We stopped eating pork and shellfish early in our involvement with Jewish life. Next we stopped mixing milk and meat at home. Other families avoid going to nonkosher restaurants or other people's (nonkosher) homes to avoid eating food from a nonkosher kitchen. Many parents, however, find that keeping their dinner table civilized and the children well nourished is challenge enough without adding further strictures about food. Whether or not you choose to adopt dietary laws, their message is a profound one. Attaining the goal of conscious and grateful eating requires attention to every aspect of eating, including our choices about what we consume and how we consume it.

AN EVERYDAY MIRACLE

Food is a sacred gift. We eat it to keep ourselves healthy and to enhance the pleasure of life's happy events. By reminding yourself and your children who the food is from (God), what it is for (to fuel us to be of service to others), and what attitude we should have toward it (both self-discipline and full enjoyment), you'll have a useful perspective for dealing with many of the food struggles that come up in your family.

Moderation, celebration, and sanctification are invaluable touchstones in this process. If you learn to practice moderation, you can approach food with interest and enthusiasm rather than obsession or fear. By celebrating a wide variety of the foods God has provided, you can let go of unreasonable guilt and teach your children both self-regulation and delight. Finally, sanctifying food by sitting down together and saying a blessing puts mealtime back in its proper place, as a means by which to appreciate your good fortune and God's bounty.

CHAPTER 8

The Blessing of Self-Control:

Channeling Your Child's Yetzer Hara

The payoff for any public speaker is audience response. That's why I love to deliver "Parent-Control, Child-Control: Where Do Wise Parents Draw the Line?" a lecture about teaching children discipline and self-control, Jewish style. The turnout is usually high, the seats quickly filling with parents whose faces reflect fatigue, tension, and end-of-the-rope frustration. I always know it's going to be a lively evening.

To break the ice I begin by telling these audiences, "Think of your child's worst trait. The little habit or attitude that really gets on your nerves. Or the medium-sized habit that your child's teacher keeps bringing up at parent conferences. Or the really big one that wakes you up at three in the morning with frightening visions of your little guy all grown up and living alone in an apartment in West Hollywood, plotting a shooting spree at the post office. Nod your head when you've come up with it."

Within five seconds, every head is bobbing.

"Good. Now you're one step ahead of where you were a moment ago, because now you know your child's greatest strength. It's hidden in his worst quality, just waiting to be let out."

I'm speaking, of course, about the yetzer hara, the evil impulse that is also the source of all passion and creativity. The yetzer hara is a warehouse for our curiosity, ambition, and potency—it's the yeast in the dough. Jewish wisdom teaches us that our child's unique yetzer hara contains the blueprint for her greatness. Our job as parents is clear-cut, if not simple. We are to identify these traits and remove "stumbling blocks before the blind" so that our children's yetzer hara can be channeled and expressed in a constructive rather than a destructive way.

Certain behaviors almost always fall into the category of unacceptable: if a child is repeatedly setting fires or torturing animals, everyone needs to worry. But many behavior problems fall into a vast gray area in which each set of parents has their own threshold of anger, concern, or alarm. Sleepless seven-year-old Miranda may be welcomed in her parents' bed anytime she has a bad dream, while in a different family a child's nighttime visits are considered intrusive and inappropriate. Will's kindergarten fib, "I didn't break it, it broke itself," may be seen by his parents as an age-appropriate and harmless way of trying to wriggle out of a tight spot, while in another family this "lie" is viewed as a serious ethical breach. In different families the same behavior will be defined as feisty or rude, sensitive or cowardly, endearing or irresponsible. But in all families there are some behaviors that cross the line of acceptability. All parents need to civilize their children.

The rabbis teach that children don't naturally behave in a civilized fashion. The British pediatrician and psychoanalyst D. W. Winnicott concurred. The normal child is not a "good" child, he writes:

What is the normal child like? Does he just eat and grow and smile sweetly? No, that is not what he is like. A normal child, if he has the confidence of his mother and father, pulls out all the stops. In the course of time he tries out his powers to disrupt, to destroy, to frighten, to wear down, to waste, to wangle and to appropriate. Everything that takes people to the courts (or to the asylums for that matter) has its normal equivalent in infancy and childhood, in the relation of the child to his own home.

Any child, then, spends a good portion of his time being bad. The parents' challenge is to teach their child how to control the energy of his yetzer hara and transform it into greatness. "Helping a child channel his yetzer hara" isn't just a euphemistic term for discipline. It means not only enforcing a set of rules but also accepting your child's temperament, respecting his limitations, and shoring up his strengths.

In order to figure out how to improve your child's behavior and channel his yetzer hara, you first need to answer two questions: Is my child's behavior normal? And what part, if any, of my child's problem behavior is a reaction to my own inappropriate attitudes and expectations?

NORMAL BADNESS

When parents come to me with worries about their child, the first thing I evaluate is whether or not the problem falls within the parameters of normal misbehavior or unhappiness. "Normal" covers a very broad spectrum, as I learned many years ago when I was a psychology intern in the Department of Psychiatry at Cedars-Sinai Medical Center in Los Angeles.

One of my responsibilities at the hospital was to administer psychological tests to children who were being evaluated upon intake to our clinic. My first month on the job, I tested a seven-year-old whose mother had brought her in to see if she might be dyslexic. After reviewing the girl's Rorschach test results, I ran to my supervisor's office. I had discovered a life hanging in the balance during the course of a routine exam. Her tests were a greenhorn diagnostician's dream.

"Look!" I said, waving the tests at him. "She saw squashed

bats, blood! And these drawings! They look so gloomy. She drew a haunted house. She talked to me about death and God. She says she often feels sad and lonely! Should we hospitalize her right away?"

My supervisor carefully examined the entire test protocol. He asked me some questions about my interview with the child and the family.

"She looks just fine to me," he finally concluded. "Might have a reading problem down the line, but seven is generally too early to diagnose dyslexia. You don't need to do anything right now, but ask her mother to stay in touch with us. And you, read this book."

He handed me a copy of *Your Seven-Year-Old: Life in a Minor Key* by Louise Bates Ames, Carol Chase Haber, and Frances L. Ilg. That was the day I learned that a normal seven-year-old's mind, and spirit, is a place of extremes and dark drama, and that a normal seven-year-old's Rorschach can look a lot like the Rorschach of a clinically depressed, suicidal adult.

Your Seven-Year-Old is one in a series of parenting books based on the remarkable research conducted over the past forty years by Louise Bates Ames and Frances Ilg at the Gesell Institute of Human Development in New Haven. On the bookstore shelf the series look like ordinary parenting books: *Your One-Year-Old*, *Your Two-Year-Old*, on up through the age of fourteen. But inside you will find sensible and reassuring descriptions of natural phases of children's development, written in a manner that conveys the authors' delight in children and their deep respect for them. Knowing what to expect at each stage is a comfort to parents with a suddenly contrary, crabby six-year-old or a morose, withdrawn seven-year-old. Over the years I have made a practice of recommending these books to parents who come to me for guidance. Occasionally I give sections to children to read as well. The children usually say, "It sounds like the person who wrote this met me already!" The books also give such a broad definition of what's normal that if your child's problems don't fit their descriptions, you might—I said *might*—have some justification for worrying.

After I get a detailed description of a child's problem behavior, I interview the mother and father more closely. I ask them if anyone else in the child's life is troubled by the behavior or attitude in question. Is the child having trouble making friends? Is he losing the friends he's got? Is the teacher complaining? Are both parents troubled by it?

In my experience, fathers tend to minimize their children's problems, saying, "I was the same way when I was his age." Sometimes this long view is right on target, sometimes it leads fathers to overlook real problems. Mothers don't typically underestimate their child's problems but their view can also be skewed: since children often show their worst side to their mothers, the mothers may draw a grimmer picture of their child's character or psychological profile than is accurate. When both parents are worried, there is a greater likelihood that a real problem exists. If parents and teacher are concerned and there is trouble with social relationships and school achievement, I'm generally convinced that we're out of the realm of normal troubles. For those families, counseling is in order. Some of the time, however, the children fall well within the normal range. Then it's time for parents to examine their own expectations, attitudes, and *mishegas*.

THE *MISHEGAS* FACTOR

They fuck you up, your mum and dad.
They may not mean to, but they do.
They fill you with the faults they had
And add some extra, just for you.

Philip Larkin

Is it inevitable, as Philip Larkin implies, that you will damage your child? Yes, to some degree, it is. Every generation of parents makes a whole new set of mistakes. Although we are not responsible for many of our children's traits, for example those that are inborn or grow out of the influence of school, peers, the media, and cultural values, research confirms that parents do have a significant impact on their children's character. Mothers and fathers usually influence their children more than any other environmental factor, so it's possible that your child's problems are at least partly a reaction to your own mishegas. This wonderful Yiddish word, which means nonclinical "craziness," is a good catch-all for the parental neuroses that can adversely affect children.

What forms of well-intentioned but misguided parenting do I see most often? There are a few common tribes: The "we are all equals" parents frustrated that their children won't willingly cooperate with rational, reasonable rules. The "on the go" parents puzzled by their child's desire to stay at home and veg out. There are the anxious parents who continually warn their children about life's dangers yet are annoyed by their fearfulness; the competitive parents irritated by their child's lack of ambition. There are the suffering families where mother and father live with simmering unspoken resentment yet wonder why their children don't seem happy. Finally, there are the "me, me, me" parents who view their children as a personal achievement but neglect to guide and control them.

The good news is that you can limit the damage you do if you are willing to own up to your mishegas. It may be that, like so many people, you got away with your particular brand of craziness until you became a parent. In an adults-only world, your perfectionism, moodiness, laziness, impatience, or desire to be liked might have been tolerated by other adults. You might have become expert at rationalizing these bad traits to yourself and others. With children, rationalizations are pointless. Instead of sympathy, you get instant karma. Are you wimpy? Your children will walk all over you if you don't toughen up. Are you moody? Your kids will be moodier. Are you prideful? Your children will test your humility every time you take them out in public. Your character traits will boomerang back at you when you become a parent, reflected in your children's behavior.

Often a parent's mishegas is invisible to the mother and father but obvious to an outsider. I recall one parenting class in which a father rose to speak about the problems his wife was having with their son, ten-year-old Jerome:

> Jerome is a terrible smart aleck. Yesterday he took ten dollars out of his mother's wallet and walked by himself to Burger King. When Beth went into his room to confront him about this, he was breaking another rule by looking at pornographic Web sites on the Internet. Most days he tells Beth that he has no homework, but when she calls the homework hotline she finds out that there's homework in every subject! At home, if she's watching the news on TV, he takes the remote and changes the channel. If she confronts him about any of this he makes a joke. So basically he steals, he lies, he cheats, and he treats his mother disrespectfully.

Did you notice that Jerome's dad, Noel, was doing the talking even though it was Beth who apparently had the big problems with Jerome? Perhaps you wondered whether Beth was in attendance that night. I did, so I asked.

"Is that the Beth in question sitting next to you?"

"Yes," said Noel. "It is."

I noticed that the long-suffering, harassed, lied-to, stolen-from, and generally ill-treated Beth was wearing a wry smile and had a twinkle in her eye. After a private session with the couple, I learned what was behind Beth's twinkle. She grew up in a home where there was lots of playful banter but little open conflict or disagreement about anything. Both as a young girl and as an adult, Beth put a premium on others' opinions of her. She wished to be seen as agreeable and didn't like to make waves. When I inquired, I learned that Beth had a long list of grievances against her boss and some against Noel, too, for taking advantage of her general willingness to go along with what others wanted.

How did Beth's mishegas—her meekness—affect her son's behavior? Her desire to be well liked by everyone inhibited her from getting angry with her equals. This stifling of her impulses led to the "kicking the cat" phenomenon. Jerome was the only one whom she saw as lower in status than she, and thus he was a safe target for her frustration. Additionally, Beth had a "wise guy" locked up inside her, a Margaret Cho that no one got to see. Instead she let Jerome put on the show and got some vicarious satisfaction out of his rude and wild behavior *even though it was directed at her.* Unconsciously, Beth was encouraging Jerome's bad behavior with the twinkle in her eye, which her son saw as clearly as I did.

Examine yourself to see how your own mishegas might be affecting your child's behavior. Are you expecting your child to do things you don't do yourself: avoid sugar, get down to homework right after school, spend time with friends you aren't in the mood to be with, sleep when you aren't tired? Where are those unrealistic expectations coming from? Gather data. Are you pumping up small problems? Ignoring big ones? Running into the same wall again and again? Stubbornly sticking to ineffective strategies? Ask the experts: check in with your friends, your child's classmates' parents, your child's teacher. If you think you need a professional opinion, see a therapist. Before clamping down on your child, find out if your view of the situation is badly distorted. The most effective first step in improving your child's behavior might be to change your own.

RECOGNIZING YOUR CHILD'S WORST BEHAVIOR
AS HER GREATEST STRENGTH

If you've honestly confessed to your own craziness and have decided whether or not your child's "badness" is normal, you are ready to work with her yetzer hara. Deborah, the mother of three girls, gave a parenting class this biographical sketch of her four-year-old daughter, Lucy:

> She's unbelievably bossy. We all call her the ballet master. When she's with her younger sister and her sister's friends, she tries to choreograph their every move: "This is a very fancy tea party! You have to sit with your legs crossed and your hands in your lap! No loud voices!" If she sees her older sister watching television, she'll ask her whether she's finished her homework.
>
> Her preschool teacher says that Lucy doesn't paint but prefers to walk around the room reminding the other children to put on their smocks, not to mix colors, and to shake off their brushes so the paint won't get too watery. She is constantly organizing and fixing. Last week we went to the library. Did Lucy want me to read to her? Of course not. Instead she found a cart with a pile of books waiting to be restacked. Lucy set right to work, neatly organizing all the books with the spines facing out.

Clearly, Lucy is no shy and amenable follower. Her authoritative nature and penchant for organizing can be wonderful assets that will serve her well throughout her life, as long as she learns to temper them with good manners. In her mother's tone, however, I sensed a helpless, genteel horror at Lucy's behavior. Lucy's forcefulness was embarrassing to her parents, and the embarrassment was preventing them from seeing the positive aspects of their daughter's personality. I proposed that they try to "reframe" their opinions of Lucy. *Reframe* is a term used by psychotherapists that means to rethink your interpretation of an event, often turning your existing opinion on its head.

"Don't view Lucy's behavior as bossy, view it as demonstrating leadership skills," I suggested. "She isn't nosy, she's extremely observant. The fact that she likes to organize the books in the library is a wholly positive trait—imagine how she could apply these skills to keeping her room clean, not to mention the rest of the house."

Parents tend to want contradictory things from their children—docile, "Gallant"-like manners along with extraordinary feats of intellectual, creative, or physical derring-do. But the extraordinary talents arise from the yetzer hara, the unruly "Goofus" side of your child's personality. It's essential that you learn to see those intense, often irksome traits as the seeds of your child's greatness.

Try thinking of:

- Your stubborn or whining child as persistent.
- Your complaining child as discerning.
- Your overeating child as lusty.
- Your argumentative child as forthright and outspoken.
- Your loud child as exuberant.
- Your shy child as cautious and modest.
- Your reckless, accident-prone, or rule-breaking child as daring and adventurous.
- Your bossy child as commanding and authoritative.
- Your picky, nervous, obsessive child as serious and detail-oriented.

Now ask yourself if your child has sufficient opportunity to express her natural tendencies in a constructive way. This is a two-part challenge for parents: first you must make sure you're not setting your child up for failure, and once you've cleared her path, you must give her tasks that make the best use of her yetzer hara.

REMOVING STUMBLING BLOCKS BEFORE THE BLIND

If you keep running into trouble with your child at specific times—getting ready for school, mealtime, homework, bedtime—it may be that you are inadvertently placing a stumbling block before him. Look for the pattern in the unacceptable behavior, and think about restructuring the situation rather than repeatedly punishing your child for not behaving the way you want him to. To reduce the opportunities for your child to misbehave, ask yourself:

- Does the trouble arise when my child is hungry? Tired? Overstimulated? When I am?
- Is his schoolwork too difficult? Too easy?
- Does my child have enough stimulating things to do? A new study of sibling rivalry shows that its primary cause is not a desire to get parents' attention but boredom.
- Is my child suffocating? If children can touch someone else in all four directions all day long they are too boxed in. All children need some time to themselves to unwind.
- Does my child have a long enough recess break at school? Does he have some time between school, homework, and bedtime to play?
- Is my child sleep-deprived?
- Does my child have a headache from eyestrain?
- Has my child been tested for hearing problems?

In general, watch for common "meltdown" situations: shopping for groceries with hungry, tired children on the way home from day care; Star-Spangled Chips Ahoy in the cupboard when you want the children to eat fruit for dessert; Super Soaker birthday parties when you've got a child who gets overexcited by a rowdy crowd; MTV on in the house when you don't want your daughter lobbying for tiny tank tops and platform boots.

Preventive Havoc

All children have a barbarous streak. Even if you remove every stumbling block, it is only fair to let them break free from their constraints now and then. The sage Abayei, orphaned from birth, was raised by a nurse he called Eim (Mother). Said Abayei: "Eim told me, 'To raise a child one needs warm water [for bathing] and oil [for anointing]. When the child is a little bigger, he needs things to break.'" When he became a parent, Abayei bought cheap, chipped plates for his own children to break. This wise father understood that all children need a messy, unstructured, unproductive free-for-all every now and then.

Does your child get enough time to horse around? To make noise? To get into trouble? To break things? Arrange to ignore some benign mayhem: send your kids to the backyard with instructions to play with the hose. Turn your back and let them get as wet and dirty as they want. At the end of the summer, let them pull out the remains of the vegetable garden, clipping and ripping the plants to shreds. Direct them to throw cans into the recycling bin. Don't say a word about the noise. If your city-dwelling children tire of genteel craft projects on a rainy day, let them bake a "cake" or poison potion using any ingredient in the kitchen, or buy a bag of party ice and let them throw it into the bathtub. Or take them to the park to play in the mud. Two five-year-olds up in their room and it's suspiciously quiet? Don't storm in immediately to make sure that they aren't showing each other their genitals or lighting matches. Give them a bit of privacy to be children, even slightly naughty ones. Is your ten-year-old choosing to zone out with CDs and some neighborhood friends on a school night or chatting it up on-line when she should be studying for the state capitals test? Let it go one time. She won't end up an elementary school dropout or in jail. You are parents, not police or undercover agents. Think of all of this as preventive misbehavior, the small temblor that releases tectonic pressure and forestalls a bigger earthquake.

Presentation Is Everything

When you ask your child to help out—set the table, clean the patio furniture, watch a younger sibling—does she perceive your request as a fun opportunity or an irritating burden? Often it depends on the way you ask. Once, when I accompanied my second grader's class on a field trip to the science museum, I had a chance to see how an expert does the asking.

The bus driver was in her mid-twenties. She was a bright vision with forty tiny braids in red barrettes, a red satin baseball jacket, and red-and-black-plaid pants. As she turned to the children I was expecting the usual slightly defeated bus driver safety-rules speech. Here's what I heard instead:

"I need some special monitors! I need some folks to help me out if anything happens to this bus and we have to get off before we get to the museum! If you're thinking of volunteering, listen closely and I'll tell you what the monitors have to do."

Now she spoke very slowly in a near whisper. The children were rapt. "You'll have to look and see which exit door is near you and lead the way for all the other children out that door. Can anybody here handle that?" Almost every hand shot up. The bus driver took her time. She scanned the bus slowly, looking at each child. Finally she picked Mandy and Alex. Both children immediately sat up straighter and beamed at the others like royalty at a coronation. The bus driver finished up her talk with the usual rules about not making too much noise or eating on the bus. At this point I realized that Mandy and Alex were the only two children seated next to the emergency exit doors, each with a teacher beside them.

During our picnic lunch I asked the bus driver about her

strategy. "The children by the exits are the ones I'm aiming for," she said. "I do that whole volunteer thing so I won't put them on the spot if they don't want the responsibility."

Brilliant. By transforming a responsibility into an honor, this young woman had set up the children to handle a crisis with dignity and at the same time held their attention while she delivered the safety rules.

CHANNELING THE YETZER HARA

At the beginning of the chapter I mentioned that it took about five seconds for the parents at my lectures to pinpoint their child's most irritating or worrisome trait. Once you've singled out this trait (or traits) and reframed it in a more positive light, it's not too difficult to come up with tasks that will be well suited to your child. Bossy—excuse me, future CEO—Lucy should be given tasks that require her to keep track of schedules and chores, organize items, and remind her mother and father of upcoming events. Her parents can make sure she has calendars, charts, toolboxes with lots of little compartments, anything that helps her to organize and control her world.

Parents need to invent the tasks or diversions and supply the tools that will channel their child's particular yetzer hara. Some of the tasks should be actual chores, while others can simply be an outlet for their energy. For example, Lucy's "real" chores could be straightening the magazines in the family room, sweeping the front porch, and setting the table. Her "yetzer" tasks could be to give her parents a few reminders every day ("Dad, don't forget to empty your pockets before you put your pants in the hamper"; "Mom, make sure to turn on the dishwasher tonight") and to teach her younger sister a new game every week. This way, even though Lucy's parents will still need to teach her manners and how to mind her own business, Lucy will have an outlet for her overweening urge to organize, remind, and lead.

There are three general rules to keep in mind when channeling your child's yetzer hara. These apply to all children, regardless of their specific inclinations.

Don't Be Overly Demanding

Avoid using the words *always* and *never*. According to Jewish law, certain *mitzvot* (commanded actions) can be performed imperfectly, yet the obligation will still be fulfilled. In American jurisprudence, this is called complying with the spirit of the law. Take your child's good intentions into account. Don't have impossible expectations such as always tell the truth, always sit at the table without squirming around in your seat, never squeeze the baby too hard when you hug her, always remember to bring home all the books you need for your homework. Reading the Gesell books (*Your Two-Year-Old*, on up) is a good way to gauge how much you can realistically expect from your child.

Remember That Success Motivates

Take a new perspective. Instead of saying, "If only she would try harder, she would do better," say, "If she did better, she would try harder." Let your children taste success. Be a talent scout. Find islands of competence. Catch them being good and mention it: "This room looks great!" "I don't know if I could have pulled off this party without all the help you gave me." "A big thank-you, Celia, for washing that smelly dog, and to you, Michael, for helping Ilana with her homework."

Make it easy for your child to succeed. Separate clothes into four categories—school clothes and party clothes, cool day clothes and warm day clothes—and let your child choose his or her outfits. Don't make a single comment about the choice unless it's a compliment. If the only thing you know your child can do well is to use a Phillips head screwdriver, loosen a half dozen screws around the house before he comes home. Tell him you need his talents.

Don't Talk Too Much

Judaism stresses the power of words. Our holiest object is a book (the Torah). On the holiday of Simhat Torah we even dance with the Torah, celebrating all the words wrapped inside. We can use words to enrich our children's lives or we can misuse them. Think about using words in moderation. Don't try to provide instant solutions to your child's problems; instead, be quiet and just listen. If you find yourself arguing with any child older than two, you are wasting your time. Their skills are better than yours. In general, talk less and act more. Be a role model, don't be a lecturer.

Sometimes removing all the stumbling blocks, recognizing the direction of your child's yetzer hara, and using all the positive spin in the world isn't effective. Your child still does things you don't want her to. Then it's time to use discipline. As with so many aspects of child-rearing, a little bit of forethought and strategy can make this chore much easier.

THE PROPER REBUKE: EXPRESSING DISPLEASURE WITHOUT HUMILIATING YOUR CHILD

In Leviticus 19:17 we read, "Do not hate your kinsman in your heart. Reprove your neighbor, but incur no guilt because of him." What does "incur no guilt" mean? Some biblical commentators say it refers to the guilt you would feel if you unintentionally humiliated the wrongdoer during the rebuke. Others see it as a reference to what can happen in relationships when people hold back strong feelings. In either case, resentment may smolder until someone explodes in anger, or a coldness may grow between people who had previously been close. A third interpretation has to do with shared responsibility. If we stand by in silence when we see someone do something we know is wrong, we share in his or her guilt.

A proper rebuke by a parent gives children a chance to learn about parental values and standards of behavior. Children also learn that it is possible to express disappointment, frustration, or hurt directly without hostility and without causing shame. Keep in mind that the difference between rebuke and criticism is your intent. Are you scolding your child because you're tired and frustrated? Does he make a good target for your distress because he is smaller than you are? Take a few seconds to ask yourself these questions before you admonish a child.

Don't expect the rebuke to come easily or feel natural. In the Talmud, Rabbi Tarfon says: "I wonder if there is anyone in this generation capable of accepting reproof." Rabbi Eleazar ben Azariah responds: "I wonder if there is anyone in this generation who knows how to rebuke properly." According to Rashi, the major eleventh-century biblical commentator, the trickiest part is delivering a rebuke that carries some sting without shaming the person being rebuked. Protecting others from shame is a central theme in Judaism. The rabbis taught that shame causes such great pain that it is akin to murder. If we cause someone to redden with embarrassment, it is as though we have drawn blood.

There are three types of sin in Judaism. The first is the *cheit*, or inadvertent sin. The word *cheit* is also a term used in archery to refer to missing the mark or aiming off course. These are sins we do by accident. The second is the *avon*, or sin committed out of the pull of desire. Although we know it is wrong, we cannot resist. The third is the *pesha*, the rebellious sin, done with the clear intention of demonstrating to God (or a parent) that he is not our master. The type of rebuke you choose should fit the nature of your child's transgression.

For the *cheit,* you can point out the error in your child's judgment and let the experience be her teacher. Psychologist Miriam Adahan calls this *rebbe gelt* (rabbi money). Rebbe gelt refers to lost jackets, spilled milk, forgetting a lunch or a homework assignment. The *consequence* of the poor judgment is the "rabbi," or teacher. It's called *gelt* because the lesson learned is worthwhile, as precious as money, and more important than whatever was lost or spilled or forgotten. Other than pointing out the error, no further rebuke is required. For this method to be effective, you must refrain from "fixing" the problem! For instance, if your child continuously forgets her lunch box, don't keep bringing it to school for her. More than one school director has told me of forgotten lunches being replaced with a sandwich messengered over from the deli. If you can refrain from stepping into the breach, your child will have a chance to benefit from the richness of rebbe gelt.

How do you rebuke for an *avon?* In the *Mishneh Torah,* Maimonides offers some helpful strategies. If you rebuke or admonish another person, you should:

- Administer the rebuke in private.
- Speak to the offender gently and tenderly. (In Ecclesiastes, too, we are taught about the importance of speaking in a soft voice: "The words of the wise man are heard in gentleness.")
- Remember that you are speaking for the wrongdoer's benefit and not out of a desire to humiliate or seek revenge against him.
- Put the rebuke in the context of your high regard for the person being rebuked.

Here's my version of Maimonides' rebuke strategy, which I've adapted from Miriam Adahan and Spencer Johnson's One-

Minute Rebuke. First, if you are too upset to speak calmly, count to ten, leave the room, or wait until later. When you've regained your composure, tell your child that you need to talk with her and go to a private place. Get down to her eye level and look directly at her. Put your hand gently on her shoulder and describe the specific behavior that is unacceptable to you: "I saw you and Leila killing ants with my tweezers."

Tell the child how you felt about what she did. Be brief. Use some face-saving comment before you rebuke, such as "I'm sure you didn't mean to," or "You probably didn't think this through." Or say something in the spirit of *es pasht nisht,* a nice Yiddish phrase meaning "this does not become you," which implies that the child's stature and past good behavior places her above the negative behavior in question: "Chloe, this isn't like you. You are usually very kind to animals."

Don't take this opportunity to start collecting thorns by giving a long history of the problem or dragging in other problem behaviors or attitudes. You don't have time, this is a one-minute rebuke. Don't predict what this behavior will lead to in the future ("I'm starting to wonder if it's safe to leave your baby brother alone in a room with you") and don't label ("You are thoughtless"). Tell your child the consequence of her behavior: "From now on until I tell you it's OK again, you are not allowed to go into my bathroom without asking." These first steps should take only a minute or two.

After delivering your rebuke, be silent for a moment to evaluate the child's reaction (remorseful, defiant, cooking up a rationalization or defense). Resist getting drawn into an argument about the size and scope of the crime.

Finally, offer an opportunity to make amends. In Judaism, the word for repentance is *teshuvah.* It means "return," both in the sense of returning to your true best self after having strayed off course and the sense of returning to God, to a divine, objective standard of goodness. As with everything else in Judaism, words and intentions are not enough. In order to do teshuvah, your child has to take some action to right the wrong she has done.

With the cheit, she can simply sponge up the spilled milk or hold the paper bag as you sweep up the broken glass. If she's lost another jacket she can contribute from her allowance to make up for a new purchase.

You can't bring the dead ants back, but your child can scrub off the tweezers and be put in charge of feeding the fish for a week. During the amends portion of the rebuke, you can ask how she would handle the situation differently next time. If she has no suggestions, offer one of your own: "If you want to play surgery, it has to be just pretend." You might also ask for her ideas about what she can do to make up for her actions. Talk briefly until you reach agreement about appropriate acts of teshuvah.

Finally, touch your child to remind her of your love and to reassure her that although her behavior has disappointed or upset you, you aren't rejecting her. If you think it's probably true, say, "I'm sure it won't happen again." Hug her and let her know that you are not harboring resentment. Then, *Kadima!* Forward! Move on with your day.

PUNISHMENT FOR A *PESHA*: WHEN A GENTLE REBUKE IS NOT ENOUGH

If your child's unacceptable behavior was intentional, if it was not a crime of passion but seems to be a *pesha*—a crime of rebellion or a testing of parental authority—punishment is necessary and justified. Just as you want to avoid shaming a child when you rebuke her, you must make sure not to terrify or abuse her when meting out punishment. At the same time, she needs to feel the sting of her misdeeds.

Judaism holds that children should only be punished if they

have been forewarned and know what to expect if they misbehave. The sages teach that God never punishes without previous warning, and as parents we are supposed to emulate God's ways. The Talmud also warns against threatening a child with future harsh punishment. The rabbis tell a story of a young child who broke a bottle on the Sabbath, and whose father threatened to box his ears when the Sabbath had ended. The boy was so terrified that he killed himself by jumping into a deep pit. Children have vivid imaginations and may harm themselves in an effort to avoid a promised punishment, so punishment should be given as soon as possible following the misdeed.

Sometimes—like in public settings—this simply isn't practical, in which case a stern look and sotto voce rebuke can be followed by a consequence when you reach home. Don't fall into the trap of having a big back-and-forth discussion at the scene of the crime. Try to refrain from announcing a punishment and then deferring it. If you don't keep your word, your children will cease to take you seriously. One small crack in the wall of your resolve and they'll be all over you like a road crew with a truckful of dynamite.

A final caveat: Don't up the ante on punishment. If you blurt out, "No TV for three days," and your daughter responds with a flippant, "Big deal," you are stooping to her level and abusing your power if you come back with, "OK, fine then! It will be no TV for a week!" You earn the privilege of leadership and respect by not taking advantage of your position.

To Find Effective Punishments, Reframe Entitlements as Privileges

I often hear parents say, "He doesn't care if I punish him. If I send him to his room he has a good time. Nothing has an effect. He doesn't care which privileges I take away."

"Oh, yes he does," I always answer. "The secret lies in your definition of the word *privilege*. If you redefine most of what your child considers entitlements as privileges to be earned, you'll have a dazzlingly large universe of effective punishments available to you."

As I mentioned back in Chapter 5, every child is entitled to certain basics. *Everything else is a privilege to be earned! Everything!* Software, fashionable clothing, sweet treats, TV, bicycles, phone use, staying up late on weekends, play dates, grilled cheese sandwiches prepared on the spot by Mom, trips to the video store . . . all the things your child believes are his birthright.

The first step in inaugurating this new worldview is a change in your lexicon. Instead of saying, "*If* you don't do X (clean up your room right now!) *then* you won't be able to do Y (watch television tonight)." Change the "If . . . then" to "When . . . then," as in: "*When* you remember to put your clothes in the hamper for three days in a row, *then* you'll be allowed to watch television in the evening after homework. I will not remind you even once. If you like, I'll be glad to help you set up a chart to help you remember. Now tell me what I said so I'll know that we both understand the rules the same way."

"*When . . . then.*" That's the key phrase. Now go listen to a CD, call a friend, or do some gardening. Your child is on his own for a while. When he remembers to cooperate, he'll earn the privileges he longs for. It's a whole new perspective.

MAKING AMENDS REPAIRS THE WORLD

The repentant sinner should strive to do good with the same faculties with which he sinned. . . . With whatever part of his body he sinned, he should now engage in good deeds. If his feet had run to sin, let them now run to the performance of good. If his mouth had spoken falsehood, let it now be opened to wisdom. Violent hands should now open to charity. . . . The troublemaker should now become a peacemaker.

—RABBI JONAH GERONDI,
thirteenth century

The purpose of discipline is to teach both new attitudes and new behaviors. Making amends is a good way to help children learn precisely what they have done wrong, because the child is required to actively undo or repair the unacceptable behavior. An Orthodox rabbi, the headmaster of a boys' school, told me how he implements this principle. When Abram twice stole cookies from Ari's lunch tray "to be funny," the rabbi required him to help out in the kitchen for a day and to bring Ari a plate of freshly baked cookies. Another student, Moshe, covered a bathroom stall with graffiti. The damage was undone when the maintenance staff repainted the entire bathroom the next day. Instead of suspending Moshe from school, the rabbi kept him there after hours and put his hands to work: Moshe cleaned up the bathrooms and graded papers until 6 P.M. The rabbi had no more trouble with graffiti from Moshe.

"I think missing an important basketball game that afternoon was partly responsible for the good effect of the punishment," he told me, "but so was the time and care we put into figuring out the right way for him to make up for the damage he did. Psychologists call this logical consequences. The Torah calls it *teshuvah*—a chance to make amends for his actions."

If your child has committed a sin of rebellion, think about how he can repair the physical or emotional damage he has caused. As Rabbi Gerondi recommended, he should try to make amends using whatever faculty he employed to commit the crime.

A LIFELONG QUEST FOR CHARACTER

Sampson Raphael Hirsch, the nineteenth-century rabbi and author, had this to say to a mother who complained that her son did not listen to her: "For ten years you did what he wanted, now you expect him to do what you want?" Clearly, we have to get into the habit of disciplining children when they are young if we want them to behave properly when they reach adolescence. Jewish wisdom emphasizes the importance of preparation. You can plan for a wholesome and safe adolescence by getting your child accustomed to discipline from his or her earliest years.

Miriam Adahan has a simple formula for effective parenting: one-third love, one-third law, and one-third sitting on your hands. The one-third love we intuitively understand. One-third sitting on your hands means that you'll turn a blind eye to lots of minor transgressions, pick your targets well, and be judicious with discipline. One-third law means that you'll be really tough and unyielding one-third of the time, perhaps much tougher than feels comfortable. The Talmud offers similar advice: when dealing with a child, "be it ever your way to thrust him off with the left hand and draw him to you with the right hand."

This push and pull is emotionally wrenching for parents. To succeed at it, we need to discipline ourselves in ways we may not have done before. This is part of the plan. Judaism teaches us that working on developing *middot* (good character traits) is a lifelong process; it doesn't stop at the bar or bat mitzvah. Raising children will help you build middot, because changing their bad behavior will probably require you to change yourself. Some of the least glamorous yet most valuable character traits, such as patience, tenacity, foresight, courage, self-control, and acceptance are won in the trenches of parenthood. As you teach your children how to control and direct their yetzer hara, you will discover strengths you never knew you had.

CHAPTER 9

The Blessing of Time:

Teaching Your Child the Value of the Present Moment

Two different rabbis have told me the same story. A mother, concerned about her child, comes to see the rabbi. "Rabbi, can you talk to my son, Jordan? He's angry all the time and I know something is bothering him. Maybe it's the divorce, maybe it's something going on with his friends. . . . I don't know, but you seem to be able to get kids to talk. Can I bring him in to see you?"

The rabbi then offers a time, say, Wednesday at 4:30.

"No, that won't work. Jordan has basketball practice."

The rabbi offers another time.

"No good again. He has his math tutor."

And another.

Guitar lesson.

The rabbi sees that this young person's appointment calendar is even busier than his own. He tells me that he believes he already knows what Jordan is angry about.

We are an ambitious and industrious generation of parents, but the combination of these two potentially fine traits pollutes our relationship to time. The future flips into the past amid a blur of weary winter-morning wake-ups, lists of spelling words and multiplication tables to help the children memorize, karate lessons, birthday parties, play dates. Torah teaches that God has put us in the role of caretakers of the world, not masters. As caretakers of the gift of time we are obligated to use it well. But what does that mean?

To most people, using time well means knowing how to squeeze more out of it. Yet managing time by squeezing it harder doesn't work when you're raising children, because the variables change too quickly. Just when you've perfected one schedule, a new troop of friends, sports, or classes pops up on the horizon. Many parents are surprised to discover that as their children grow older, organizing their lives gets more, not less, time-consuming. There's more homework, more social pressures, the soccer games are farther away. As activities pile up, parents scramble to improve their time-management skills, usually to little avail.

Time can be seen as a resource to be utilized or a treasure to be enjoyed. Judaism asks parents to do both. If we focus our energy exclusively on scheduling activities and monitoring homework, we won't get to treasure the moments we have with these cosmic creatures, our children. We won't hear their amazing observations, or notice their radiant beauty. We won't stop moving long enough to see them or hear them.

A major complaint of adolescents is that nobody listens to them. The habit of listening, and of expecting to be listened to, needs to start early. If we are always distracted, our children will perceive us as half listening and they'll stop trying to talk to us. That's one sad consequence of our accelerated lifestyle, but there are so many others. Amid all the hurry it's hard for children to learn essential life skills: vegging out, contemplating life, relieving boredom by entertaining themselves, and feeling a general sense of peace and contentment. If kids are not taught to reflect on things, how can they weigh issues, actions, consequences? Plato said it best: "The unexamined life is not worth living." Examining one's life takes time.

Time is holy currency in the Jewish religion. Christians talk about being a "vessel God can use." I like this idea of life as

holy service. In Christian theology, each person has the opportunity to do God's work on earth in appreciation for the antici-
pated gift of life after death. Judaism focuses on the present. *The
reward for doing God's work is the quality of your life while you're here.*
God gave us free will to choose our actions wisely, to make the
most of our time on earth. We've been given the opportunity to
leave this place better than we found it; to cherish the moment;
to treasure time as well as manipulate it. The big paradox is that
slowing down the clock takes as much effort and concentration
as getting things done. In order to use time well we must work to
protect it as assiduously as we guard our children's health or pro-
mote their education. How? Judaism has a blueprint for rest,
reflection, and renewal. It is called Shabbat.

SHABBAT: THE MYSTICAL POWER
OF A WEEKLY DAY OF REST

More than Israel has kept the Sabbath, the Sabbath has kept
Israel.

—AHAD HA'AM

The rabbis were mindful of the dangers of a hurried life. Fortunately, they had a powerful antidote ready-made. God had commanded it right up front. Just minutes after creating time itself,
God created a means of protecting it.

God worked very hard. In six days he made the heavens
above, earth, day, night, man, woman, hummingbirds, fruit
trees, lizards, bees, all the mighty throng. God then sized up his
efforts: "God was pleased, he saw that his work was good."
Check out this attitude. None of our perfectionistic, it's-never-
good-enough anxiety, no workaholism, no 24-7. He liked what
he saw. Now watch what happens next.

"On the sixth day God completed all the work he had been

doing, and on the seventh day he ceased from all his work. God blessed the seventh day and made it holy because on that day he ceased from all the work he had set himself to do." There's the critical phrase—"all the work he had set himself to do." The job he planned for himself had a beginning *and an end*. When he was finished, he stopped and rested for a whole entire day. Not long after this, God commanded everybody else to do the same thing. "Six days you shall labor and do all your work, but the seventh day is a Sabbath of the Lord your God."

Each of the 613 commandments enumerated in Talmudic tradition is there because people were violating them left and right. Otherwise, why bother commanding? God's great insight into the nature of the beings he created was his recognition that it wouldn't be easy to get people to stop working. Not working would take as much or even more self-discipline and planning as working. His people would have to succumb. They would not go gently.

Part of God's strategy was to get everybody involved. He recognized that if others were working, people would feel guilty or tempted to join in. His prescription wouldn't work unless everyone was taking the same medicine, so he made a broad sweep and decreed that everyone was required to rest. "You shall not do any work—you, your son or your daughter, your male or female slave, or your cattle, or the stranger who is within your settlement."

Finally, God amped up the importance of Shabbat by making it a sign of the covenant: "The Israelite people shall keep the Sabbath, observing the Sabbath throughout the ages as a covenant for all time." Sign of the covenant? What's the big deal? Why so much fanfare?

The answer lies in the mystical power of a day of rest. The Hebrew word for *rest* in the phrase "And God rested" is *vayinafash*. *Vayinafash* is a form of the word *nefesh*, which means "soul." In the rest of Shabbat our souls are renewed. Rabbi

Abraham Joshua Heschel, the great modern scholar and philosopher, calls Shabbat a "cathedral in time" rather than in space. In our tradition we attach ourselves to sacred events, rather than to possessions or places.

We think of Rosh Hashanah and Yom Kippur, the days of the year yielding a bigger synagogue turnout than any others, as the holiest of holy days. The powerful blare of the ram's horn can seem like the spiritual highlight of the religious year. But the tradition in some synagogues is to abstain from blowing the shofar when Rosh Hashanah falls on Shabbat. Why? Because according to Jewish law, on Shabbat you are forbidden to carry musical instruments, and Shabbat takes precedence over Rosh Hashanah. A prescribed weekly day of rest and renewal ranks above a high holy day.

In *The Art of Jewish Living: The Shabbat Seder,* Dr. Ron Wolfson explains the rules we follow to accomplish the work of spiritual renewal:

> What is forbidden on Shabbat is any act that changes the physical world. When we rest on Shabbat, we stop manipulating nature, we stop building and moving and changing the physical. This makes Shabbat a time to focus on the eternal, on that which cannot be changed through human action. Even nature is given a day free from the interference of humankind. Much of the job of preparing the home for Shabbat is done so that we do not have to "work" during the holiday.

Rabbi Marc Sirinsky, in *Ecology and the Jewish Spirit: Where Nature and the Sacred Meet,* compares Shabbat's sense of timelessness to river rafting or being in the wilderness. Preparing for such a trip—finding the right maps, inspecting equipment, packing the car—is so much trouble you wonder if it's worth the effort. You have to work so hard to prepare to stop. But once on the river, with no watches or other obligations, time can unfold and expand in a natural rhythm. Rabbi Sirinsky says that in "river time," as in Shabbat, we have a chance to experience the *neshamah yeterah,* the additional soul. What is the nature of this additional soul? Traditional Jewish mystical writings teach that "with the Sabbath-soul [the *neshamah yeterah*] sadness and anger are forgotten. Joy reigns on high and below." During Shabbat and in nature, where God's handiwork is most palpable, we have a chance to capture this feeling.

The neshamah yeterah can enter us at many other times as well. One night Emma was rinsing off a blue plate before putting it in the dishwasher. It was covered with melted raspberry sorbet. "Mom, look! Come and see! It's just like a sunset. It's amazing." A green bowl that had held a salad was in the sink. Pale lettuce leaves floated near the top. "Look, it's like a pond with lily pads!" I put my arm around her and looked at all this kitchen cleanup beauty through her eyes. I felt the second soul closing in on us.

There are peak spiritual moments that happen in a family spontaneously. The prescient, poetic observations our children make, the questions they ask as they are climbing out of the bath or playing with their toast, cannot be pumped out of them or choreographed. The way time stops when a glistening bullfrog hops onto the driveway or when your child has a long and tender talk with a grandparent ushers in the neshamah yeterah without effort. But the idea of guarding the Sabbath teaches us to increase the odds that we'll find ourselves in these moments, that they will be prolonged rather than fleeting, and that we don't have to leave them entirely to chance.

HOLY DOWNTIME AT MY HOUSE

In parenting classes, I recommend using Shabbat as a model of sanctifying time. I introduce the topic by telling the story of how my family's Shabbat ritual evolved slowly, in baby steps. We started with small changes. One Friday night about twelve years ago we lit some candles, stumbled through a blessing, kissed each other, said, "Good Shabbos," and went to the local Thai restaurant for a shrimp dinner. Nothing radical. The next week, we said kiddush (blessing for the wine) over some Manischewitz Concord grape and then went back to the Thai restaurant. A month or two later, I baked a challah and we blessed it and stayed home for dinner. A year and a half later we were home every Friday night for a full Shabbat dinner. We said the blessings over everything: the candles, the children, motherhood, the sacred day.

Over the years we have revised our rules of Shabbat observance to fit the needs of our family as the children have grown and matured. When they were in early elementary school we were stricter than we are now. We used the car only to go to and from synagogue. At that time my husband and I appreciated spending the morning in synagogue away from the children, praying, singing, and socializing with friends. Only in shul could we find the time for the spiritual renewal we needed each week. We also appreciated spending the afternoon at home with the children and their grandparents with no competing agendas, no phones, no mail, no errands.

Now that the children are bigger we are looser about Shabbat, but the one thing that remains unchanged and inviolable is our leisurely Friday night dinner. It is a Jewish practice to embellish a mitzvah, or commanded action, and to make it as beautiful and pleasant as possible. This concept is called a *hiddur mitzvah* and the prototypical example is the Shabbat table. We use silver instead of the weekday utensils. We put flowers on the table. We serve wine and grape juice—an exotic with too much sugar and stain potential to be a regular weekday staple in our house. We dress up and invite a guest or two.

Everyone in the family knows that however busy we are during the week, this uninterrupted time together on Friday nights lies ahead. We don't answer the phone. We don't hurry on to the next activity. We whisper the "blessing over children" softly in their ears, a prayer with the beautiful sentiment, "May the divine light shine upon you and bring you peace."

My husband, Michael, recites the Eishet Hayil, the "Woman of Valor." This prayer begins "A good wife, who can find? She is more precious than rubies." We go around the table and share our good news, each person explaining to the rest what we are grateful for that week.

Sometimes we use family Torah discussion guides (they come as weekly faxes or e-mails by subscription) to pose ethical dilemmas to the children, such as, Do you think it's right to give mice the flu to test vaccines? Here we introduce the Jewish idea of dominion (leadership) and stewardship (responsibility) toward other species. Should a temple accept money for a new building that was given by a man who runs a company that uses child labor in other countries? What if the families in those countries wouldn't have enough to eat if the children didn't work? We discuss Jewish ideals of charity and justice. We end by singing the *birkat hamazon,* the grace after meals.

Accepting Shabbat restrictions on everyday activities offers us a deeper freedom than we would have if we didn't make the day distinct. Our Friday dinner and slow-paced Saturdays have positive reverberations for the rest of the week. Yet, as important as Sabbath is to the stability of family life and the preservation of Jewish traditions, the principles behind it are not meant to be relegated to a single day. The idea that each moment must be used wisely, that each has the potential for holiness, should extend to the other six days of the week as well. How do we start down the path of all this Shabbat-think? Of resisting our impulse to squeeze the precious essence out of time? The first step is to recognize which elements of contemporary life pose the biggest obstacles.

HURRIED PARENTS:
THERE'S NO PLACE LIKE WORK

Jackie is an architect. She told our parenting class that she was starting to come home later and later. No office romance. Just a sense of dread. After asking her lots of questions, we pieced together what in the movie business is called "the back story."

When Jackie arrived home from her office she felt like she needed a whistle, a bullhorn, and a mechanical claw to keep the line moving efficiently. She walked from room to room picking things up off the floor and shouting commands to her children. "Stop watching television! Finish your homework! Eat supper! Clear the table! Take out the garbage! Get in the bath! Stop playing with the bubbles and wash your hair! Get out of the bath! Get in bed! Hurry up and start sleeping! Wake up and wash up! Find your backpack! Go outside and wait for the carpool!"

Weekends provided no respite from this pressure. Chores not done during the week piled up. There were birthday presents to buy minutes before the parties started, Little League games to cheer at, homework projects to finish, and, for Jackie, a pervasive sense of unease that she wasn't doing enough, wasn't connecting, wasn't really close to her children.

When Jackie arrived at work the scene was altogether different. It was quiet and neat. Her grown-up buddies were there. They celebrated birthdays together, drank coffee, worked on projects that interested her. There were no tiny snippets of construction paper on the floor, and if there had been, it wouldn't have been her job to pick them up. At work she was making an important and measurable contribution. She built things. She was appreciated. She got paid. She started to come home later and later.

Arlie Russel Hochschild, author of *The Time Bind: When Work Becomes Home and Home Becomes Work*, writes about how people have started to see work as a place to relax. When two working parents spend long hours away from home, home becomes a workplace, one in which there is too much to accomplish in the few hours before bedtime. Reviewing Hochschild's book, Nicholas Lemann summarized the fallout for kids: "Children are subjected to factory style speed-ups, hurried from one place to another all day and made to squeeze all their emotional needs into the hour or less that their parents have to spare in the evening."

Like the parents who were profiled in *The Time Bind*, Jackie had never consciously acknowledged that she enjoyed work more than home. She only knew that when she was home she felt irritable, powerless, and guilty about her inability to do a better job of it all. When I told her that slowing down was hard work and that is why God had to command it, I saw the light of recognition in her eyes.

"I knew it," she said. "I should cut down to two-thirds time at work. I'm not home enough! That's the problem."

"Cutting down might be part of the solution, but your attitude and goals when you're at home are just as important as how much time you spend there," I replied. "It's a funny contradiction. If you're ambitious at home in the same way you're ambitious at work, you won't succeed. Your 'product' at work is a perfectly engineered, functional, beautiful building. The product you're after at home is to create an environment where four tired human beings can not only get the homework done and the teeth brushed but also unwind and, through sharing food and conversation, restore their connection to one another."

In order for this restoration to take place, parents have to exercise tremendous discipline, but not the kind of reach-the-goal discipline that you exercise at work. At home you will do your job best if you are, superficially at least, inefficient. Although it might ease your general sense of anxiety to load the dishwasher and return phone calls the instant you get home, control the urge. You're doing your job better if you let the dishes and phone calls wait while your daughter tells you, in one breathless download, about how her teacher's son once got lost on a camping trip and they couldn't find him for four hours.

"A really messy home is not a restorative home, and I'm not advocating living in squalor," I told Jackie. "But you and your family will all appreciate being at home a lot more if something besides cleanup detail and logistical planning take place there."

THE TOO WIRED FAMILY

Have you noticed how the forms that you have to fill out for school keep getting longer? Mother's e-mail address, beeper number, cell phone, fax machine number, and then Dad's. A nice, safe feeling. In case of emergency we can be reached by the school. But we can also be reached by employers, employees, clients, friends, and relatives. We are available all the time.

There is much that is positive and exciting about all this access. When Susanna came home from sleepaway camp and logged on, she immediately received a message from a camp friend halfway across the country. They were delighted to be in touch after being apart for twenty-four hours. I, too, have chummy e-mail relationships with people with whom I otherwise might have more formal or sporadic contact. These are the blessings. But there is a price for being so wired up: sometimes my house beeps like a hospital ICU, and the once relatively impermeable walls of my home have been made permeable. In an article titled "The Age of Interruption," author Michael Ventura observed:

> Interruption is increasingly taken for granted—both the right to interrupt others and the expectation that one will be interrupted in turn. The individual's time, already experienced as a cross between a labyrinth, a cage and a treadmill, is now vulnerable to fragmentation without warning from any direc-

tion. All of this makes for efficient communication and contact but it also allows the outside world of work into our homes at all hours.

During Shabbat, many people feel that it's legitimate to expect others to grant them a reprieve from interruptions. After awhile your friends and associates will accept that you don't answer the phone or take care of business on Friday evenings or Saturday, and they'll stop calling. You've gotten holy "permission" not to be available. But if the word of God is the only force powerful enough to overcome the cultural pressure to answer the phone, you'll still be enslaved during the rest of the week. Without self-imposed limits on intrusions you won't have a chance to be nourished or to nourish the other members of your family. You'll be too wired.

KEEPING BUSY TO WARD OFF DESPAIR

We're busy at work and wired at home, victims of the mixed blessings of the computer age and our lifestyles. Of course, we're not exactly helpless. We could turn off the fax machines and cell phones anytime; we could cut down on the overtime at work and endure a messy house for the sake of a few extra moments with our family. Why don't we? British psychologist D. W. Winnicott had a theory about that. He wrote about "the manic defense against despair," an apt description of what motivates some of our frantic activity.

Winnicott believed that when people feel existential anxiety, an easy and effective way to squelch that feeling is to keep busy. Today, powerful triggers for despair are only a click of the remote away. As I'm writing this, the news is full of predictions about drastic environmental changes due to global warming. You might react to this news by thinking about what you could do to help, or you might have a largely unconscious reaction that goes something like this: "I want to get awareness of this reality out of my mind as soon as possible. It's so scary to think of my children living on a planet that's undergoing cataclysmic changes. There's nothing one person like me can do to fix a global-sized problem, so I'll schedule everybody for a few more classes." As I said, this is an *unconscious* process. Winnicott believed that we speed up our lives unintentionally in order to escape feeling helpless in the face of overwhelming problems or inner struggles.

This may explain why the idea of a whole day of rest is terrifying to so many people. We're not afraid of losing time but of having time to reflect. Without the usual distractions and interference, we may have to confront feelings of disappointment, loneliness, frustration, panic, helplessness, and exhaustion, and our fear that we are not strong enough to make the changes we need to make.

HOMEWORK: THE TIME BANDIT

With willpower and a clear sense of mission, we can change some of the behavior that robs us of time with our families. But there is one particularly insidious force that confounds and frustrates nearly every family I meet. It's homework. Beginning in kindergarten or first grade and accelerating steadily through twelfth grade, homework consumes the evening hours, cranks up household tensions, and turns freewheeling kids into nervous grinds.

It wasn't always this way. Homework in this country is currently at its highest level ever. Researchers at the Institute for Social Research at the University of Michigan found that the amount of homework given in elementary school tripled from 1981 to 1997. In the early decades of the century, progressive educators in many school districts banned homework in primary schools in an effort to discourage rote learning. The Cold War—specifically the launch of *Sputnik* in 1957—put an end to that, as lawmakers scrambled to bolster math and science education in the United States to counter the threat of Soviet whiz kids. Students frolicked in the late '60s and early '70s as homework declined to near–World War II levels. But fears about U.S. economic competitiveness and the publication of *Nation at Risk*, the 1983 government report that focused attention on the failings of American schools, ratcheted up the pressure to get tough again. In the 1990s there were many alluring reasons for increasing the homework load yet again. Parents' sense of uncertainty about the future led them to accept a homework burden that, without these fears, might seem clearly ridiculous.

Everybody points fingers. Teachers complain that parents, already anxious about college admission, demand lots of homework. They say that if they don't assign it, parents feel cheated, as if they've visited the doctor and gone home without a prescription. Parents complain that schools are requiring homework to help prepare children for the batteries of standardized tests that will rank schools and teachers. I suspect that some parents are using homework as a low-cost, wholesome baby-sitter. Since children can't run free in the neighborhood after school, homework seems like an appealing alternative: more time doing homework means less time watching television.

But just as taking more vitamins than you need doesn't make you healthier, upping the homework load doesn't yield much that is helpful to children. The University of Michigan study showed no improvement in scores on standardized tests as an outcome of greater homework volume. More homework doesn't generate greater academic skill, it generates a greater number of children with headaches, stomachaches, bad dreams, and a bad attitude toward school. And, of course, it creates more tension at home over how and when to get it done.

Lana, the mother of a college freshman, told our parenting

class about the arduous route her son Scott had taken to one of the nation's most prestigious universities:

> Scott was an excellent high school student. He took a full load of AP classes. He was accepted at the University of California at Berkeley, but after two months he was back home and enrolled at the local community college part-time. He was totally burned out. As I look back on it, I think the problems started in middle school. He was both cloistered and stressed. He couldn't go anywhere by himself, but he had to burn the midnight oil studying. By high school he became a machine. He was incredibly productive and seemed to get so much satisfaction from his achievements that we didn't realize how much normal life he was missing.

We can't take our cues from our children. Lana said that she and her husband didn't realize how much "normal life" Scott was missing, but to Scott, life *was* normal. His parents were in a position to compare his life with other, less pressured lives, but Scott, enrolled with a classful of fellow superachievers, was not. When I hear stories like his, my heart aches for all the boys and girls who toil late into the night, burdened with workloads most adults wouldn't tolerate for a week. Parents who came of age in the '70s and '80s, when the homework load was lighter and the overall atmosphere less punishing, owe it to their children to make sure they experience at least some of the freedom that is an essential part of youth.

With academic trends shifting every decade or so, parents can't afford to base their goals for their children solely on grade point averages, test scores, and activities that will look good on a college application. The children have too much to lose. A good way to set your child's schedule and your own expectations is to rely on the trusty Jewish principles of moderation, celebration, and sanctification. Homework is fine, in moderation. Just watch to see that the work isn't crushing your child's celebration of his own youth or ruining your chance to savor the time you have with him.

TAMING HOMEWORK

In our era, parents believe they need to be involved in order to manage both the volume and the high level of creativity demanded by the New Homework. Unfortunately, hitting the books is rarely the most fruitful way for parents and children to spend time together. And while creative assignments such as creating family trees and fashioning a working volcano out of papier-mâché can be delightful, too much parental involvement raises the stakes for everyone. Your Casey's Native American diorama with its three twigs from the backyard and a brown clay papoose might look pretty pathetic next to Jackson's with its cellophane stream and teeny Christmas bulbs illuminating the water. But that may be far more painful for you than for Casey. When you jump in to do too much of the work, your child may end up with the most A's or the most dazzling project but you're not giving him a gift. Instead you may be robbing him of a sense of real pride and the chance to achieve on his own. And you can't fool teachers. They always know who did what.

How can you translate the Jewish principle of moderation into real-life homework assignments? In my view, homework should increase by ten minutes for every grade level, starting with kindergarten. So a first grader should be able to get through her homework in no more than twenty minutes, a fifth grader in no more than one hour.

It's easy for me to recommend this formula, but what should you do if the teacher assigns more homework than this recommended limit? The first step is to talk to the teacher and see how long she thinks the assignments should take the student to complete. Many children will drag a half-hour assignment out for ninety minutes, especially if the work is too hard or too boring or if she is using homework as a target for rebellion. Ask yourself some questions: How much time is my child wasting procrastinating or worrying? Does my child understand what needs to be done and does she have the skills and tools to do it? Brainstorm with the teacher to try to figure out what's causing a problem if short assignments take your child a long time.

When Susanna was in third grade, her teacher offered us a solution that worked well for the battles we were having about homework. At the time, she was going through a period of grave homework resistance. I nagged. I cajoled. I threatened to take away privileges. I wanted to give up. Her teacher, Louise Robbins, recommended a homework strategy to me. "First, let's modify her assignments by eliminating some of her vocabulary homework. Susanna doesn't need to write sentences for all the vocabulary words because she almost always gets them correct on the tests and it's probably tedious for her to write a sentence for each one. Let her choose the words she thinks she doesn't know and only write sentences for those. If her grades drop we'll reinstate the longer assignment.

"Second, tell her that she can work 'only until seven-thirty' or 'only for another half hour.' You choose the limitation. Don't ask her if she's finished. If she doesn't complete everything, let me handle it."

We found that this approach tipped the whole power struggle by putting the conflict between Susanna and the homework (and her teacher and eventual grades) instead of between Susanna and her parents. It also showed her that we valued time for a bedtime story or a full night's sleep as much as we valued getting homework done. Susanna, now in middle school, is efficient and organized about her work, but occasionally it will pile up. We use the same strategy. We warn her ahead of time,

"Lights out by ten even if you're not done with your work, so plan ahead."

If your child is as efficient as possible and the homework load is still overwhelming, you need to lobby on her behalf. Talk to the teacher. If there is no change in the homework load, move on to the principal. Sometimes school administrators are unaware of the cumulative load put on students by teachers, specialists in enrichment subjects, and coaches. If the school is entirely unsympathetic, consider switching.

And think about your goals in raising your children. These days children do seem to need to work very, very hard to get into the top universities. Consider early on that your child can have a full, rich life and contribute to the world without going to an Ivy League school. Talk with your spouse about how your values mesh with your child's innate drive, temperament, and interests.

One elementary school principal told me a story I've never forgotten. Brooke attended the same high-pressure, high-homework-demand school as her very organized, academically driven sister, Lauren. Brooke scraped along, often handing assignments in late or incomplete. When her parents decided to switch her to a less pressured school her mother said, "In the new school they do third-grade-level math in third grade and no one is ashamed of it. They're still working on addition and subtraction! Brooke is doing beautifully and she's very happy there."

Brooke came back to visit the principal three months after starting the new school. The first thing he noticed was the color in her cheeks. "She looked like a different child," he observed. My bet is that Brooke's future will be rosier too, even if she never takes any AP classes.

THE TIME-SAVERS:
EVERYDAY METHODS TO GUARD TIME

Aside from taming homework, there are changes you can make immediately to enhance the finite time you have with your children. The ideas that follow are easy to insert into your daily routine.

Find Time to Connect

What do you do when your child talks to you? Chances are, you keep doing what you were doing before she started in. This is especially true for parents of chatterbox children. But no matter how severe your child's logorrhea, *once each day*, pay attention. Even if it's just for two minutes, stop everything else you are doing, get down to her eye level, and put your hand on her shoulder. Look at her. Listen to her. If she's not used to this she may ask you why you're mad at her. Reassure her that you are just interested, just listening to what she's saying.

Before too long your children will be teenagers. They may no longer prefer your company to that of their friends. If you've got a spare moment, sit down beside your child. "Mom, why are you sitting here?" she may ask. "Everything is so hectic, I just missed being near you," you can reply. Or, instead of one final sprint through the spelling list, say, "No more homework tonight," and offer a back rub before bed. Be like Eva's mom in Chapter 6, who loved to wash her daughter's long, copper-colored hair. Find the most precious trait of each of your children and let them know how much you cherish it.

Let Them Dawdle

Often your children will have to do things more quickly than is natural for them. Try to balance this high-pressure time with time that is leisurely. One day a week, give your child three hours to put on one sock, undress and dress all the Barbies, put on the other sock halfway, listen to a CD. Every night leave time for bedtime rituals and getting enough sleep. This means starting far earlier than you may be in the mood to begin, but that's not your child's fault. He is entitled to this. Most four- or five-year-olds, especially those who have been away from parents all day long, need an hour and a half to brush teeth, get into pajamas, settle into bed, and be soothed by story or song.

Don't Do Things You Hate

A mother once asked me to help her figure out the right length of time she should spend "watching" her son play Nintendo.

"Do you like to watch him play Nintendo?"

"No, but he likes me to do it."

"But I don't," I said. "I don't like you to do it. It is bad for you and for him. What else does he want you to do?"

"Shoot hoops."

"Do you like to shoot hoops?"

"I don't mind."

"What do you like to do to relax?"

"I love to watch baseball on TV."

"Does he?"

"Oh, he loves it too."

"Well, there you go."

Work hard to find things that you and your child *both* enjoy. This way, when you stop the clock and spend some time together, you'll both want to do it again. Children used to "recite" to entertain adults. I like Gershwin songs. By the time Emma was eight, she could sing "They All Laughed" with Ella Fitzgerald's phrasing and "Nice Work If You Can Get It" with Peggy Lee's. She loved to entertain us and we loved to listen to her. Find pleasures to share with your child.

Make Sure Your Children Have a Chance to Get Bored

I once had a yoga teacher who, while we were doing the hard stretches, cautioned the class, "Don't fear the pain." As soon as she said that, I felt comforted and started breathing again. I progressed with the posture.

I thought of my yoga teacher when I listened to young Gracie. Gracie, age seven, didn't like the laid-back, slow-paced summer camp her parents sent her to. She complained to her counselor, "This camp is so boring. There's nothing to do. Once when I was six, I was bored just like this." Gracie feared the pain. Why? Because when she got bored at home her parents always helped her find a plug-in form of entertainment. Here at camp Gracie was adrift. Faced with the challenge of finding something to do, she was in a panic. She hadn't learned any boredom management skills.

Parents have a paradoxical mission. We have to work hard not to provide our children with interesting things to do. Children need a chance to build up their boredom tolerance muscle. If you adopt an "I know you'll find something to do soon" attitude and think of boredom as a positive opportunity instead of something to be gotten rid of, children have a better chance of learning how to entertain themselves.

Treat daydreaming and fooling around as valuable activities. Being messy, noisy, silly, goofy, and vegging-out are as essential to the development of your child's mind and spirit as anything else he does. Allow him the pleasure of staring out the window, of throwing a ball around without a uniform or a team or a score, of counting raindrops without turning it into a multiplication quiz. An advantage to adopting this attitude is that you won't have to work so hard. If you don't spend time doing screamingly boring things like watching someone play Nintendo, you might feel like giving someone a back rub.

Find Time to Reflect and Plan

The psalmist said, "Number our days that we may gain a heart of wisdom." Without time to think and plan and examine our lives, we become slaves instead of masters. Through thoughtful discussion, parents can teach their children to shape life policies in advance. In southern California, we don't wait until the earthquake comes to buy extra flashlights and water. Up north, people clean the gutters and downspouts before the rainy season. We are prepared for the forces of nature that we know are inevitable.

Acting spontaneously in the middle of situations that feel like a flood or earthquake may mean getting hurt. Judaism always teaches us to be prepared and has given us the mitzvot, 613 specific policies and plans for action, to govern our daily decisions. Taking time to talk together can help you clarify what you believe as a family and what behaviors follow from these beliefs. Shabbat dinner is the ideal place to have these discussions.

GUARDING TIME FOR CHILDHOOD:
LET SEVEN BE SEVEN

All of the suggestions above are aimed at getting you and your children to slow down your day-to-day activities and learn to cherish the moment more often. As parents, we must also tackle another challenge: slowing down the pace of childhood itself.

Children are very anxious to grow up quickly—to see grown-up movies, wear grown-up clothes, talk like grown-ups, watch grown-up TV. Some parents would prefer to get their children all grown up fast. I've even witnessed parents challenge their kids: "So you want to be a teenager now? Fine. Go ahead!" Why do they say it? First, because the kids want it so badly, and second, because it feels safer for children to be grown up than to be innocent. If they're tough, sassy miniadults, then they're not vulnerable little kids out in the hard world.

Our children are exposed to more of life than we were. At day care, in school, in the neighborhood, and on teams, they meet a greater variety of people than we did. They know about ethnic, racial, religious, and economic groups different from their own. Because of this exposure many are worldly and tolerant. They understand agendas. If it's Thursday they know not to get on the school bus but to wait for the carpool to take them to religious school or gymnastics. Children of divorced parents learn to keep track of their belongings in two different households. But does this mean they're more mature?

Karen Ivy has taught fourth grade for thirteen years. Here's what she says about her students: "Fourth graders now are like fourteen-year-olds. Their parents let them see R-rated movies as long as they aren't violent, but the children don't have the experience to make sense of what they are seeing. Some kids are still like Rebecca of Sunnybrook Farm, but others are growing up too fast. They get jaded because they haven't had to wait for anything." Waiting requires time. Naturally, our children don't want to wait, not when everything in our culture is urging them onward. A small case in point: television commercials aimed at seven-year-olds feature children older than seven because toy manufacturers recognize our children's passionate desire to emulate bigger kids, to be grown up.

But a seven-year-old is not nine or ten, he is seven. A seven-year-old is young and innocent and shy and mighty. A seven-year-old completely overvalues his own power and wisdom. Part of our job as parents is to enforce seven-year-oldness in seven-year-olds—to demand it and to protect it. If a seven-year-old has all the information, privileges, and responsibilities of a ten-year-old, seven will be lost to him.

MARRIAGE FIRST, THEN CHILDREN

Most of this chapter has been devoted to showing you how to enhance the time you spend with your children. There is one element, however, that is even more important to their well-being than the time you share. It's your marriage.

In the frantic race to get so much done, I see marriages neglected more than children. We're so anxious about and connected to our children that it's not unusual for a couple to tell me they haven't been out alone together in five months. They don't like to leave the children, they say. On the face of it this doesn't make a lot of sense. What couple wouldn't want to take a romantic break from child-rearing once in a while? But along with the pride and excitement of parenthood come changes that can drive couples apart and into the arms of their children.

Parenthood tests a marriage as few other circumstances will. For the first time, a couple can't simply work out their problems with each other because there's always one extra person (or more) involved. After children, disagreements crop up where there were none before—fundamental differences about priorities, money, stability, discipline, schooling, religion. It's sometimes easier to avoid newfound differences than to struggle through them. Instead of a friend, your spouse becomes a target for secret bitterness. You can feel like a martyr and soothe your loneliness in the company of the children.

Being too busy or too devoted to the kids is an excellent way of avoiding real time with your partner, during which you'd have to face and resolve your difficulties. Without time and attention, the marriage becomes an edifice riddled with termites. As your children grow older and everything gets more complicated, the first thing to give way will be your weakened marriage.

Time alone with your spouse can weatherproof your relationship, protecting it from the storms of raising a family. Getting out of the house one evening a week is a good start. Even more important, try to get away from home and kids altogether for a night or two on a regular basis. In order to reconnect emotionally with your mate, you need to be on different turf, even if it's just a resort a few miles out of town.

In a new setting, all the positive aspects of your partner have a chance to get cued—the way he engages people, the way he notices plants and flowers, the way she loves the water, her sense of humor. Alone with each other, you can remember why you elected to make this journey with this particular human being. The differences will still be there, but when you get around to discussing them, they'll be balanced by warm feelings and memories of good times you've had recently, not five months or five years ago.

Getting away together is also the best way to think clearly about your lives. Many schools and businesses sponsor a retreat for the administration at least once a year. Why do they go to Lake Arrowhead instead of just brainstorming in the conference room? Because these organizations recognize that in order to do your best thinking, you need three things: a new environment, somebody else to prepare the meals, and the opportunity to take a walk in the woods (or on the streets of San Francisco, if that's what works for you). The family is as important an enterprise as a business, and the leaders of the family need to get away too. Just as Moses and Aaron retreated to the Tent of

Meeting to escape the demands of the Children of Israel, a mother and father need to escape their children once in a while. This is incredibly beneficial for the children, because when you return, you're more of a team again. You're not so resentful, you're not such a martyr. If you can get away long enough to reflect, you might decide to rid yourselves of some of the activities that have been taking up so much of your family's time.

BEFORE IT'S TOO LATE

Guarding time is not for the lazy or weak. It takes fierce devotion and commitment to protecting time alone with your spouse, uninterrupted family time, bedtime, downtime, and time around the table on Friday night. If we can guard this time, we are doing holy work and offering the children something that no one can buy. We are offering them ourselves, and we are showing them the path to a rich and meaningful life.

One evening as we sat in the living room after Shabbat dinner, Emma went back to the table and sat quietly by the tray holding the still burning candles for fifteen or twenty minutes. "What were you doing there, Emma?" we asked her. She showed us the poem she had written.

CANDLELIGHT

Come here
come here and stay for awhile
to look at the beauty of the candles
to see the candle burn away
and to see their beauty burn away
Come here
come here to look at the light
to see its brightness

to see the happiness in the light
to see it grow and
to see it burn away
Come on before it's gone!

CHAPTER 10

The Blessings of Faith and Tradition

Losing Your Fear of the G Word and Introducing Your Child to Spirituality

One day shortly after Emma turned eight she asked me one of those Big Questions: "Who put the money under my pillow? Did you? Did Dad? Tell me."

"I don't think the tooth fairy would appreciate hearing you talk about her this way," I responded. I gave this duplicitous answer because I suspect that a child still asking this question may want reassurance more than the truth. I've seen plenty of children over ten still collecting good-sized piles of cash from the tooth fairy. To both parent and child, belief in the tooth fairy feels like a safe and gentle little fiction. It's not like questions about God. It's not fraught.

Not long after the tooth fairy question, Emma asked the Special Hug question. "*How* does the sperm get to the egg in the Special Hug?" This one was fraught, but I'd been waiting for it. I was out of the starting gate in seconds. "I'm glad you asked me that question, Emma. Sit right here and let me get some books that have the answers and we'll have a nice talk." When it comes to sex, most parents are nervous but prepared. We arm ourselves for the challenge with scientifically accurate information. We might add a plug for our own values, having figured out in advance the spin we want to put on our sexual history.

A few more months passed. Then Emma asked me the hard one. She was saying her bedtime prayers and was about to mention God when she hesitated.

"I'm not sure I can say it anymore, Mom," she confessed.

"Say what?"

"God."

"Why?"

"Because I don't know if I can believe in God anymore."

"Why is that?"

"The monkeys, Mom. Which is true, Adam and Eve or the monkeys?" I wanted to wind the clock back to the tooth fairy, but this was just the beginning. Emma was on a roll. "And miracles. Were there really any? Maybe they got across the Red Sea in some little boats. Did you ever think of that? Has there ever been a miracle? Have you ever seen one?"

I couldn't resist. She was so passionate and serious. "You, Em, are a fine example of a miracle."

"What about Susanna? Isn't she a miracle too? That's not what I mean. I mean a *real* miracle."

The particular subject matter of Emma's heartfelt question is part of my life's work, but answering her wasn't easy for me. I know I'm not alone. Many thoughtful parents avoid the topic of God because they aren't sure what they believe and don't want to teach their children something that might harm or confuse them. Yet if we want to take any part in keeping our children's curiosity alive and keeping the religion of Judaism vibrant, we have to plunge into the waters of theology and take a swim.

FEAR OF THE G WORD

"First I want to thank God."

"This wouldn't have been possible without God."

"I want to thank the Higher Power we choose to call God."

A few years ago, I heard these breezy credits being given by various singers and musicians during acceptance speeches at the televised Teen Choice pop music awards. None of the young performers hesitated to name themselves as fellow travelers, to cozy up to the G word in a relaxed and friendly fashion. Were it only so easy for the parents I meet! Alissa, the mother of two boys ages eight and two, admitted, "It took me until my second child to work up the courage to use the word *God*. I was so self-conscious. I actually began in the dark, saying the *Shema* at night with Gabriel as I tucked him in. It was another six months before I could say the G word in daylight."

Rabbi Adin Steinsaltz, the modern scholar and author of *Simple Words,* believes he knows why we have so much difficulty with the concept of God. Part of the problem, he writes, is a consequence of our need to anthropomorphize: "It is hard to have an emotional relationship with something that is entirely different, so we use anthropomorphic images to help us. . . . We depict everything in our own image . . . we elevate the low and lower the high. We do it with animals, we do it with trees, we do it with inanimate objects because that is how we can relate emotionally."

We lower God and call God "he" (or "she") not because God is like a person but because we only know how to express things in human terms. As children, we envision an old white guy with a long beard sitting on a throne up in heaven. He makes the world in six days flat, creates a gigantic flood that swallows up everything but one little floating zoo, splits the sea in the nick of time, causes manna to fall from heaven (medieval Torah commentary says that it tasted like whatever each person wanted it to), and, finally, God hands over all the laws anyone would ever need to Moses on Mount Sinai. The Bible's vivid, magical stories and good-guy-versus-bad-guy themes suit the way children's minds work beautifully, but the action hero–sorcerer version of God gets stale pretty quickly for adults. When we're struggling with existential questions about the reasons for our own and global suffering and looking for ways to understand human cruelty and pain, the vaporous bearded guy in the big chair doesn't offer answers. What happens? We start "not believing."

In most areas of life we revisit concepts with increasing depth and complexity as we grow up. First we learn about the "special hug," and throughout life we keep learning more about how to balance instinct, desire, loyalty, and mature relationships. Questions of love and sex are explored in fiction, in movies, and in hours of discussion among friends and between lovers and spouses. In early elementary school we learn that the heart pumps our blood around our body; in middle school we learn about the double circulation system, arteries, veins, and capillaries; in high school we learn about meiosis and mitosis. As we grow old we learn about angina and myocardial infarction.

How many of us have continued to mature in our understanding of God? For most of us, the learning stopped short, right after Moses got the tablets. We have never had much help getting beyond the divine-mover-and-shaker idea. Even many of the more advanced thinkers among us stopped their formal religious learning at thirteen. We lack the concepts, language, or skills we need to answer our children's questions and our own. What we are "not believing" in is a small child's concrete, anthropomorphic idea of God and a literal reading of Bible stories. The paradox is that this is not what Jewish theology teaches about God in the first place.

DO, AND YOU WILL UNDERSTAND

In Judaism, doubting God is built into the theology. The word *Yisrael* literally means "person who struggles with God." Abraham Joshua Heschel once wrote that Judaism does not ask its followers to take a leap of faith, it asks them to take a leap of action. You aren't expected to work out your theology before you begin to live a Jewish life; *na'aseh venishmah*—"we will do and we will understand."

First you do. You are welcome to take your doubts along. You light Shabbat candles and see how their glow affects your family's dinner. Before and after Grandpa's bypass surgery, or when Abigail's strep test is positive, or Uncle Jordie is sick with AIDS, you say the blessing over the sick, *refu'ah shelemah* ("may there be a complete recovery of mind, body, and spirit") and witness how having something active to do with her sadness and worry helps your child cope. You build a sukkah, use palm fronds for the roof, and eat dinner outside for a week and see how lovely it can be to spend time as a family out-of-doors after dark for six days running. The night your daughter gets her braces on and she's feeling proud but her mouth is aching, the whole family joins hands to celebrate her milestone by singing the *shehecheyanu,* the prayer for "firsts." In Judaism you are taught to "be" as a blessing. Every day, you mine the details for opportunities to elevate, to sanctify, to make order and find meaning. From your actions, you begin to learn God's wisdom and see the mark of God's touch.

A medieval proverb says, "If I knew God, I would be God." You don't need to know the "right" answers in order to talk to your child about God. You can let her know that you haven't figured it all out yet, but you want to continue the conversation all through your life together. If you accept the invitation of your children's questions, you can pick up where your own education stopped. You can join them in learning.

GOD AND SCIENCE: A CHILD'S VIEW

What I most wanted to communicate to Emma at the moment she confronted me with the conflict between science and religion was my appreciation of her question. I told her that both ideas—the monkey idea and the Adam and Eve idea—were true, but in different ways. Her question was not an "either/or" question but an "and/also" question.

"God does exist," I told her, "but God is so different from science that we can't use the same parts of our mind to understand them. If we wanted to prove to people that there was no God we could say, 'How could Noah fit all those animals in the ark? What kept the predator animals from killing the gentle herbivore animals? How come Noah and his wife didn't jump overboard to escape the smell?' It's easy to make the story sound silly. If we think literally about the story of Noah, or Moses and the burning bush, or the parting of the Red Sea, we can use science to make fun of the idea of God.

"But God and science aren't in a competition," I continued. "To teach about science we use the laws of logic and instruments like a microscope. To teach about God we use different laws, like the Ten Commandments, and we use stories instead of instruments to show how the laws work. To test and measure God we use the part of our mind that sees beauty in nature and goodness in people.

"As far as I know, the world *was* created through a process that took billions of years," I said. "And yes, humans did evolve from apes. But the story of God making the world in six days isn't about using chemical tests to date the age of rocks so we can figure out how old the world is. The story of creation is there to remind us of the laws of living: that working hard is important, that resting is important too, and that we should always try to do things carefully and in the right order. The story of the parting of the Red Sea is about how hard it is to leave and go somewhere new even if the old place was terrible. The story of the burning bush is about being ready and willing to hear the voice of God at unexpected times in unexpected places. God wants us to follow the examples in these stories, and that's why they are written in the Bible.

"We can think of the world around us as God's science laboratory," I told Emma. "Have you noticed the way that, every single time, night follows day and the seasons follow each other in perfect order, the way the ocean has waves and fish have scales and it's never, ever the other way around? Did you know that the wings of some moths have markings that look like an owl's face, so that predators will stay away from them? If you think about it, all of these things can be explained in the 'and/also' way, as parts of science *and* parts of God's amazingly great design. Science teaches us about the patterns and systems all around us. Science makes God's incredible world credible.

"Rabbi Rembaum at our synagogue says that science tells us how things work and Torah teaches us why it's important. Other people say that science gives us a map to the stars and religion gives us a map to heaven. Religion teaches us how to be good people and how to take care of the two big gifts God has given us: the gift of life and the gift of the great wide world." For that moment, Emma understood.

THINKING ABOUT GOD AS A VERB

Parents introduce their children to new adults by telling them what the person does: "That man's name is Marty and he brings us our mail." "Dr. Kaplan is going to give you some medicine to help you get rid of your sore throat." Rabbi Harold Kushner, the author of *When Bad Things Happen to Good People*, writes, "Little children don't need theology, they need to meet God." The best way to introduce your child to God is to point out what God does.

One day a few summers ago my family and I were gliding along in the swan boats on the lagoon in the Public Garden in Boston when one of our fellow passengers, a girl about seven years old, called out in delight, "Look, Mom! Jesus sure decided to put a lot of beautiful plants on the edge of the little island!" I was struck by how assured this little girl felt about the power of the divine hand. If you want your child to meet God, you'll need to show her frequently that God is close to her, too. It gets easier when you remember that unseen things can be very real. You can give examples as you notice them.

"Can you see love?" you might ask your child. "Love is something we know is real, but we can't see it. I *show* my love for you by the way I tuck you into bed at night, bandage your knee when you fall, and make you tomato rice soup when it's cold outside. To meet God we have to be like detectives and look for clues. Just as a candle hidden from view sheds its glow all around, we can see God in God's reflection: in the good things people do for one another, in the miracles of nature, in our ability to change and grow."

Children, with their natural affinity for wonder and joy and their lack of self-consciousness, can be a good guide to finding out what God does. When Susanna was five, I accompanied her to a birthday party in the park on an overcast Sunday morning. The party was to be held in old train cars, theoretically a charming setting but in reality crowded, noisy, dimly lit, and poorly ventilated. I was crabby, wishing for a cup of coffee, more of the Sunday newspaper, and the quiet and privacy of home. As we walked up the hill from the parking lot to the park entrance, Susanna tugged on my hand.

"Look!" She pointed toward the sky. "Rainbows!" There, perfectly framing the metal arch at the park entrance gate, were two complete rainbows. I had heard of double rainbows but never before seen one. The rainbows lit up a Jewish button in my mind.

"Su! It's time to say *shehecheyanu*, the prayer for special moments." (Later, I learned that there is even a specific blessing for rainbows.) We held hands and sang the prayer in Hebrew: "Blessed are you, Lord our God, ruler of the universe, who has granted us life and sustained us and brought us to this moment." Together we thanked God for his beautiful paintbrush. I wasn't crabby anymore.

OK, GOD EXISTS, BUT WHO WROTE THE BIBLE AND WHAT DOES IT HAVE TO DO WITH ME?

"Those Jewish prayers were written by important people," Emma commented to her father one Saturday.

"What difference does it make that the people were important?" he asked.

"If they weren't important people, then the prayers wouldn't really be prayers, they would be little poems."

Emma's observation coincides with what most Jews believe about the origin of the Torah. Morrison David Bial, in his book *Your Jewish Child*, writes, "These people [who wrote the Bible] wanted to record their history and to create a society guided by laws and ethics. It is easy to see that they were inspired by God, because the things that they wrote thousands of years ago are still important today." Others, like Abraham Joshua Heschel, said that God himself revealed the divine word at Sinai but that these revelations were transcribed by human beings. Whether you answer your child's questions by telling him that these stories and characters are real or legendary and mythic, the most important point to communicate is that the Bible is a very special book, one that belongs on its own shelf. Fairy tales, Brer Rabbit stories, and Greek myths are treasures of a different sort. The Bible is a holy text, one that is read more often and by more people than any other book that has ever been published.

The Hebrew Bible is divided into fifty-four weekly portions that are read in order each year. Other readings are added at the holidays. At every spot on the planet where Jews worship together, the same stories are read on the same day, both in

Hebrew and in the native language of the local people. The text knits our scattered people together. Every year of your life, as you encounter the same characters and walk through the same dramas—the Golden Calf, the story of the twelve insecure spies, Naomi and her loyal daughter-in-law Ruth, the evil Haman and brave Queen Esther—you get a chance to understand them in a more mature way. You also get a chance to apply their teachings to the changing problems you face.

Showing children how the Bible relates to their lives gets easier the better you know the stories. Danielle's fifth-grade teacher at her Jewish day school asked Danielle to lead tours for prospective students and their parents. At the dinner table Danielle told her family the news and reported that she had turned down the offer. Her father gently drew her out about her reasons. Now that she had her braces, Danielle didn't like to smile at new people, and she believed that a tour guide should smile throughout the whole tour. She was also afraid that the visitors would ask her questions about the school and she might give them wrong answers. Talking further, her father learned that his conscientious daughter also believed that she would be responsible not only for encouraging students to apply to the school but for how well they did once they were enrolled!

Danielle's amiable and Torah-knowledgeable father, Dov, told her that by not wanting to be a tour guide she was following in a long Jewish tradition:

Moses didn't exactly feel up to the jobs he was given either. When God spoke to him from the burning bush and told him to go to Pharaoh and free the Israelites from slavery, Moses tried every tactic he could think of to get out of the job. First he said, "Who am I to pull off such a huge coup—getting Pharaoh to agree to a plan that won't benefit him in any obvious way?" When this didn't work, Moses tried another tactic: "OK—who should I say sent me? If I say 'the God of your fathers' sent me, they'll say, 'Yeah? So what's his name?'" God was reassuring and supportive but didn't accept Moses' reservations. Finally, Moses talked about his own personal weaknesses. "I'm no good at speaking in public. I stutter and can't think well on my feet." This was no problem for God, who suggested that Moses' brother Aaron, so articulate that he was a virtual talk show host, could help him.

So, Dani, you're a good Jew, you're following in a long tradition.

Ultimately, Danielle and her Dad came up with some terms. Danielle would agree to try being a tour guide with the teacher's understanding that if she was miserable she wouldn't have to continue. She would ask last year's tour guides about the hardest questions they had had to answer and she would ask her teacher if she could bring along another student to help her if the groups were larger than eight people. Danielle led tours all year. She continued to feel a bit uneasy and shy about her braces, but she was glad that she had overcome her stage fright enough to take a chance at doing something she had been terrified to try.

GOD'S LAWS OF HUMAN KINDNESS

Children can also see God at work through the structure of Jewish law. When my husband injured himself in a skiing accident three years ago, Cis, the head of the temple mitzvah committee, called to ask what the committee members could do to help us. Drive the children to school? Bring dinners? I told her we were fine, that we appreciated the call but didn't need any help. She insisted. I remembered that this was the mitzvah of *bikkur holim*, visiting and helping the sick.

The word *mitzvah* does not mean "good deed" but actually

means commandment. In Judaism giving to the poor or needy or caring for the sick is not charity, it is justice. By helping others, you set the world straight when it has tipped against an individual or group. Cis's offer was different from one of friendship, courtesy, or social service. She was asking us to give her an opportunity to fulfill a holy obligation mandated by God. What right did we have to refuse?

I ended the conversation by agreeing to call Cis back as soon as I figured out how the committee could help us. Soon I had to go away on a business trip. Michael was still in pain and walking with crutches, so he couldn't take responsibility for the children's dinners over the weekend. I called Cis, and the committee set to work. Every night that I was gone, someone arrived with a homemade meal. The children told me about these dinners. Persian rice with lima beans and dill. Homemade brownies. Tiny, fluffy turkey meatballs. They told me about the women who brought the dinners: one a neighbor, one a friend, and one a temple member whom none of us knew. I was honored to be part of this specific extended family and grateful to be part of a community that counts bringing food to a temporarily disabled family as a holy obligation. I was glad that my children got a chance to meet God through the meatballs and lima beans and the members of the mitzvah committee.

If you don't belong to an organized community, you can still say the prayers, do the rituals, and teach your child about God's laws of human kindness. Eventually, however, you might begin to feel that your own private spiritual path is lacking in some of the richness that organized religion has to offer. What if you don't remember the prayers, songs, and traditions from long-ago family get-togethers or the Hebrew classes you took when you were ten? There is a place you can go to learn what you never knew or have long forgotten. It's the place that, until recently, many of us have avoided like the plague. It's synagogue.

IT'S NOT GOD I HAVE A PROBLEM WITH, IT'S HIS PEOPLE: RESISTANCE TO ORGANIZED JUDAISM

Instead of welcoming organized religion as a bridge to spirituality, many parents I meet shy away from it. The reasons they give? It's too rigid, hypocritical, unfamiliar. It's too patriarchal. For some, it's too Jewish. One woman recalled the moment she first consciously recoiled from her religion:

> When I was a teenager my mother took me to see *Fiddler on the Roof* and whispered proudly in my ear, "These are your people!" I cringed. I had always liked the intelligence and sense of humor of the Jews I knew, but I held myself apart from so many other qualities I perceived: clannishness, arrogance, loudness, and lack of refinement. *No, Mom,* I thought to myself, *these are not my people.*

A great many Jews share this woman's reluctance to embrace her roots. Some had unhappy parents who were psychologically scarred by the Holocaust, the Depression, or their experiences as immigrants. These adults view Judaism as a religion of victimhood, the realm of the permanent outsider. Others had parents who, involved in the Socialist and labor movements of the 1930s to 1950s, were determined to downplay their religion. Nina, a mother in one of my classes, recalled:

> I never went to Hebrew school. I had a few years of Sholom Aleichem Kindershul, which gave me a love of folk dancing, Mottel stories, and the ability to sing the Vilna Partisan's song in Yiddish. But the word *God* was forbidden at Kindershul; my grandpa was a labor organizer, and my dad is a former Communist.

For these reasons and a host of others, hundreds of thousands of baby boomers drifted away from Judaism. They might never have looked back if they hadn't had children. These parents arrive at my classes full of ambivalence yet feeling that they owe their sons and daughters more in the way of spirituality than a menorah and a yearly seder. By a wide majority, the people in these classes are mothers. They're able to voice their hopes and misgivings clearly, but I've noticed that when they talk about their husbands, a more complete picture of the family emerges. Here is what some of these women have told me about trying to bring their husbands back to the Jewish fold:

Walter saw his family's suburban temple scene of the late 1950s and '60s as shallow, primarily social, and not at all spiritual. It ruined Judaism for him. Now he stays at the office late on Friday evenings even though he knows how much I would like to have a Shabbat dinner with the children.

My husband, Neil, was raised in a Conservative family. They parked around the corner and walked to shul; they were kosher at home where it was convenient but ate shrimp with lobster sauce at the Shanghai Lucky Palace every Sunday night. He saw this kind of Judaism as hypocritical, and it left him bitter. He'll give in and go to High Holy Day services, but only because I beg him to.

When I first met my husband, Howard, he told me he had been raised in an Orthodox home and described how he hated it. He and his brother used to go into the attic on Saturdays and flip the lights on and off to rebel and express their resentment over all the restrictions. Howard felt that Judaism was oppressive, that it was rammed down his throat. He associates it with narrow-mindedness and a ghetto mentality. He can't imagine depriving our kids of Friday night sleepovers for the sake of a Shabbat dinner or voluntarily going to synagogue to pray.

Because my husband never went to Sunday school, he doesn't have any religious skills. Larry is rarely in situations where he's a clumsy beginner, and I think he feels self-conscious about what he doesn't know, which is everything—prayers in Hebrew, the format of the synagogue service, even the songs. The children are better at the routine than he is. It's awkward for him at services. He stands in the back and shuffles his feet. He can't wait to go home.

Blythe, who converted to Judaism when she married Nathan, had this to say:

My husband is against my taking Judaism seriously and trying to make a Jewish home for our children. He sees going to synagogue as another obligation, another place to drive to in our overly busy lives. He complains, "I married a beautiful shiksa and you're turning into my grandmother."

Although the examples above are about men, I've seen mothers struggling with every issue I've just described. Women often have another objection to traditional Judaism: its patriarchal nature. Even in liberal, egalitarian Jewish circles, women sometimes have areas that chafe. An artist named Jody told the class:

It's hard for me to read prayers other people have written because they don't express what I'm feeling in an authentic way. I find myself drawn more to the practice of meditation and studying the teachings of the Dalai Lama than to Judaism. And Marija Gimbutas and her goddess theology seem a lot more creative and empowering to me than the patriarchal religion I happen to have inherited. I've really derived so much more benefit from reading, meditating, and listening to lectures and tapes about Eastern philosophy than from sitting in stilted services and reading from an uninspiring prayer book.

With baggage like this, it's not surprising that so many parents want to tiptoe around organized religion. Not only are they ambivalent themselves, they rarely agree with each other about how their children should be taught. Every marriage, even those between two Jews, is a mixed marriage. Each partner inevitably has his or her own, often quite righteous, view about religious faith and practice, about what is proper to say to the children about God, and about whether the children should be allowed to go, forced to go, or barred from going to Sunday school. Each believes that anyone to their right is a zealot and anyone to their left is a philistine.

Marriage between two Jews often yields two unequal, negative attitudes about Judaism. When a Jew marries someone of another faith, both partners may find themselves drawn back to the religious traditions of their childhoods, yet a surprising number of these mixed marriages yields a different kind of dilemma: the born Jew drags his or her feet while the other spouse is enthusiastic about becoming more involved in Judaism. Rather than try to resolve their differences and forge a shared set of convictions, some parents give up and opt instead to buy spiritual life insurance for their children. They try to pass the torch of the tradition directly to their sons and daughters without feeling the heat of the flame themselves.

THE FALSE SOLUTION OF PEDIATRIC RELIGION

Amy was frustrated because she had to nag her son Jason daily to study his *haftarah* chanting in preparation for his bar mitzvah. I'd known her for several years, so I felt that I could push her. "Why should he study it?" I asked.

"Because I'm not just throwing him a big thirteenth-birthday party with tons of presents. This is a religious occasion. It's about becoming a Jewish adult."

"A Jewish adult like you?"

"No, precisely *not* like me. That's the point. My parents didn't offer me this; I had no religious upbringing. Temple Emanuel is great. The program at the religious school is creative and interesting, and I know Jason likes it. He has no right to complain."

"What do you do while he's at religious school?"

"I swim at the pool in the Jewish community center across the street."

"And this makes you a member of the Jewish community?"

She got my point.

Jonathan Omer-Man, a Los Angeles rabbi and educator, calls Amy's approach "pediatric religion." Others have called it "carpool religion" (children get shuttled to Sunday school while parents stay home) or "dry-cleaning religion" (you send them to the experts to be spiritually cleaned and pressed). It's more painless and requires less effort than joining in yourself, but it rarely sticks. Religious school alone won't accomplish the two things you may most hope to give your children: a lifelong commitment to ethical and spiritual teachings and a legacy that they can pass on to your grandchildren.

Children can learn to play tennis whether or not you play. They can even become champions. They can learn desktop publishing and how to do refined Web searches, but learning values and developing a sense of the holy must start at home. The Hebrew word for parents, *horim*, shares a root with the word *morim*, teacher. You are your child's first teacher. If you turn the religious and spiritual education of your child over to professionals, he may lose what he needs most—your touch, your life experience, and your angle on the issues. By carting a child off to religious school when there is no whiff of religion at home—no Shabbat candles, no prayer, no discussion, no rituals—parents send the message that religion is good for children but irrelevant for adults; that it is something to be outgrown, like cartoons.

This is not a new problem. The great, uncompromising Hasidic leader Rabbi Menahem Mendel of Kotsk said, "If you truly wish your child to study Torah, study it yourself in their presence. They will follow your example. Otherwise they will not themselves study Torah, but will simply instruct their children to do so."

I believe that these words are true. Yet, despite the fact that bringing Judaism into my life has yielded astonishing blessings, I have not achieved unambivalent enthusiasm for organized religion. I still carry baggage. It bears the labels "Dislikes being part of a group," "Squirms when sincerity verges near the corny," and "Finds getting through the day hard enough without extra restrictions or obligations." Sometimes the goodness of the congregants at my synagogue makes me feel venal, cynical, and selfish by comparison. Sometimes the idea of ritual and religious obligations annoys or exhausts me. But I continue to study, hold a Shabbat dinner every Friday night, say the prayers, and perform the rituals. Susanna has already had her bat mitzvah, and in a few years Emma will follow suit. My husband and I don't want our daughters to use this rite of passage as a door *out* of Judaism, so I keep up with the traditions, making sure they evolve as my children get older.

The traditions continue to bring benefit to us purely on an adult level as well. The people we've met because of our involvement with Judaism have broadened our social world and challenged us intellectually and spiritually. The respite and warmth of our leisurely Friday night dinners, the roundtable of gratitude even when we are feeling demoralized, our shared lexicon of Jewish ideas and biblical personalities all add to our adult relationship as well as guiding us as parents.

"GOOD ENOUGH" RELIGION

There are many appealing spiritual pathways for adults. Eastern religious and meditative practices provide relief from a pressured, materialistic world; feminist spirituality is personally empowering and validating; Talmud and Kabbalah (which we are not supposed to even begin to study until we are forty years old) are intellectually provocative and exciting. But what's good for adults is not necessarily good for children. In Chapter 7, I mentioned "muesli-belt malnutrition," the low-fat, high-fiber diet that is healthy for middle-aged adults but fills up young children before they get the protein they need to grow. It's the same with religion. Abstract concepts and hours of meditation don't work for them. Children need to visualize God; they need stories and heroes and simple ethical guidelines.

The medium is the message. Emotions are evoked and memories etched not with brilliantly argued points of theology but through the senses. This is why religious rituals are designed explicitly to appeal to our senses: the beauty of candle flames; the fragrance, color, texture, and taste of challah; the lovely sight and smell of the *bessamim,* sweet spices held in a delicate, silver filagree box or tiny, carved wooden tower that you wave under your nose at the conclusion of Shabbat; the sound of ritual prayers and songs. Children's delight in the world of the senses is always waiting to bubble out, so religious rituals have a natural and easy appeal for them.

By definition, *organized* means standardized, systematic, and planned. Organized doesn't mean spontaneous and creative. A synagogue is not a one-stop shopping center for all your spiritual needs, but the payoff of the organized part of Judaism is the built-in structure for service to others, for shared grief and sorrow, for singing, praying, studying old books, and gaining time-tested wisdom. The best Jewish communities provide just the kind of high-protein, colorful, meaty religion that children need to see, touch, eat, smell, and sing about.

I tell the parents in my classes that instead of sizing up the sermon, the rabbi, or the service, they may benefit more from sizing up what Jews call *kavanah*, a Hebrew term that means spiritual focus. You measure your kavanah not by asking, "How was the sermon?" or "What do I really think of this rabbi?" but by asking yourself, "How well was I able to take something of value from what was said? Did I *dan l'chaf zecuth*, judge on the side of merit, give the benefit of the doubt, to the congregants? Was I generous or stingy in my judgments?" Like D. W. Winnicott's good enough mother, ask yourself, "Is this place, are these people, is this sermon good enough?" Save your hyperdiscriminating self for the new Korean restaurant or the latest movie.

Rabbi Mordecai Finley, who heads congregation Ohr HaTorah in Los Angeles, tells his congregants that he loves to listen to his wife, Meirav, play Mozart on the piano. He doesn't resent Mozart because Mozart composed the music and he didn't. He just enjoys the beauty. He knows how hard it is to learn how to read music and to play an instrument; he realizes that it takes more patience and perseverance than talent, that you have to practice for a long time before it sounds any good. Rabbi Finley makes an analogy to liturgy that speaks directly to Jody, the artist who said that the prayers didn't express her feelings, and to Larry, who felt like a beginner. "The prayers are the tradition and the instrument is your heart," he instructs. You can't drop in and expect to be showered with holy feeling, but if you work hard at it for a while, you'll be rewarded by hearing the music.

L'DOR VA DOR —
FROM GENERATION TO GENERATION

In Volume 15 of the *Encyclopedia Judaica* there is an entry describing the life and works of Rabbi Joseph Ha-Levi Soloveichik, the head of an important Lithuanian rabbinic dynasty. Eight generations back on my mother's side we were Soloveichiks. My mother was raised in America with no religion. By the time she was twenty-one she had declared herself an atheist. My father's father held closely to the Judaism he had brought with him from nineteenth-century Poland. He was a founding member of his Orthodox shul in Brighton Beach. On his deathbed he warned my father, "This religion will die with me." For a long time it looked like my grandfather's prophecy would come true. He knew how hard it would be for the generation that followed his to carry on.

Like so many educated, serious Jewish adults, I was close to strolling right past a tradition of great psychological, spiritual, and intellectual riches without even knowing it existed. I am still surprised to find myself a bearer of Jewish tradition in my family. In 1999 I was Scholar-in-Residence at Leo Baeck Temple, the same place where I attended my first family service ten years earlier, a complete outsider, calling my mission "cultural anthropology" instead of religion. Now I am a psychologist who has left the practice of psychotherapy to do preventive mental health work: to teach, to guide families back to their faith, to help parents look at their children's anxieties and desires using a different lens.

In my practice I saw so many loving, sensitive, smart parents looking in the wrong places to remedy their families' distress. Stuck in the short view of parenting, they measured their children's mettle by sizing up their mood, their grades, or their social standing. When we take a longer view, we measure differently. We look at children's capacity for reverence, for gratitude, and for compassion. If they fall short, we step back to figure out why. We recognize that these qualities don't kick in by default among the math tutor, the birthday party, and the soccer game. Building strength and self-reliance in our children requires an investment of our time and thought, it requires planning and discipline, it requires a long view both backward to our heritage and forward to the future.

For me Judaism provides a legacy of teaching and ritual that has proven to be both profound and practical. You and your family may choose a different path than that of your forebears, but if you don't want to get caught up in the anxiety, materialism, and competition all around us, you must choose some path to walk on with your children. You must name it, follow it, and plan the curriculum for their spiritual education as thoughtfully and intelligently as you plan their academic education.

Because of the time it takes for starlight to travel to earth, some of the stars we see glowing in the sky have burned out long ago. It's the same with parenting. The children we touch pass the light we kindled in them on to their children, and it goes on glittering. When Emma was in third grade, Michael overheard her friend Mara challenge her, saying, "There is no God, you know."

"Yes there is," replied Emma.

"Then how could he let so many of *your* people die in the Holocaust?" (An interesting pronoun since Mara is also Jewish.)

"God didn't do that, bad people did. And God can't do everything. It's impossible. But he did one thing. He gave you and me the gift of life, and it's our job to use it and make the world better than we found it. The people who killed people didn't use their gift the right way."

Like all children, Emma turns out to be a natural theologian. At nine, she understands important things about life. And because of her confidence, there's a chance that she'll pass these lessons along to her children.

Notes

EPIGRAPH

"Better a broken bone" . . . Lady Allen of Hurtwood was a leader of the post–World War II adventure playground movement in Europe. Quoted in Janny Scott, "When Child's Play Is Too Simple," *The New York Times*, July 5, 2000.

CHAPTER 1

35 "A rabbi told his congregation" . . . Quoted in Joseph Telushkin, *Jewish Wisdom* (New York: William Morrow, 1994).

37 "It is not your responsibility" . . . The Ethics of the Fathers 2:21. The Ethics of the Fathers (Pirke Avot) is easy to find. It is inserted in the text of Jewish prayer books, for example, *Ha-Siddur Ha-Shalem: Daily Prayer Book* (New York: Hebrew Publishing Company, 1997), and is also published separately in various editions.

CHAPTER 2

43 unfairly "generic" demands . . . Michael Thompson, Ph.D., lecture presented at Curtis School, Los Angeles, November 17, 1998.

52 landmark study of temperament . . . Stella Chess and Alexander Thomas, *Temperament and Development* (New York: Bruner/Mazel, 1977).

54 "good enough mothering" . . . Donald Winnicott, *Babies and Their Mothers* (Reading, Mass.: Addison-Wesley, 1987).

58 "I have never met a boy" . . . Quoted in Roald Dahl, *Boy: Tales of Childhood* (New York: Viking, 1988).

CHAPTER 3

63 "When a person honors the parents" . . . . Talmud, Kiddushin 30b.

63 "Better that my people" . . . Jerusalem Talmud, Hagigah 1:7.

63 the burgher Schmuel . . . There are many versions of this story. Mine is adapted from Penninah Schram, *Stories One Generation Tells Another* (Northvale, N.J.: Jason Aronson, 1987).

66 cruel, crazy, or criminal . . . Moses Maimonides, *Mishneh Torah: Maimonides Code of Law and Ethics,* abridged and translated from the Hebrew by Philip Birnbaum (New York: Hebrew Publishing Company, 1974).

70 "Train a child in the way that he should go" . . . Proverbs 22:6.

72 best to treat the Fifth Commandment as a chok . . . Rabbi Noach Orlowek, *My Child, My Disciple* (Jerusalem: Feldheim, 1993).

73 a set of basic standards . . . Laws concerning the honor of parents can be found in Vol. IV, Chapter 143, in Rabbi Solomon Ganzfried, *Kitzer Shulhan Aruch: Code of Jewish Law* (New York: Hebrew Publishing Company, 1993), 19. The Shulhan Aruch (set table) is the standard legal code of Judaism. It was first compiled by the great Sephardic rabbi Joseph Caro in the sixteenth century.

80 "Where are you?" . . . Genesis 3:9.

80 prohibition against startling another person . . . Rabbi S. Wagshal, *Guide to Derech Eretz* (Southfield, Mich.: Targum Press, 1993).

83 Anthony Wolf, *Why Did You Have to Get a Divorce? And When Can I Get a Hamster?* (New York: Noonday Press, 1998).

84 if the Jewish people demonstrate the virtue of derech eretz . . . Tanna Devei Eliyahu (Rava 11) in Rabbi S. Wagshal, *Guide to Derech Eretz* (Southfield, Mich.: Targum Press, 1993).

86 (hospitality to guests) . . . Biblical and talmudic laws of hospitality are summarized in Chapter 2, "Welcoming Others with a Pleasant Countenance," in Rabbi S. Wagshal, *Guide to Derech Eretz* (Southfield, Mich.: Targum Press, 1993).

87 "You shall not go up and down as a talebearer" . . . Leviticus 19:16.

87 God . . . punish Moses' sister, Miriam . . . Numbers 12:1–11.

CHAPTER 4

90 "A father is obligated to teach his son how to swim." Talmud Bavli, Kiddushin 29a (Brooklyn, New York: Artscroll Mesorah Publications, 1977).

95 the goal of psychoanalysis . . . Sigmund Freud, *Studies on Hysteria,*

Vol. 2, in the *Standard Edition of the Complete Psychological Writings of Sigmund Freud*, translated into English by James Strachey (New York: W. W. Norton, 2000).

96 the "wave pattern" of emotions . . . Miriam Adahan. *Raising Children to Care* (Jerusalem: Feldheim Publishers, 1988).

98 Josepha Sherman, *A Sampler of Jewish American Folklore* (Little Rock: August House Publishers, 1992).

100 a scouting party of twelve spies . . . Numbers 13:27–33.

101 One of the oldest urban myths . . . Joel Best and Gerald Horiuchi, "The Blade in the Apple," *Social Problems* 32 (June 1985): 488–99.

103 Barry Glassner, *The Culture of Fear: Why Americans Are Afraid of the Wrong Things* (New York: Basic Books, 1999).

104 Jane M. Healy, *Failure to Connect: How Computers Affect Our Children's Minds for Better or Worse* (New York: Touchstone, 1999).

105 "It can knit the world together." I heard this statement made by Rabbi Schneerson in a taped lecture. His general teachings are available in Simon Jacobson, *Towards a Meaningful Life: The Wisdom of the Rebbe, Menachem Mendel Schneerson* (New York: William Morrow, 1995).

108 a Buddist preschool in Kyoto . . . Joseph Tobin, David Wu, and Dana Davidson, *Pre-school in Three Cultures: Japan, China and the United States* (New Haven: Yale University Press, 1989).

110 ministering angels . . . Jacob Neusner, *Genesis Rabbah* (Providence, R.I.: Brown Judaic Studies, 1985), 8:5.

110 "Let kids make cheap mistakes." Barbara Colorosa, Videotape: *Winning at Parenting . . . Without Beating Your Kids* (Littleton, Colorado: Kids Are Worth It, 1989).

113 not to put a stumbling block before the blind . . . Leviticus 19:14.

CHAPTER 5

116 endowed at birth . . . Talmud, Sanhedrin 91b.

117 The men of the Great Synagogue . . . Talmud, Baba Yoma 69b.

120 "Logic is like a sword" . . . Samuel Butler, *The Notebooks of Samuel Butler, 1874–1883* (out of print).

124 "have plenty of everything" . . . Deuteronomy 28:7.

CHAPTER 6

133 "Mrs. Corry" . . . P. L. Travers, *Mary Poppins* (San Diego: Harcourt Brace, 1981. Originally published 1943).

134 "Anyone whose wisdom exceeds" . . . Eleazar ben Azariah, *Pirke Avot*, 3.22.

134 "Whoever occupies himself with Torah only" . . . Talmud Bavli, Avodah Zarah 17b.

134 "the Baal Shem Tov traveled" . . . Yitzhak Buxbaum, *Jewish Spiritual Practices* (Northvale, N.J.: Jason Aronson Inc., 1990).

141 "Humans are the only creatures" . . . Donald Akutagawa, Ph.D., and Terry Whitman, Ph.D., *Parenting Insights Magazine* (No. 14, 1996).

146 slavery as responsibility without authority . . . Wilfred R. Bion, "Experiences in groups," *Human Relations*, vols. I–IV, 1948–51. Reprinted in *Experiences in Groups* (London: Tavistock, 1961).

147 To entice them . . . Moses Maimonides, *Mishneh Torah: Maimonides Code of Law and Ethics*, abridged and translated from the Hebrew by Philip Birnbaum (New York: Hebrew Publishing Company, 1974).

CHAPTER 7

159 "the Jewish mother betrays" . . . Jenna Weissman Joselit, *The Wonders of America: Reinventing Jewish Culture: 1880–1950* (New York: Hill and Wang, 1994).

163 "muesli-belt malnutrition" . . . Sheila Kitzinger and Celia Kitzinger, *Tough Questions: Talking Straight with your Kids About the Real World* (Boston: Harvard Common Press, 1991).

164 "food lust" . . . Yitzhak Buxbaum, *Jewish Spiritual Practices* (Northvale, N.J.: Jason Aronson, 1990).

171 "Grief can take care" . . . Mark Twain, *Following the Equator: A Journey around the World*, Vol. 2 (New York: Harper and Brothers, 1988).

171 "Everybody wants to save time" . . . Bobby Calder, "Snacking Today: Anytime and Anyplace," *The New York Times*, July 30, 1999.

172 a person who eats in public . . . Talmud, Kiddushin 40b (Brooklyn, N.Y.: Artscroll Mesorah Publications, 1977).

172 eat slowly and chew the food well . . . Talmud, Berakhot 54b (see reference above) and *Kitzer Shulhan Aruch* 32:17 and 32:4. Rabbi Solomon Ganzfried, *Kitzer Shulhan Aruch: Code of Jewish Law* (New York: Hebrew Publishing Company, 1993).

177 "which we find revolting" . . . (*Kitzer Shulhan Aruch* 33:9).

182 "The dietary laws" . . . Jacob Neusner, *Genesis Rabbah*, 44 (Providence: Brown Judaic Studies, 1985).

CHAPTER 8

186 "What is the normal child like?" D. W. Winnicott, "Aspects of Juvenile Delinquency," *The Child, the Family and the Outside World* (London: Penguin, reprinted 1965).

188 Louise Bates Ames and Carol Chase Haber, *Your Seven-Year-Old: Life in a Minor Key*. Gesell Institute of Child Development Series (New York: Dell, 1995).

189 "just for you" . . . Philip Larkin, "This Be the Verse," *Collected Poems* (New York: Farrar, Straus & Giroux, 1988).

196 cheap, chipped plates . . . Talmud, Baba Yoma 78b.

201 "capable of accepting reproof" . . . Babylonian Talmud, Arakhin 16b.

202 Moses Maimonides, *Mishneh Torah: Maimonides Code of Law and Ethics,* abridged and translated from the Hebrew by Philip Birnbaum (New York: Hebrew Publishing Company, 1974).

202 "rebbe gelt" and "One-Minute Rebuke" These two concepts are described by author and psychologist Miriam Adahan in her excellent Jewish parenting book, *Raising Children to Care* (Jerusalem: Feldheim, 1988). Her formulation of the One-Minute Rebuke is adapted from the original concept of parenting-book author Spencer Johnson.

205 father threatened to box his ears . . . Babylonian Talmud, Semakhot 2:5–6.

208 one-third love . . . Miriam Adahan, *Raising Children to Care* (Jerusalem: Feldheim, 1988).

208 "be it ever your way" . . . Talmud, Sotah 47.

CHAPTER 9

211 "More than Israel" . . . Ahad Ha'am, early Zionist leader, quoted in Joseph Telushkin, *Jewish Wisdom* (New York: William Morrow, 1994).

213 "cathedral in time" . . . Abraham Joshua Heschel, *The Sabbath* (New York: Noonday Press, 1991).

213 Ron Wolfson, *The Art of Jewish Living: The Shabbat Seder* (Woodstock, Vt.: Jewish Lights, 1996).

213 Marc Sirinsky, *Ecology and the Jewish Spirit: Where Nature and the Sacred Meet,* Ellen Bernstein, editor (Woodstock, Vt.: Jewish Lights, 1998).

214 "the Sabbath-soul" . . . Zohar 2:204. The Zohar is the central text of Kabbalah. An excellent edition is by Daniel Matt, *Zohar: The Book of Enlightenment,* Classics of Western Spirituality series (New York: Paulist Press, 1988).

217 Arlie Russel Hochschild, *The Time Bind: When Work Becomes Home and Home Becomes Work* (New York: Henry Holt and Company, 1997).

218 "factory style speed-ups" . . . Nicholas Lemann, "Honey, I'm Not Home," *The New York Times Book Review* (May 11, 1999).

219 Michael Ventura, "The Age of Interruption," *The Family Therapy Networker,* January–February 1995.

220 "manic defense against despair" . . . D. W. Winnicott, paper read before the British Psycho-Analytical Society in 1935, in *Collected Papers* (London: Tavistock, 1958).

221 homework . . . tripled from 1981 . . . Michael Winerip, "Homework Bound," *The New York Times Magazine* (January 3, 1999).

230 "Number our days" . . . Psalms 90:12.

CHAPTER 10

239 Adin Steinsaltz, *Simple Words* (New York: Simon & Schuster, 1999).

240 a leap of action . . . Abraham Joshua Heschel, quoted in David J. Wolpe, *Teaching Your Children About God* (New York: Henry Holt, 1993).

241 "we will do and we will understand" . . . Exodus 24:7.

243 Harold Kushner, *When Bad Things Happen to Good People* (New York: Schocken Books, 1989).

243 For a full discussion of the concept of God-in-Action, see Chapter 3, "Children Ask About God," in Harold Kushner, *When Children Ask About God* (New York: Schocken Books, 1971).

245 David Bial Morrison, *Your Jewish Child* (New York: UAHC Press, 1998).

Recommended Reading

This is a highly selective list of helpful books for parents. I've left off the big names and popular classics—David Elkind's *The Hurried Child*, Mary Pipher's *Reviving Ophelia*, Rabbi Harold Kushner's *When Bad Things Happen to Good People*—and included lesser-known books that are both practical and inspiring.

*   *   *

My children are already asking questions about Judaism that I'm not sure how to answer. What books can help me out?

Edwards, Anne. *A Child's Bible* (New York: Pan Books, 1973).

> When I first began my Jewish studies I was so unfamiliar with the Bible stories that I needed the colorful illustrations and simplified story lines of a children's Bible to help me keep track of the dense, confusing lists of characters and settings. Unlike many greatest-hits-only Bibles for children, this small-sized 370-page paperback contains almost all of the stories. It is inviting and practical for both unschooled adults and curious children.

Plaut, Rabbi W. Gunther. *The Torah, A Modern Commentary* (New York: Union of American Hebrew Congregations, 1981).

> Every home needs an annotated copy of the adult Bible. After my introduction through the children's Bible, I graduated to the book commonly known as "Plaut." Although this volume is laid out in a way that is awkward to navigate, it's worth a bit of extra effort. The explanations and essays are wide-ranging—from Rashi (the greatest medieval Jewish commentator on the Torah) and the Talmud to Shakespeare, the Koran, Hasidic tales, Edna St. Vincent Millay, Thomas Mann, and Arthur Koestler. Plaut's is the edition of the

Torah used by the Reform movement, and it provides a wonderful foundation.

Strassfeld, Michael. *The Jewish Holidays* (New York: Harper and Row, 1985).

This is my favorite book on holiday rituals. The author describes the history and traditions of each holiday, the mystical meaning behind the practices, and the flow of the spiritual calendar: "In Sukkot there is a transformation from the stern judge of Yom Kippur to the sheltering mother of Sukkot. . . . Sukkot is a reminder not to become entombed in our homes, a reminder of a different kind of shelter made of openness and faith." The book is also practical. For example, the author provides a shopping list of the materials you'll need to build a sukkah in your backyard and instructions for making your own shofar out of a ram's horn.

Telushkin, Joseph. *Jewish Literacy* (New York: William Morrow, 1991) and *Jewish Wisdom* (New York: William Morrow, 1994).

Put together these two volumes and you have a 1,300-page modern Jewish encyclopedia that will take up only four inches of horizontal space on your bookshelf! Rabbi Telushkin's work is comprehensive, accessible, and fun to read. The subtitle of *Jewish Literacy* is: *The Most Important Things to Know About the Jewish Religion, Its People and Its History*, and the claim is true, almost everything is here. "What is the Kabbalah?" "What do Reconstructionist Jews believe?" "I know about the three kings, frankincense, and myrrh but what is the real story of Hanukkah?" You'll find the answers you seek in *Jewish Literacy* in clear, digestible bites.

Then turn to *Jewish Wisdom* for ethical and spiritual teachings. "Do Jews believe in life after death?" "What is the Jewish view about divorce? Abortion? The death penalty?" I highly recommend the section called "Between Parents and Children" in *Jewish Wisdom*. It is full of common sense from the Torah.

* * *

How do we start to celebrate Shabbat?

Heschel, Abraham Joshua. *The Sabbath* (New York: Noonday Press, 1991).

Friends and neighbors (and your children!) will tempt you to keep up a frenzied round of activities right through the weekend. Starting with a good understanding of the philosophy behind the observance of Shabbat can bolster your commitment to holy downtime. No one argues this more convincingly, or more poetically, than the modern scholar and philosopher Abraham Joshua Heschel. This small book, now half a century old, is a beautifully written meditation on one way to slow our pace and take the time to appreciate our gifts, to reflect on our choices, and to plan for the future. Rabbi Heschel sums up Jewish theology succinctly: Judaism is a religion aimed at sanctifying time rather than space, objects, or achievements.

Wolfson, Ron. *The Art of Jewish Living: The Shabbat Seder* (Woodstock, Vt.: Jewish Lights, 1996).

OK, you've made a commitment to slowing down for part of the weekend and to bringing the light of Shabbat candles into your family life. Where do you begin? What are the nuts and bolts? Dr. Wolfson will guide you through the rituals and explain what everything means. Your children may be delighted to learn that the lyrics of "Shalom Aleikhem" (Peace Be with You), the traditional melody sung after lighting the candles on Friday night, welcome two ministering angels, the messengers of God, who visit every home as the family ushers in the Sabbath. You may be moved to learn that starting in the Middle Ages it became a tradition for parents to bless each child on Shabbat using the same fifteen-word priestly benediction that was used in the ancient temple service in Jerusalem. Yet another example of the home as altar presided over by parents acting in God's image.

*   *   *

Where can I read more about Judaism and parenting?

Danan, Julie Hilton. *The Jewish Parents' Almanac* (Northvale, N.J.: Jason Aronson, 1994).

The Jewish Parents' Almanac is a treasure chest—many books rolled into one. Julie Hilton Danan, a Jewish educator and writer living in San Antonio, Texas, covers a wide range of topics, from child development from a Jewish perspective (the early elementary school years are the right time to teach children the concept of *tikkun olam*, our responsibility to form a partnership with God in repairing the world), to Jewish cultural literacy, to family mitzvah projects. The essay "Parenting as a Spiritual Path" is outstanding.

Salkin, Rabbi Jeffrey K. *Putting God on the Guest List: How to Reclaim the Spiritual Meaning of Your Child's Bar or Bat Mitzvah* (Woodstock, Vt.: Jewish Lights, 1993).

This book won the Benjamin Franklin Award for best religion book of the year, with good reason. Using unusually graceful, friendly, and lively prose, Rabbi Salkin integrates Jewish theology with an understanding of the real world in which we are raising our children. On our idolatry of the fast track he says, "Princeton, the headquarters of the Education Testing Service, has replaced Jerusalem as our Holy City." On perfectionism: "Don't let the rite get in the way of the passage." And Jewish legacy: "Our task is not only to inherit memory but to create memory." He recommends that Jewish education continue beyond bar and bat mitzvah and suggests that parents ask their children questions about their own Jewish leadership readiness, such as, "Will you know how to run the seder when Grandpa and Grandma and Daddy and I are gone?"

Twerski, Rabbi Abraham, and Dr. Ursula Schwartz. *Positive Parenting* (Brooklyn, N.Y.: Artscroll Series, Mesorah Publications, 1996).

Rabbi Twerski is a psychiatrist and leader in the field of substance abuse counseling. This is the first book I've found to tackle modern parenting problems (ADD, single parenting, child abuse) from the perspective of Jewish law and Orthodox beliefs. The authors illustrate their theories with Hasidic stories, rabbinic teachings, and vivid examples from family life.

•   •   •

What are good books about normal child development?

Ames, Louise Bates, with coauthors. Gesell Institute of Child Development Series. *Your One-Year-Old, Your Two-Year-Old*, and on up through *Your Ten- to Fourteen-Year-Old* (Dell Publishing Company, New York).

Don't be scared off by the publication dates—some of the books in this series are more than twenty years old, but the authors' generous and sensible descriptions of typical behavior for each age still hold. It's also illuminating to see how much the culture has changed. In *Your Eight-Year-Old*, published in 1989, the authors write, "Personal space is expanding for the eight-year-old. Your child can now walk home by bus from a somewhat distant point. His walking area within his own neighborhood is so wide that it is sometimes hard to locate him."

Unfortunately, today our eight-year-olds can't roam quite so freely. This makes the need to give them "expanded personal space" more of a challenge but just as important. All the books in the series contain reassuring descriptions of the *natural* phases of development. For example, the subtitle of *Your Seven-Year-Old* is *Life in a Minor Key*, a comfort to parents with a gloomy, introspective young person moping around the house. Then on to *Your Eight-Year-Old: Lively and Outgoing* and *Your Nine-Year-Old: Thoughtful and Mysterious*. These are exceptional books about child development, because the authors are deeply respectful of children and reassuring to parents, and their prose style is a pleasure to read.

Hallowell, Edward M., and Michael Thompson. *Finding the Heart of the Child: Essays on Children, Families and Schools* (Washington, D.C.: National Association of Independent Schools, 1993).

Edward Hallowell is a national expert on ADD and the author of *Driven to Distraction*. Michael Thompson is the author of *Raising Cain*, a best-seller about boys' development. Together they have written a collection of essays for educators that speaks equally eloquently to parents about a wide range of topics, including: what it's like to have Attention Deficit Disorder, our expectations and goals for our children, normal sexual feelings between adults and children, and how to distinguish normal from abnormal behavior. I always include this book on the reading lists I distribute at my lectures, whether I'm speaking to teachers, parents, or rabbinical students. It is forthright and inspiring.

Healy, Jane M. *Your Child's Growing Mind: A Practical Guide to Brain Development and Learning from Birth to Adolescence* (New York: Doubleday, 1994).

Dr. Healy blends information about the stages of child development with new findings on the growth of intelligence. She warns against early pressure to read and overuse of computers and television, and supports the "brain building" potential of real-life experiences.

•   *   •

What are some good books about raising children in a changing world?

Coles, Robert. *The Moral Intelligence of Children: How to Raise a Moral Child* (New York: Random House, 1997).

The Pulitzer Prize–winning psychiatrist and Harvard University professor interviews children and tell us what he has learned. This is Dr. Coles's first "how to" book directed specifically at parents and teachers. His description of the roots of adolescent cynicism is enlightening. One of the best traits of this developmental stage—a well-developed conscience and natural desire to have something to believe in—can turn into arrogance, fault-finding, and a loss of idealism when adolescents see too many contradictions in their world. What guidance can parents of younger children draw from Dr. Coles's findings? Now is the time to clarify our values and confront contradictions in the way we are raising our children.

Damon, William. *Greater Expectations: Overcoming the Culture of Indulgence in Our Homes and Schools* (New York: Simon & Schuster, 1995).

This is an exposé of the "cult of self-esteem" and the problem of emotional blackmailing of parents by children. Dr. Damon offers parents guidance for meeting the challenge of raising children with wholesome ambition in a world of middle-class comfort and convenience.

Glassner, Barry. *The Culture of Fear: Why Americans Are Afraid of the Wrong Things* (New York: Basic Books, 1999).

A thoughtful professor of sociology at the University of Southern California has written this calming antidote to our collective paranoia. Armed with a careful analysis of the statistics on crime, child abduction, and cybersmut, Dr. Glassner makes a convincing argument that the children are safer than we imagine.

Hardyment, Christina. *Perfect Parents: Baby-Care Advice Past and Present* (Oxford: Oxford University Press, 1995).

Things change. Things stay the same. Christina Hardyment offers readers the long view in her witty and sobering account of the advice given to parents by experts from 1750 to 1995. The only one fully spared is Bruno Bettelheim.

Kitzinger, Sheila, and Celia Kitzinger. *Tough Questions: Talking Straight with Your Kids About the Real World* (Boston, Mass.: Harvard Common Press, 1991).

This (sociologist) mother-and-daughter team have written the most sophisticated "how to" book I've found about raising children in today's world. They cover a wide range of topics, including food, lies and secrets, sex, politics, and religion. In the section on talking to children about death they recommend *Charlotte's Web* (death is made bearable through the continuance of life in the form of the spider's offspring), *The Little Prince,* and the books of C. S. Lewis.

Postman, Neil. *The Disappearance of Childhood* (New York: Vintage Books, 1994).

In this set of essays, Neil Postman, a culture critic, describes how and why television and mass media create precocious children. He then contrasts the superficial maturity of modern children, who know all about sex and violence, with the childlike nature of adults who strive to emulate the young.

Rosenfeld, Alvin, and Nicole Wise. *Hyper-Parenting: Are You Hurting Your Child by Trying Too Hard?* (New York: St. Martin's Press, 2000).

A psychiatrist and journalist have written this convincing sermon for loving, ambitious parents who forget that childhood is a period of preparation rather than full-fledged performance. The authors address the problems of overscheduling, overenrichment, and using children's achievement as a badge of our own success. An excellent book.

Siegler, Ava. *What Should I Tell the Kids? A Parents' Guide to Real Problems in the Real World* (New York: Dutton, 1993).

A practical guide to telling a child hard stuff: that parents are divorcing, that a parent is gay, that there's a suicide in the family, or that a parent is an alcoholic. This book is particularly useful because Dr. Siegler offers hypothetical dialogues between parent and child and then deconstructs what's being communicated.

*　　　*　　　*

Can you recommend any children's books that teach about self-reliance without being preachy or dull?

Fleischman, Paul. *Weslandia* (Cambridge: Candlewick Press, 1999).

Wesley is an outcast until a wind blows strange seeds into his garden. Giant red plants grow, providing him with clothing, shelter, food, bug repellent, a good income, and lots of new friends. Without a bit of help, Wesley creates an entire civilization and a whole new life. This witty tale of an unusually inventive and resourceful young boy is masterfully illustrated by Kevin Hawkes. My children instantly fell in love with this book.

Hoberman, Mary Ann. *The Seven Silly Eaters* (San Diego: Browndeer Press/ Harcourt Brace, 1997).

This is a beautiful and amusingly illustrated modern children's story told in rhyme. The authors use the problem of picky eating as a metaphor for the trap good-intentioned parents fall into when they become enslaved by children's whims.

Dr. Seuss. *Horton Hatches the Egg* (New York: Random House, 1940).

I love this story of an elephant who means what he says and says what he means, a model of clear communication, integrity, and responsibility.

Steig, William. *Brave Irene* (New York: Farrar, Straus and Giroux, 1986).

Vot a mensch, this Irene! Mrs. Bobbin, a dressmaker, has made a beautiful dress for the duchess to wear to the ball. When Mrs. Bobbin falls ill, her small daughter, Irene, offers to bring the dress to the palace herself. Mother protests because of the snowstorm brewing outside. "Irene put on her fleece-lined boots, her red hat and muffler, her heavy coat and her mittens. She kissed her mother's hot forehead six times, then once again, made sure she was tucked in snugly, and slipped out with the big box, shutting the door firmly behind her." The happy ending, with its new friends, ginger cake, oranges, pineapple, and spice candies, doesn't kick in until Irene has suffered real adversity, including despair and a brush with death. This is a story of love and courage.

* * *

Nothing scares me more than the idea that my teenager will get involved in drugs or be prematurely sexually active. What can I read to get a running start?

Bartle, Nathalie. *Venus in Blue Jeans: Why Mothers and Daughters Need to Talk About Sex* (New York: Dell, 1998).

Meet America's cultural split personality about sex. Sexual imagery is on every billboard, advertisement, and music video, but parents are still uncomfortable talking about the subject, both because of natural reticence and out of fear of encouraging sexual activity by spilling all the details. Dr. Bartle reports on numerous studies revealing that our sophisticated, articulate children know much *less* than we think they do about sex and emphasizes the importance of talking openly to children—offering them a *context* for all the sexual *content* in the world around them.

Wolf, Anthony. *Get Out of My Life but First Could You Drive Me and Cheryl to the Mall? A Parent's Guide to the New Teenager* (New York: Noonday Press, 1991).

Using a droll tone—"most teenager disobedience lies in the realm of sleaze and deception" (rather than direct disobedience)—Dr. Wolf helps parents interpret teenagers' unique style of communication and explains what to do once you understand their messages. Also recommended: Dr. Wolf's 1998 book, *Why Did You Have to Get a Divorce? And When Can I Get a Hamster?*

*   *   *

You recommend putting marriage before children. How exactly can such a thing be accomplished?

Wallerstein, Judith, and Sandra Blakeslee. *The Good Marriage: How and Why Love Lasts* (Boston: Houghton Mifflin, 1995).

You can begin by appreciating that without tending, no marriage can flourish. The authors of this admirable study of fifty happily married couples tell us that many marriages are "good enough." They explain that "there is no love without hate, no admiration without envy, no sexual closeness without sexual threat and insecurity, no change without resistance." In describing the variety and range of "good" marriages—from friendship without high passion to the constant fighters who are deeply bound together— Judith Wallerstein and Sandra Blakeslee reassure the reader that it's not necessary to repeat a pattern of parental marital unhappiness and that there is no single correct formula for a successful marriage.

Index

Parents' Discussion Guide

This guide was originally developed to help parents who would like to participate in a parenting class using the concepts in *The Blessing of a Skinned Knee* as a foundation. There are many ways you can benefit from the ideas in the guide, however, and I invite you to use it for:

- Book club discussion groups
- Grade-level parent meetings at your child's school
- Faculty in-service workshops
- Community center or neighborhood parent support groups
- Individual guidance while reading *The Blessing of a Skinned Knee*

SETTING UP A PARENTING
CLASS OR DISCUSSION GROUP

If you're interested in gathering a group of parents together to discuss issues of concern, below are some general guidelines you may find useful.

Size and Participants

Parent discussion groups can range from a minimum of six members for informal parent support groups to twenty participants for professionally led parenting classes. With fewer than six members you run the risk that typical rates of attrition, plus one or two parents home with a sick child or a competing commitment, may leave the group with only two members, which is intimate but without the potential for the same vitality and shared learning that a larger group affords. My favorite group size is twelve. Classes work best when the parents have children in the same age range: early elementary, later elementary, middle school, or high school.

When and Where

Groups/classes can meet in members' homes, at synagogue, church, or after drop-off or pick-up at school. Weekdays usually work best, but another good option is a Saturday or Sunday morning class that meets while children are in religious school. When possible—if the class is sponsored by a synagogue or school—provision of on-site child care is a wonderful asset and will increase enrollment.

Length and Frequency

No mater how dedicated and enthusiastic, every group needs ten minutes for the arrival of stragglers and for settling in and warming-up. An hour and forty-five minutes to two hours is an ideal class length. With less time, the class is not worth the effort of investing in child care and travel.

Weekly meetings for six consecutive weeks work well for parenting classes with a designated leader and structured curriculum. *Havurot* (family friendship groups) and leaderless support groups often meet less frequently (biweekly or monthly) but continue for months or even years. I led one group that lasted for two years. My colleague, parent educator Marilyn Brown, has a continuously running class that began with mothers of new babies and toddlers and now consists of mothers of pre-teens.

Rules for Parenting Classes/Groups

No one would want to attend a parenting class that followed Robert's Rules of Order, but some guidelines for conduct and attendance will help things to run smoothly. During the first meeting, the group can decide whether or not a set of explicit guidelines is needed. Here are some rules other groups have adopted:

- Meeting times will be established during the first meeting and won't be changed to accommodate the schedules of individual group members.
- No taping of the group for spouse or friends.
- Each group member is obligated to call if they are unable to attend and leave a message with the leader or designated person in charge of organizational details.
- Since latecomers distract others, everyone will make the commitment to be on time.
- For classes held at the school the children attend: the topics of the administration, teachers, and curriculum are off limits.
- Maimonides teaches us to rebuke and at the same time to elevate. Translated to parenting class etiquette, this means that we phrase comments in positive terms, do not criticize one another, and respect the opinions that diverge from our own.

- Parents agree to keep what is said in the group confidential. Confessions, harangues, and problems will not be repeated outside of the groups.
- No one should be pressured to reveal anything about themselves or their family if they choose not to. If group members are responding to questions "around the table," any member can decline to speak by saying, "I pass."

CURRICULUM FOR SIX-SESSION PARENTING CLASS/GROUP

Each class has:

- a central topic
- one or two chapters of required reading to be completed before the class
- a reflection assignment to be thought about before the class
- a quote or quotes of the day to be written on a board or read aloud before each class
- a list of discussion questions that will be handed out at the beginning of each class

Each member can review the reflection and discussion questions before each class. I've intentionally provided more questions than even the most ambitious and organized group can cover in a two-hour class. The leader or group members can select from among the questions listed based on each particular groups' interests and concerns.

Name tags should be provided for all participants for the opening sessions.

What You Should Expect from a Jewish Parenting Class

Martin Luther King, Jr. described the goal of his ministry as comforting the disturbed and disturbing the comfortable. A Jewish parenting class should also accomplish these goals. A Jewish parenting class examines the everyday challenges of child rearing from the perspective of the *beit din* (the ancient court of Jewish law). Every decision we make as parents has not only psychological dimensions but moral, ethical, and spiritual ones as well. Using a Jewish perspective to understand parenting problems gives us a long view and reveals the underpinnings of the problem, not just the surface cuts and scratches. In a Jewish parenting class, the goal is not to put a Band-Aid on the current difficulty—to simply comfort the disturbed—but to stretch ourselves by learning basic Jewish principles of living.

You should expect to leave a Jewish parenting class with:

- A deeper understanding of Jewish thought
- An understanding about how our culture handicaps and confuses parents who are trying to raise self-reliant, compassionate, optimistic children
- Guidelines about defining appropriate expectations for children
- Insights about how your own psychological needs may be hampering your child's growth
- Insights about your individual child: his or her temperament, natural endowments, interests, and inclinations
- Resources for finding basic information about different stages of your child's social development

A good Jewish parenting class is profound but never solemn or staid. *Pilpul* (from the Hebrew, "pepper") is a dialectical method of Talmudic study and debate, consisting of drawing out the broadest range of logical possibilities in the text. The purpose of *pilpul* is both to deepen the participants' under-standing of the applications of the law and to sharpen their wits. Disagreements, laughter, tragic stories, laughter, juicy sto-ries, laughter, teasing, and tenderness—a good Jewish parenting class is peppery.

SESSION ONE
TOPIC: Helping our children realize their potential without cre-ating stress.

Reading Assignment
Chapter 1. *How I Lost One Faith and Found Another*
Chapter 2. *The Blessing of Acceptance: Discovering Your Unique and Ordinary Child*

Reflection Assignment
Look at a photo album with pictures of you when you were your child's age. Try to recall your natural interests and pas-sions at that time. Think about how the expectations of your family and the environment you were living in helped these inclinations flourish or wither.

Quotes of the Day
"If your child has a talent to be a baker, do not ask him to be a doctor." (Hasidic)

"When I reach the world to come, God will not ask me why I wasn't more like Moses. He will ask me why I wasn't more like Zusya." (early Hasidic leader, Rabbi Zusya)

Begin the first class with introductions around the table. Par-ticipants should share the names, ages, and grades of their chil-dren and mention any topic they hope to cover in the course of the six meetings.

Discussion Questions

- Think about your natural child's talents, inclinations, passions. How would you describe her nature? Is she like you? Different in tempo, interests, volatility?
- What opportunities does your child have to express his natural inclinations?
- Are there telltale signs (bedwetting, fears, apathy, irritability, sleeplessness, nail chewing, hair-pulling) that you may be pressuring your child to achieve at a high level in areas in which he is not endowed?
- Reflect on whether you are accepting "good enough" or looking for perfection from your child? From yourself as a parent?
- Think of a family where the kids have turned out well. Ask them for guidance about their expectations (for grades, for music practicing, for help around the house) of their children. Share what you learn with the group.
- Share strategies you've used for resisting the "flu bug" of competition with other group members.

SESSION TWO

TOPIC: Granting our children freedom: Where do wise parents draw the line?

Reading Assignment

Chapter 3. *The Blessing of Having Someone to Look Up To: Honoring Mother and Father*

Chapter 4. *The Blessing of a Skinned Knee: Why God Doesn't Want You to Overprotect Your Child*

Reflection Assignment

When you were growing up how did you address your parents and their friends? How did you address teachers? If you were required to be more formal than your children are, what were the advantages and disadvantages?

Think back to your childhood. On a summer night, were you able to play outside until dark without adult supervision? Could you ride your bike freely in your neighborhood? Recall the bones you broke, the adventures you had. What were the benefits of this degree of freedom? Any harm? Compare your experiences to your child's current level of freedom.

Quotes of the Day

"When a person honors the parents, God says, 'I consider it as though I lived with them and they honored me.'" (Talmud, Kiddushin, 30b)

"Do not to put a stumbling block before the blind." (Leviticus, 19:14)

Discussion Questions

Take an inventory of honor by asking yourself these questions:

- Do you allow your children to interrupt you when you are on the phone?
- Do you have a designated place at the dinner table? Do the children sit in your place?
- Do your children consistently contradict you?
- Do they talk back to you in public?
- Do you give your children enough opportunities to help out? To demonstrate thoughtfulness? To take care of you?
- Do they respect your privacy? Do they enter your room or take your things without asking?
- Do your older children commandeer the remote? Tie up the phone line? Forget to give you phone messages they have taken?
- What are your family's rules of *hakhnasat orchim* (hospitality to guests and on playdates)? Compare your ideal to your real situation.
- Do you set an example in the way you treat your own parents?

- Share strategies around the table for combating rude talk and entitlement. Share consequences and rewards that have been effective.
- What creative ways have group members found to give children freedom while still keeping them safe?

SESSION THREE
TOPIC: Giving and receiving.

Reading Assignment
Chapter 5. *The Blessing of Longing: Teaching Your Child an Attitude of Gratitude*

Chapter 6. *The Blessing of Work: Finding the Holy Sparks in Ordinary Chores*

Reflection Assignment
When you were growing up, did you have as much stuff—clothes, books, vehicles, athletic equipment, and toys—as your children do? Was the stuff in as many places in the house? Did your family try to repair things before replacing them? If yes, what lessons did this teach you? What chores did you do? How did you help your parents in other ways? What did you learn from having these responsibilities? What did you sacrifice?

Quotes of the Day
"He who has one hundred wants two hundred." (Jewish saying)

"Slavery is responsibility without authority." (British psychoanalyst W. R. Bion)

Discussion Questions
- Make a list of those things you believe your child is entitled to and those that are privileges to be earned. Compare lists with other group members.

- Does your family have a ritual for expressing gratitude?
- Do you let your children know what makes you grateful towards them?
- Do you frequently lift your spirit by going shopping? How often do you buy something and then regret it or find you already have the same or a similar thing at home?
- Does your child know which charities to which you contribute? Does she know why you've chosen them?
- What chores does your child do daily? Weekly? Do you need to nag or remind?
- What methods have group members found to encourage their children to take initiative about helping out at home?

SESSION FOUR
TOPIC: Discipline.

Reading Assignment

Chapter 8. *The Blessing of Self-Control: Channeling Your Child's Yetzer Hara*

Reflection Assignment

Take a moment to think about the way your parents disciplined you. Were they *laissez-faire* parents? Guilt-inducing? Overcontrolling? Trial and error? What aspects of their techniques of discipline were constructive and helped you develop self-control and a sense of security? What aspects caused you to feel anxious or rejected?

Quotes of the Day

"Be it ever your way to thrust your child off with the left hand and draw him to you with the right hand." (Talmud, Sotah 47z)

"What is the normal child like? Does he just eat and grow and smile sweetly? No, that is not what he is like. A normal child, if he has the confidence of his mother and father, pulls out all the stops. In the course of time he tries out his powers to disrupt, to destroy, to frighten, to wear down, to waste, to wrangle, and to appropriate. Everything that takes people to the courts (or to the asylums for that matter) has its normal equivalent in infancy and childhood, in the relation of the child to his own home." (Pediatrician and psychoanalyst D. W. Winnicott).

Discussion Questions

- Think of your child's worst trait: anything from a little annoying habit or attitude to a big problem that has his teachers exasperated or deeply concerned. Then reframe it—think of this trait as your child's greatest strength. What are the good aspects of the trait? How might it benefit your child now and in adulthood?

- Ask yourself which aspects of your child's environment are obstacles to this trait being expressed positively: An overly busy schedule? Inappropriate expectations for school performance? Sleep deprivation? Poor organization of his room, desk, supplies? School work that is too difficult? Too easy? Not enough playtime or downtime?

- Examine your discipline strategy: Are you pumping up small problems? Being inconsistent? Making empty threats? Sticking with an ineffective approach?

- Which consequences for misbehavior and which rewards for compliance and good attitude are most effective? Share discipline strategies with other group members.

SESSION FIVE
TOPIC: Food and eating.

Reading Assignment

Chapter 7. *The Blessing of Food: Bringing Moderation, Celebration, and Sanctification to Your Table*

Quotes of the Day

"The Jewish mother betrays an unusual amount of concern about the problem of feeding her children. In general, she should stop worrying so much about how much they eat and what they wear." (A 1923 article in *Froyen Zhurnal*, a Yiddish advice magazine for newly arrived immigrants)

"Since the destruction of the Temple, every table in every home has become an altar." (Talmud, Pesachim 4b)

Reflection Assignment

What are your most pleasant childhood memories of the tastes, smells, and presentation of food? What were your holiday food rituals? What are your least pleasant memories of food tensions or battles with your family?

Discussion Questions

- Explore the attitudes towards food that you bring from your childhood. Did you grow up with destructive attitudes that you don't want to pass along to your children? Are there memories you wish to preserve?
- Take an inventory of the example you set for your children. Do you eat leftovers from their plates? Do you eat standing up in front of the pantry where the crackers and cookies are kept? Do you frequently eat in the car?
- Are you so afraid of having fats and sugar in the house that you deprive the children of a normal range of foods?
- What are your children's favorite foods? Do they know what foods you love?
- Are you teaching them how to cook?

SESSION SIX

TOPIC: What are our goals in raising our children?

Reading Assignment

Chapter 9. *The Blessing of Time: Teaching Your Child the Value of the Present Moment*

Chapter 10. *The Blessing of Faith and Tradition: Losing Your Fear of the "G Word" and Introducing your Child to Spirituality*

Quote of the Day

"If you truly wish your children to study Torah, study it yourself in their presence. They will follow your example. Otherwise they will not themselves study Torah, but will simply instruct their children to do so." (Rabbi Menahem Mendel of Kotsk)

Reflection Assignment

As a child, how much time did you have to daydream and reflect? What activities did your family do together that you enjoyed? What religious education and worship opportunities did you have as a child? Did you feel frustrated and oppressed by them? Confused? In what ways did they enrich your life?

Discussion Questions

- Has your home life gotten so pressured that you often prefer to be at work?
- What would be the obstacles to a "tech free" (no computer, no beeper or cell phone) day of the week at home? What would be the benefits?
- What aspects of your childhood religion do you want to pass along to your children? A predictable cycle of ritual events and celebrations? A lens on right and wrong, fate and justice? Sounds, odors, tastes, and beautiful images? What was missing from your childhood experience that you would like to provide for your family?
- Does lack of skill or self-consciousness prevent you from taking part in religious rituals?

- What obstacles are in the way of finding a community that shares your religious or spiritual beliefs? Geography? Snobbery? Shyness? Finances?

Class is over! Say goodbye, trade e-mail addresses, consider continuing your learning as a group by finding a rabbi or Jewish educator to teach you from Jewish texts or plan a parenting book discussion group using the list of recommended readings at the back of *The Blessing of a Skinned Knee*.

FOR THE BEST IN PAPERBACKS, LOOK FOR THE

In every corner of the world, on every subject under the sun, Penguin represents quality and variety—the very best in publishing today.

For complete information about books available from Penguin—including Penguin Classics, Penguin Compass, and Puffins—and how to order them, write to us at the appropriate address below. Please note that for copyright reasons the selection of books varies from country to country.

In the United States: Please write to *Penguin Group (USA), P.O. Box 12289 Dept. B, Newark, New Jersey 07101-5289* or call *1-800-788-6262.*

In the United Kingdom: Please write to *Dept. EP, Penguin Books Ltd, Bath Road, Harmondsworth, West Drayton, Middlesex UB7 0DA.*

In Canada: Please write to *Penguin Books Canada Ltd, 90 Eglinton Avenue East, Suite 700, Toronto, Ontario M4P 2Y3.*

In Australia: Please write to *Penguin Books Australia Ltd, P.O. Box 257, Ringwood, Victoria 3134.*

In New Zealand: Please write to *Penguin Books (NZ) Ltd, Private Bag 102902, North Shore Mail Centre, Auckland 10.*

In India: Please write to *Penguin Books India Pvt Ltd, 11 Panchsheel Shopping Centre, Panchsheel Park, New Delhi 110 017.*

In the Netherlands: Please write to *Penguin Books Netherlands bv, Postbus 3507, NL-1001 AH Amsterdam.*

In Germany: Please write to *Penguin Books Deutschland GmbH, Metzlerstrasse 26, 60594 Frankfurt am Main.*

In Spain: Please write to *Penguin Books S. A., Bravo Murillo 19, 1° B, 28015 Madrid.*

In Italy: Please write to *Penguin Italia s.r.l., Via Benedetto Croce 2, 20094 Corsico, Milano.*

In France: Please write to *Penguin France, Le Carré Wilson, 62 rue Benjamin Baillaud, 31500 Toulouse.*

In Japan: Please write to *Penguin Books Japan Ltd, Kaneko Building, 2-3-25 Koraku, Bunkyo-Ku, Tokyo 112.*

In South Africa: Please write to *Penguin Books South Africa (Pty) Ltd, Private Bag X14, Parkview, 2122 Johannesburg.*